THIRSTY LAND INTO SPRINGS OF WATER

Negotiating a Place in Canada as Latter-day Saints

Thirsty Land into Springs of Water

Negotiating a Place in Canada as Latter-day Saints

BROOKE KATHLEEN BRASSARD

UNIVERSITY OF TORONTO PRESS
Toronto Buffalo London

© University of Toronto Press 2025
Toronto Buffalo London
utppublishing.com
Printed in Canada

ISBN 978-1-4875-0633-9 (cloth)   ISBN 978-1-4875-3388-5 (EPUB)
                                   ISBN 978-1-4875-3387-8 (PDF)

Library and Archives Canada Cataloguing in Publication

Title: Thirsty land into springs of water : negotiating a place in Canada as Latter-day Saints / Brooke Kathleen Brassard.
Names: Brassard, Brooke Kathleen, author
Description: Includes bibliographical references and index.
Identifiers: Canadiana (print) 20240537289 | Canadiana (ebook) 20240537300 | ISBN 9781487506339 (hardcover) | ISBN 9781487533878 (PDF) | ISBN 9781487533885 (EPUB)
Subjects: LCSH: Church of Jesus Christ of Latter-day Saints – Alberta – History – 19th century. | LCSH: Church of Jesus Christ of Latter-day Saints – Alberta – History – 20th century. | LCSH: Latter Day Saints – Cultural assimilation – Alberta – History – 19th century. | LCSH: Latter Day Saints – Cultural assimilation – Alberta – History – 20th century.
Classification: LCC BX8617.C3 B73 2025 | DDC 289.371 – dc23 | 289.37123/4 – dc23

Jacket illustration: *One Hundred Years in the Promised Land* by Jessie Ursenbach (Oil painting, 24 x 18 1/16 inches; Alberta Foundation of the Arts). Courtesy of the Ursenbach Family.
Jacket design: Rebecca Lown

We wish to acknowledge the land on which the University of Toronto Press operates. This land is the traditional territory of the Wendat, the Anishnaabeg, the Haudenosaunee, the Métis, and the Mississaugas of the Credit First Nation.

University of Toronto Press acknowledges the financial support of the Government of Canada, the Canada Council for the Arts, and the Ontario Arts Council, an agency of the Government of Ontario, for its publishing activities.

This book has been published with the help of a grant from the Federation for the Humanities and Social Sciences, through the Awards to Scholarly Publications Program, using funds provided by the Social Sciences and Humanities Research Council of Canada.

 Canada Council for the Arts   Conseil des Arts du Canada

ONTARIO ARTS COUNCIL
CONSEIL DES ARTS DE L'ONTARIO
an Ontario government agency
un organisme du gouvernement de l'Ontario

 Funded by the Government of Canada   Financé par le gouvernement du Canada

 MIX
Paper | Supporting responsible forestry
FSC® C016abs

Contents

List of Illustrations   vii

Acknowledgments   ix

Abbreviations   xv

1 Introduction   3

2 Families   27

3 Women   55

4 Business   89

5 Politics   107

6 Architecture   128

7 Conclusion   147

Notes   165
Bibliography   213
Index   241

Illustrations

0.1 Cardston Alberta Temple   x
1.1 Portrait of Charles Ora Card   8
3.1 Early view of Cardston, looking north   66
4.1 Knight Sugar Factory in Raymond, postcard published by Rumsey & Co., ca. 1910   103
5.1 John H. Blackmore, Social Credit poster   120
6.1 The Cardston Alberta Temple, West Gate, ca. 1925   144
7.1 Hans Peterson's headstone   149
7.2 Thomas R. Leavitt's headstone   150
7.3 Noah Shurtleff's headstone   151
7.4 Austin G. Russell's obelisk   151
7.5 Fanny Caldwell's headstone   154
7.6 Helen Shaffer's obelisk   155
7.7 Olinda Pierson's grave marker   156
7.8 The Christensen family grave marker   158
7.9 The Redfords' gravestone   159
7.10 The Hurds' gravestone   159

Acknowledgments

I am an outsider. This is often one of the first things I must acknowledge when asked about my area of research. When I explain that my research focuses on Latter-day Saints, the immediate follow-up questions is, "Are you a member?" It is usually an instant reaction to hearing my area of interest, as if any boundaries disappear when I utter the term "Mormonism" or "The Church of Jesus Christ of Latter-day Saints." Even though curious minds have asked me this question dozens of times, I still respond with the immediate, shocked, stern reply: "No! I'm not a member." As if I am still not used to the question, as if I am still angered by the question, and still feel offended that they would think I was a member just because I study the religion. But people are curious. Mormonism, or, more officially, The Church of Jesus Christ of Latter-day Saints, is still shrouded in mystery and misunderstanding. Therefore, I rationalize these personal questions with the belief that they are surprised an outsider, with no personal commitment to the faith, would devote so much time and energy to its history and public understanding. They are curious. As was I when I began this journey, as an undergraduate student at the University of Lethbridge, living just an hour car ride away from Cardston, Alberta, the epicentre of Canadian Mormonism.

The Cardston Alberta Temple is at the heart of why I study The Church of Jesus Christ of Latter-day Saints (Figure 0.1). My roommate at the time was from the area surrounding Cardston, and on a drive to her hometown, we stopped at the temple. She, like myself, was not a member of the Church, but had grown up with many Latter-day Saint friends and classmates, so her understanding of the religion far outstretched that of my own experience at the time. It was night-time and the lights of the temple allowed visitors to see it from a great distance, but up close it was even more impressive. Impressive and confusing.

Figure 0.1 Cardston Alberta Temple.
Source: Author's photograph

It looked like nothing you would expect to see in a southern Albertan town with a population under 4,000. It was a beautiful, glowing, stone fortress. A fortress on various levels, as I soon discovered, that I was not allowed to enter. Thus, my journey to understand the Church and Latter-day Saints really began as an exercise to answer two questions. The first being why I was not allowed inside the temple; the second being why this type of building, located in this small, rural town, looked the way it did.

At the time I was formulating these questions, I carried a bias against The Church of Jesus Christ of Latter-day Saints. As someone raised in a family of conservative Christians, new religious movements, like the Church, were only discussed under the umbrella of "cults." A lack of respect and a lack of genuine understanding followed Latter-day Saints and members of other new religious movements, and so my childhood introduction to the religion was one of fear and misguidance. I started exploring religious studies scholarship on new religious movements and the Church and realized I had experienced a very specific version of Mormonism, as (mis)understood by many mainstream Christians.

Acknowledgments xi

Luckily, over the course of my education and this project, I made the acquaintance of many Latter-day Saints who helped clarify any preconceived misjudgments I had made or carried with me from childhood, and I have been most fortunate to call many of these Saints my good friends. Barbara Jones Brown and family, and Heather Stone and family, thank you for your patience and endurance of my endless questions. You have welcomed me into your homes, lives, and families and treated me as close to an honorary Latter-day Saint that one could possibly be, without the temple recommendation, of course.

Numerous institutions provided financial support that allowed me to complete research in Utah and Alberta. Specifically, the Government of Alberta through the Alberta Historical Resources Foundation provided the means to complete my research trip throughout southern Alberta. As well, the Canadian Corporation for Studies in Religion granted me a Doctoral Travel Scholarship that funded a research trip to Salt Lake City and the Church History Library. In addition, I appreciate and acknowledge support by the Ontario Graduate Scholarship Program through funding from the Province of Ontario and the University of Waterloo.

My summer at Brigham Young University through the Neal A. Maxwell Institute for Religious Scholarship and the Mormon culture summer seminar provided financial and scholarly engagement that initiated my research in the L. Tom Perry Special Collections and Church History Library. I am forever grateful to Dr. Richard Bushman and Dr. Claudia Bushman for facilitating this seminar. In addition, The Charles Redd Center at Brigham Young University awarded me a Fellowship in Western American History that further aided the completion of research in their special collections, and I sincerely thank them for their support.

The Church History Library, L. Tom Perry Special Collections, Glenbow Museum, Galt Museum & Archives, Raymond Pioneer Museum & District Historical Society, Cardston & District Historical Society, Cardston Court House Museum, Card Pioneer Home, and Magrath Museum helped make this project possible. I feel very fortunate for their support and this project greatly benefited from the labour of hardworking volunteers, staff, librarians, and archivists.

In addition, I owe a big debt of gratitude to the mentors of and my cohort in the American Examples program through the Department of Religious Studies at the University of Alabama. Thanks to funding from the Henry Luce Foundation, this program created a collaborative working group of scholars of religion in America, and I had the opportunity to workshop some of the research connected to this book project. A very special thank you to Michael Altman for reading and critiquing this book, and to Russell T. McCutcheon for hosting a special workshop on first book projects. Their mentorship, along with all the other American Examples mentors and cohort members, pushed me to consider larger theoretical questions surrounding my research focus and the implications this research has on broader issues.

The following journals and press kindly granted me permission to reprint excepts from previously published work. Excerpts from chapter 2 first appeared in my articles "Prairie School in the Prairie: An Architectural Journey through Mormon History in Southern Alberta 1888–1923," in a 2016 issue of the *Journal of Mormon History* 42, and "Vines, Gates, and Temples: Using Cemeteries to Understand Mormonism in Canada," in a 2018 issue of the *Journal of the Society for the Study of Architecture in Canada*. Portions of chapter 3 were previously published in "The Last Best West: The Politics of Co-operation among Latter-day Saints in Southern Alberta," in *Business and Religion: The Intersection of Faith and Finance*, edited by Matthew C. Godfrey and Michael H. MacKay, and published by Brigham Young University Press and its Religious Studies Center in 2019.

This manuscript comes from the research I completed at the University of Waterloo in the Department of Religious Studies. During my time at the University of Waterloo, many individuals supported my progress through the PhD program. Thank you, Fiona McAlister, for making sure we graduate students never had to worry about administrative details because you always had it expertly covered. Thank you to both Dr. Doris Jakobsh and Dr. Mavis Fenn for being kind, patient, supportive role models and for providing guidance and mentorship throughout this long, difficult journey. I am deeply grateful to the outstanding support, mentorship, and community provided by the University of Waterloo's Department of Religious Studies, fellow graduate students, and my PhD cohort. I would never have survived the first year of the PhD program without the friendship of Laura Morlock who adopted me into her family, became a best friend, and forced me to eat and rest, in addition to listening to all my research questions, problems, and ideas. Thank you, Katie Riddell, for befriending this anti-social first-year PhD student and taking me under your wing. Your scholarship and friendship have been one of the best parts of my Waterloo experience. Pam Andrews, my former roommate/life partner and complete opposite, thank you for teaching me how to be an adult. I am so lucky you moved to Waterloo and needed a place to live.

A special thank you and appreciation to the University of Waterloo Interlibrary Loans and, specifically, to Ted Harms. Ted handled my many requests with promptness, proficiency, kindness, and clarity. While the university libraries housed many helpful resources, it was

Ted and the Interlibrary Loans department that provided the meat of my secondary sources. Without them, my research would have lacked many monographs and edited volumes that came from outside the province. I so appreciate the hard work of all the librarians, library staff, and archivists that made this research possible.

I would never have finished my revisions without two supportive writing groups. First, a huge thank you to the Waterloo Writes community, the Writing and Communication Centre, Maša Torbica, and Nadine Fladd. Our weekly Virtual Writing Café sessions were lifelines during COVID-19 lockdowns and motivated me to finish this book. A special thank you to Nadine for regularly meeting with me to discuss writing strategies and for providing thoughtful, detailed feedback on drafts. Also, thank you to Western University's FIMS Writes community and the welcoming environment of our Wednesday morning writing sessions I attended while completing my MLIS from 2021–2022.

Dr. David Seljak and Dr. Douglas E. Cowan provided challenging and necessary critiques of this manuscript throughout the writing and revising process. Thank you, Dr. Seljak, for pushing through my often-painful grammar and spelling mistakes. Thank you, Dr. Cowan, for gifting me your books on Mormonism when you moved offices, and for lending your expertise, time, and attention.

I took a risk moving across the country to start a doctoral program with a supervisor I had spoken to only twice over the phone, but from the first dinner at his home, before classes had even begun, to the surprise practice comprehensive exam that left me in tears, I knew I had made the right decision. Thank you to Dr. Jeff Wilson for mentoring me and supervising my journey through course work, comprehensive examinations, and the dissertation process. You expertly handled my anxieties and neuroses and provided continuous encouragement when I needed it. I am incredibly lucky to have you as a mentor and friend. Thank you.

Finally, thank you to my family. My parents and brothers have been unfailingly supportive of my sometimes-rocky academic choices. I am eternally grateful to my partner Joel Countryman for his never-ending faith and confidence in my intelligence and abilities. He never let me give up on this project even when I wanted to quit. I am also deeply grateful to our zoo – Gwen (RIP), Isadora, Logan, Jubilee (RIP), and my writing partner Oreo – for forcing me to go outside, walk, breath, and cuddle.

Abbreviations

AFA	Alberta Farmers' Association
ARCC	Alberta Railway and Coal Company
AWI	Alberta Women's Institutes
BNA	British North America
CCF	Co-operative Commonwealth Federation
CPR	Canadian Pacific Railway
CRA	Co-operative Retrenchment Association
FLDS	Fundamentalist Church of Jesus Christ of Latter-day Saints
JMH	Journal of Mormon History
LDS	Latter-day Saint(s)
LTPSC	L. Tom Perry Special Collections
NWMP	North-West Mounted Police
NWT	North-West Territories
TGGA	Territorial Grain Growers' Association
UFA	United Farmers of Alberta
UFWA	United Farm Women of Alberta
YLMIA	Young Ladies Mutual Improvement Association

THIRSTY LAND INTO SPRINGS OF WATER

Negotiating a Place in Canada as Latter-day Saints

Chapter One

Introduction

The soil was a rich alluvial, the most abundant of soils.[1]

We were learning to love our new Canadian home. It was different in many respects from our Utah home. We did not have the conveniences and comforts of the homes we had left, but as rapidly as possible we were beginning to acquire them, and we always had the Rockies to the west as a reminder of the land we had left ... This prairie country with the surrounding hills and mountains was first known as Buffalo Plains. The white of the bones contrasted strikingly with the blood-red of the fragrant, large prairie rose that grew everywhere over the prairie close to the ground. We had never seen this variety of rose before. It seemed to be something the prairie itself had bred.[2]

The title of this book comes from chapter 35, verse 7, of Isaiah: "And the parched ground shall become a pool, and the thirsty land springs of water: in the habitation of dragons, where each lay, shall be grass with reeds and rushes." Latter-day Saints interpret this chapter to mean that "In the day of restoration, the desert will blossom, the Lord will come, Israel will be gathered, and Zion will be built up."[3] While many might read and think of the Latter-day Saint experience in Utah, with the evolving meanings of Zion and the globalization of the Church, the passage also applies to their experience in Canada. In the late nineteenth and early twentieth centuries, Latter-day Saints in Canada not only literally brought water to "parched ground" through several irrigation projects in southern Alberta, but also, with time, flourished, or blossomed, like healthy vegetation from watered soil. Where once there was no water, water shall abound; where once there was no Church, Latter-day Saints shall prosper.

But it was not that simple. The ground resisted. It presented weeds and roots. Sometimes the tools broke. Canadian society, specifically the region that became known as southern Alberta, did not, at first, welcome Latter-day Saints with open arms. Society remained skeptical and indifferent to the new religion and its members. The ground remained parched. The Latter-day Saints, searching for acceptance, but not willing to give up all the practices and beliefs that made them different from their Canadian neighbours, had to work the land, sometimes gently, sometimes roughly, to find the springs of water, or acceptance.

This book examines how Latter-day Saints integrated into Canadian society by analysing several sites of negotiation, including marriage, gender, business, politics, and the built environment. The process of negotiation for member of The Church of Jesus Christ of Latter-day Saints was a complicated and messy procedure that oscillated between assimilating, resisting, and finding the right balance between acceptable and different. Latter-day Saints living in what would become the province of Alberta from the late nineteenth century to the early twentieth century integrated into Canadian society and maintained their "peculiar" identity through negotiations, evidenced in their families and marriage practices, their gendered roles, their business styles and political participation, and their architectural design and gravestone choices. Mainstream Canadian society forced the newcomer to decide what they would adopt, reject, or adapt, and this book will show that process for one minority religious group. The topic of Latter-day Saint integration in Canada is significant because it fills two gaps in previous scholarship. This book will not only add the Canadian context, which is often absent in Mormon studies discourse, but also insert the Church into narratives of Canadian history and religious studies where it, too, is an often forgotten subject.

Historical Background

Before we can begin to understand the struggles and successes of the Church in Canada, we must understand the Church's origins and what led members to settle in what was called at the time of their settlement the District of Alberta in the North-West Territories.[4] Most readers will likely think of Utah when they think of the Church. However, even though Utah did become the Church's main location, it was not always the centre of the new religion.

The American Revolution accelerated an erosion of tradition and the expansion of independent thinking in the former British colonies. Separated from Great Britain, the isolated United States "made it possible for religious outsiders to see their own destiny as part and parcel of the meaning of America itself," and this ideology weakened the upper class and likewise their religious institutions.[5] In *The Democratization of American Christianity*, Nathan O. Hatch, discussing Joseph Smith Jr. (1805–44), writes, "In a land of democratic promise and burgeoning capitalist expectation, Smith was born into a family in 1805 that never was able to break the grip of poverty, wearisome toil, and chronic dislocation."[6] They lived in New York state, surrounded by religious revivals and an assortment of denominations and sects, none of which helped the Smith family in their search for stability, spirituality, and prosperity. By 1830, Joseph Smith Jr., earlier claiming he possessed gold plates – engraved plates containing a record of ancient teachings – and the tools to translate them, published the *Book of Mormon*, a narrative written in biblical prose, set in the New World, as a fifth Gospel. In the new text,

> Smith also projects a distinctly populist vision that suggests how God will restore the ancient order of things. He is violently anticlerical but confident that God will reconstitute the church according to popular norms. The *Book of Mormon* has its own preferential option for the poor, not as persons to be pitied, but as those whom God has chosen to empower.[7]

As a rising religious leader, Smith set forth in motion the formal organization of the new religious movement to be known as The Church of Jesus Christ of Latter-day Saints.[8] About five months after the publication of the *Book of Mormon*, Joseph Smith Sr. (1771–1840), father of the Church's founder, and his youngest son Don Carlos Smith (1816–41) carried the controversial text and new religion into Upper Canada. The provinces of Upper Canada and the Maritimes offered up hundreds of converts to the growing religious organization. As the centre of Mormonism moved, British North America lost many of these converts to locations such as Kirtland, Ohio, and Nauvoo, Illinois, but their ties to the future nation of Canada remained strong.[9]

One such convert, who would eventually become the Church's leader, was John Taylor (1808–87). He started his life in Milnthorpe, Westmorland, England, was christened in the Church of England, and later became an adult member of the Methodist Church. His parents relocated to Upper Canada around 1830, and Taylor joined them in Toronto in 1832 where his connections to Methodism led him to his first wife Leonora Cannon (1796–1868) whom he married in January of 1833. Growing dissatisfaction with the Methodist Church and a meeting with Latter-day Saint missionary Parley P. Pratt (1807–57) opened the Taylors to learning about the new church. According to Church history, Pratt baptized John and Leonora in 1836 in Black Creek, at Georgetown, Ontario. The following year, Joseph Smith Jr. (1805–44) travelled to Upper Canada and soon called John Taylor an apostle, an ordained leader, of The Church of Jesus Christ of Latter-day Saints, which required his relocation to Missouri. Taylor eventually became the third president and prophet of the Church in 1880.[10] Taylor offers an example of how converts in British North America tended to leave and join the Latter-day Saints in the United States especially as the Church moved west. As well, Taylor demonstrates a lasting connection between the Church and what would become Canada.

Violent opposition to Smith and his followers chased the growing church to Kirtland, Ohio, and Jackson County, Missouri, but the group did not find peace in either location. Eventually they established another community in Illinois, calling it Nauvoo, but in 1844, after openly preaching the doctrine of plural marriage (the custom of a man marrying more than one woman) and destroying a dissident group's paper press, authorities arrested Joseph and Hyrum Smith. A mob stormed the jail and killed Joseph and his brother. Not without conflict, Brigham Young (1801–77) took control of the Church and instigated a further westward migration, to the territory to be known as Utah. From 1847 to 1857, almost a hundred towns came into being because of Latter-day Saints' efforts in Utah, but the public announcement of plural marriage in the summer of 1852 added more problems for the Church during this time of settlement.[11]

Despite the Civil War, Congress managed to pass the Morrill Anti-Bigamy Act into legislation in 1862. The Act made marriage to more than one wife a crime and disincorporated The Church of Jesus Christ of Latter-day Saints. Non-Latter-day Saint Americans labelled plural marriage a form of white slavery and, in 1882, US President Chester A. Arthur signed the Edmunds Act and removed the right to vote from those practising the doctrine of plural marriage, in addition to mandating fines and imprisonment. The Church did not change their beliefs or practices, and thus the House passed the Edmunds-Tucker Act in 1887. As Terryl Givens explains,

> The bill dissolved the church, its Perpetual Emigrating Fund, and its militia, the reconstituted Nauvoo Legion. Church property was confiscated, and an obedience and loyalty test oath stripped virtually all Mormons of their political rights ... A few months later, Church President John Taylor died in hiding, and for the next three years, the Mormons endured more imprisonments, bankruptcy, dismembered families, and virtual criminal status for membership in their church.[12]

It was during this turmoil that Church leaders sent members, in particular men with more than one wife, into the North-West Territories to wait out this conflict with the US government.

When the Latter-day Saints faced severe pressure from the United States government, President Taylor looked back to his time in Canada and suggested that the Church search Canadian territory for a place where the Saints might find peace from prosecution for their practice of plural marriage. Following the efforts of Charles Ora Card (1839–1906), Latter-day Saints began settling in the District of Alberta in the North-West Territories in 1887 (Figure 1.1). Many of these settlers were involved in non-monogamous relationships but tended to bring only one spouse to the new Canadian communities. Before, the Church sought converts and encouraged gathering in Ohio, Missouri, Illinois, and Utah. Now, the in-gathering of the Saints began to shift to a scattering of Zion's seeds out into the world. The permanent residency of Latter-day Saints in Canada was the first such experiment. Once more, the Saints were in a diaspora, starting over, separated from their Church headquarters and families, but this time on the Canadian prairies.

Latter-day Saints were outsiders from the beginning. Givens clarifies:

> Hostility to Mormonism emerged long before – and would persist long after – Mormonism's practices of centralized gathering, economic communalism, or polygamy. From the start, opponents were contemptuous of Mormonism's ill-suitedness to embody the sacred or the sublime ... From the prophet's [Joseph Smith's] pedestrian background and name ... to his church's relentless pragmatism ... to the specificity and proximity of the Book of Mormon's origin and story.[13]

They remained outsiders in a new environment when the select few made homes, starting in 1887, in the District of Alberta, North-West Territories.

Latter-day Saints did not enter empty land. In the late 1770s, the Hudson's Bay Company (HBC) and North-West Company (NWC) competed to establish fur-trading posts on land that became the province of Alberta. The two companies merged in 1821, but the fur trade turned unprofitable by the early 1860s. In 1867, the Dominion of Canada was formed, and two years later the Government of Canada, ignoring the people already living in western Canada, purchased Rupert's Land and the North-Western Territory from the HBC and created the North-West Territories. Between 1871 and 1877,

Figure 1.1 Portrait of Charles Ora Card.
Source: Church History Library

the Canadian government negotiated seven treaties with Indigenous peoples across the territory. Canadian historian Alvin Finkel writes, "For the federal government, the important objective was to ensure that the Native peoples' defence of their traditional territories did not stand in the way of plans to create a European commercial agricultural economy and society in what they called western Canada."[14] The production of whisky above the Montana border caused the prime minister to send the new North-West Mounted Police westward and, with the arrival of law and order, the treaty process moved forward and "civilization" was safeguarded.

Religiously, the Latter-day Saints entered a very Christian land. In 1881, the North-West Territories, with a total population of 56,466, contained over 4,000 Roman Catholics, over 3,000 Anglicans, and a collection of Lutherans, Methodists, and Presbyterians.[15] After dividing the Territories into districts, the following census resulted in more focused statistics from the District of Alberta specifically. By 1885, Christians made up approximately 55 per cent of the population in the District of Alberta, with a total population of 15,533.[16] In 1891, the total population of the District of Alberta reached 25,277 (the North-West Territories had over 66,000 inhabitants) with 23 per cent Roman Catholics, 18 per cent Church of England, 15 per cent Presbyterian, 10 per cent Methodists, 10 per cent Lutherans, and a small variety of other Christian denominations.[17] The Latter-day Saints arrived in a region with a population that was over 53 per cent Protestant. They were also arriving after a wave of immigration from Ontario that included mostly British Canadians, but also a scattering of non-British immigrants who were establishing agricultural settlements throughout the prairies.[18] Immigration from places like Germany, Ukraine, Sweden, and Iceland eventually strained British prairie institutions, but the hegemony of the English-speaking, Protestant majority continued to dominate prairie society, and minorities assimilated while trying to maintain some of their cultural heritage.[19]

Industrially, the North-West Territories relied on agriculture. According to the 1891 census, the most common occupations were farmers (7,798), stock-raisers (703), labourers (922), cabinet and furniture makers (508), and government officials (1,029).[20] In addition, coal mines, ranching, natural gas reserves, and railways lured settlers to the District of Alberta. The federal government divided the prairies into townships (36-square mile sections) and, after reserving land for the Canadian Pacific Railways, British male subjects and settlers received a homestead of 160 acres. In *Will the Real Alberta Please Stand Up?*, Geo Takach states that "the notions of starting afresh on the frontier and struggling to survive unleashed a bias against entrenched power, inherited privilege, and the haughty attitudes that went with them."[21] The experience and feelings described by Takach match the attitudes of the first Latter-day Saints in New York state learning the populist vision of Joseph Smith Jr. Democracy and independence replaced tradition, power, and privilege. While this still defines some Albertans, according to Takach, Tamara Palmer Seiler also acknowledges the land, vast and open, and Alberta's rural heritage: "Alberta's traditional character emerged from the period of agrarian settlement, characterized by farm life, small-town life, and a strong sense of community."[22] Albertans had to battle central Canada and what they perceived as morally bankrupt institutions, while Latter-day Saints had to negotiate their own social, political, and economic challenges in their new Canadian home.

Integration of a Minority Religion

This book examines how Latter-day Saints integrated into Canadian society, specifically in an area that became the province of Alberta, from the late nineteenth century to the mid-twentieth century, by studying several sites of negotiation, including architecture, gender roles, politics, business, and marriage. Inspired by the Americanization thesis promoted by scholars, such as Thomas G. Alexander, Armand L. Mauss, Ethan R. Yorgason, and Kathleen Flake, who argue that Latter-day Saints assimilated into the American mainstream society by the mid-twentieth century, one might expect to find a parallel progression of Canadianization and a clear distinction between American and Canadian Latter-day Saints by the 1950s.[23] These and other previous studies that measure the different ways and levels of assimilation guide the research of this book into categories such as politics, economics, marriage, architecture, and gender, searching for a Canadian mirror to the American story. However, there is no singular element that differentiates American from Canadian Latter-day Saints and so my search for a "Canadian Mormonism" shifted, and in this book I concentrate more on Canadian society (and less on "American Mormonism") and Canadian narratives, and how Canadian Latter-day Saints negotiated their identities in these Canadian contexts as a type of integration rather than Canadianization. The key to offering a critical analysis of negotiation, especially with a case study featuring Latter-day Saints, was to focus on the tension between integration and peculiarity/particularity.[24] Beliefs, traditions, and practices unique to Latter-day Saints and the Church – characteristics that drew borders around themselves and maintained an identity of peculiarity – provided enough tension between the Saints and outsiders to keep them separate and different, although in a generally inoffensive way because the Latter-day Saints successfully represented themselves as valuable settlers and labourers who posed little threat to the status quo in Canadian society.

As this book will show, Latter-day Saints living in southern Alberta from the late nineteenth century to the mid-twentieth century integrated into Canadian society and maintained their "peculiar" identity through negotiations evident in their architecture, business style and politics, gendered roles, and family and marriage practices. Integration was a negotiation. Mainstream society forced the newcomer to decide what they were willing to give up, maintain, or innovate in their own traditions as well as what they would adopt, reject, or ignore in their adopted society. Depending on the group's level of success, they might also maintain some tensions with the dominant society and keep a distinctive identity that the dominant group(s) would find acceptable. The process of negotiation, however, takes time; it is multi-dimensional, messy, and complicated.

This study addresses questions pertaining to Canadian and religious identities, immigration, and integration. First, what beliefs, traditions, and practices unique to the Church, characteristics that drew boundaries around themselves in order to maintain an identity of peculiarity, provided enough tension to keep Latter-day Saints both distinctive, but also relatively harmless in the eyes of the Canadian public? How did Latter-day Saints embed themselves in the social, economic, and political structures of Canada, and how did they adapt Mormonism to Canadian circumstances?[25] The Canadian context, the Latter-day Saint experience in southern Alberta, and the growth of the Church in Canada reveal a process of negotiation. There exists a tension between integration and otherness. Latter-day Saints balanced these tensions on some levels by maintaining their distinctiveness while at the same time blending into Canadian expectations.

Literature Review

The research questions fuelling this book connect back to the original Americanization thesis developed by Mormon studies scholars, historians, geographers, and sociologists studying the assimilation of the Church and its members. The histories of the assimilation of The Church of Jesus Christ of Latter-day Saints often feature a narrative tracing the practice of plural marriage, theocracy, and economic communalism to a shift in the twentieth century that involved "embrac[ing] patriotism, the Protestant work ethic, and the mores and respectability of the American middle class ... [when Latter-day Saints] had found a way to integrate their theology with their nation."[26] Scholars tracing this transformation argue that Latter-day Saints assimilated into American mainstream society by the mid-twentieth century. Tracing assimilation is important because Latter-day Saints went from being hated outsiders to the stereotypical American standard, which eventually culminated in what newspapers coined "The Mormon Moment" (i.e., Latter-day Saint Mitt Romney's 2012 presidential campaign). If the Americanization thesis promoted by scholars such as Bowman, Mauss, Alexander, Yorgason, and Flake is accurate, then one might ask whether there is a similar narrative of Canadianization.[27] At the very least, what is the Canadianization thesis? When and how did Latter-day Saints assimilate into Canadian mainstream society? Did Canadian society change the Church? Did the Church have any impact on Canadian society? Most scholars analysing the Americanization of the Church do not include Canada in their analysis. However, even when Canada is acknowledged or included, there are still issues. For example, sociologist O. Kendall White, Jr., in his article on the nation-state and the Church, concludes that Canadians and Americans are not that different because "since Canadian Mormonism is firmly under the wing of the central church, it would experience great difficulty and probably has little interest in developing its own forms."[28] If White had consulted primary sources from Canadian Latter-day Saints, he might have discovered the subtle differences between Canadian and American Latter-day Saints.

Why is the Canadian part of Latter-day Saint and the Church's history significant? Mormon studies scholars seem to focus on the American Church and paint the story of a singular type of Mormonism, but new studies, especially those emphasizing the global reach of the Church (i.e., global Mormon studies), are starting to recognize that there are different manifestations of Mormonism.[29] The evidence shared in this book suggests that the Americanization thesis does not adequately explain the spread and integration of Latter-day Saints into Canada. Even though it shares a border with and is an ally of the United States, Canada is a separate country with different values, histories, politics, and customs, so it should be fair to hypothesize that Canadian Mormonism would look and act a bit differently than American Mormonism. These differences and similarities are worth discussing if we are to understand the Church as a global religion.

In his Tanner Lecture for the 2012 Mormon History Association Annual Meeting, Canadian historian David B. Marshall observes the lack of Canadian content in the field of Mormon studies, stating, "There are no studies indicating how the Mormons in Canada integrated and assimilated while struggling to maintain their 'peculiar' identity."[30] This book begins to explore the question of how Canadian Latter-day Saints negotiated their identities in the Canadian context. Previously, Mormon studies scholars have shed some light on the Church's history and development in Canada in various articles, monographs, and edited collections. Published 30 years ago, *The Mormon Presence in Canada* offers chapters exploring public reactions to the arrival of Latter-day Saints in Canada, comparing Canadian and Mexican experiences, studying roles of women in the settlement process, and arguing that Mormon is an ethnic identity.[31] Similarly, *Regional Studies in Latter-day Saint Church History: Western Canada* provides another collection of essays particularly relevant to the study of the Church in southern Alberta. Specifically, Andrew H. Hedges's study of landscape, climate, and interactions between surrounding cultures, like the Kainai Nation, in addition to Mary Jane Woodger's chapter on spiritual gifts in Alberta, add important perspectives to understanding the Latter-day Saint experience in southern Alberta.[32] Most recently, the Church's publishing company produced an edited volume titled *Canadian Mormons: History of the Church of Jesus Christ of Latter-day Saints in Canada*, written and edited by active Church members, presenting historical summaries of the Church in specific regions. This collection tells the history of the Latter-day Saints without tackling difficult or controversial topics and without offering a deep, critical analysis of the implications of Latter-day Saint immigration and identity formation.[33] My study is different because it puts Latter-day Saints in southern Alberta at the centre of the story about the Church, immigration, identity, and integration, and asks how all these come into contact with different sites of Canadian society like business and politics, gender, families, and architecture.

Marshall continues his overview of Canadian scholarship and Mormonism by noting that "despite overriding concern with regionalism, multiculturalism, and ethnicity in Canadian historiography, the history of the Mormons has not attracted very much attention ... The landscape of Mormon historiography in Canada is virtually barren."[34] The history of The Church of Jesus Christ of Latter-day Saints in Canada matters because the history of religion in Canada is a complex, diverse story, and the Latter-day Saints make up part of that larger story, but historians and religious studies scholars have yet to dedicate more than several academic articles, a few footnotes, and a couple sentences to the Church when discussing religion in Canada. Anglo-Protestant and French-Catholic narratives dominate the histories of religion in Canada. Scholars of Canadian religion and history must take into consideration the stories of non-dominant peoples, such as Mennonites, Latter-day Saints, and Indigenous peoples, in order to uncover new narratives and hear from suppressed or ignored voices. Furthermore, such studies not only have inherent value, but they help contextualize and give nuance to our understandings of those dominant groups. For example, W.E. Mann devotes his attention to non-dominant groups in the book *Sect, Cult, and Church in Alberta* as part of a series on the Social Credit movement, but completely ignores the Church in his study of "religious developments in Alberta against the background of frontier expansion and community instability ... [in order] to understand the social roots of resurgent sect and cult movements."[35] Despite this absence, Mann confirms the importance of Alberta. Alberta is significant because of its history of religious non-conformity and various religious groupings (such as Latter-day Saints, Hutterites, and Mennonites, for example). Furthermore, Alberta offers examples of the influential role of sectarian religion in the political and social development of the region and country.[36]

Surveying the scholarship of the history of religion in Canada, I found few scholars included The Church of Jesus Christ of Latter-day Saints in their research, studies, or publications. In *The Church in the Canadian Era*, John Webster Grant allotted one sentence to the Latter-day Saints when he observes after the Second World War that "the Mormons, who had not previously expanded far beyond several colonies in southern Alberta, began to be visible in all parts of Canada."[37] The presence of Latter-day Saints in British Columbia, Alberta, Manitoba, and Ontario indicated that Grant's observation was a slight exaggeration. Likewise, in their book about the religious history of Canada, Nancy Christie and Michael Gauvreau examine the changing, rather than declining, roles of churches in Canadian society and identify the period 1880 to 1910 as one of the most conflictual periods in Canadian religious history because of sectarian splitting, gender antagonism, theological disputes, and rural/urban conflicts.[38] But Latter-day Saints and the prairie provinces are not a part of this narrative.

Western Canada, especially the prairie provinces, and non-dominant groups, such as The Church of Jesus Christ of Latter-day Saints, are excluded from most histories of religion in Canada, but some scholars do research and write about the west, the prairies, and minority religions. Anthony W. Rasporich and Sarah Carter offer some insight into understanding both the Church and the western provinces. Rasporich, comparing utopian settlements in the prairie provinces, observes that the survival of these religious groups relied on preserving particular socio-economic features of their unique cultures. The distinctive aspects that the Latter-day Saints tried to preserve in Canada, argues Rasporich, were plural marriage, nuclear farming villages, and cooperative economic organizations.[39] These are three significant sites where integration and negotiation play out and will be addressed later in this book. Likewise, Carter's study of plural marriage and polygamy among the Kainai and Latter-day Saints in southern Alberta provides further understanding of identity construction, legal implications, and minority groups in the prairie west. The works of Carter and Rasporich are among the rare few that consider the Church in southern Alberta in detail.

In *A History of Christianity in the United States and Canada*, a standard survey about religious history in North America, Mark A. Noll keeps the Church and Canada separated by dedicating a couple of pages to the Church in a chapter featuring other religious "outsiders" and concentrating any analysis of Christianity in Canada to mostly eastern regions of the country, except for his brief discussion of Social Credit in the 1930s.[40] Not all, but most historians and religious studies scholars currently studying the history of religion in Canada tend to ignore Mormonism. This book offers new narratives to add to the greater Canadian story of religious diversity. Indeed, it attempts to decentre the eastern provinces as the only site of Canadian religious interest. What does Canadian look like when, rather than Canada being what follows in the wake of the frontier, Canada is itself the frontier? What does it look like when expansion comes not from the east but the south? Latter-day Saints living in southern Alberta from the late nineteenth century to the mid-twentieth century integrated into Canadian society and maintained their "peculiar" identity through negotiations evident at various political, social, and cultural sites. Canadian and southern Albertan society forced the Latter-day Saints to abandon, keep, and change some of their "peculiarities" as well as add, deny, or ignore parts of mainstream culture. This book will demonstrate the balance of tension that kept them both distinct and acceptable as a new religion on Canadian soil.

Crossing and Dwelling

How did Latter-day Saints in Canada balance their social, cultural, and religious distinctiveness with integration into Canadian society? An examination of architecture, marriage practices, gendered roles, business practices, and political participation show how Latter-day Saints balanced the distinctive parts of their identity as members of a minority religion navigating a new homeland. Thomas A. Tweed offers a theory of religion for the religious life of transnational migrants that we can apply to the Latter-day Saint experience in Alberta. To begin, let us consider Tweed's definition of religion: "Religions are confluences of organic-cultural flows that intensify joy and confront suffering by drawing on human and suprahuman forces to make homes and cross boundaries."[41] Most influential to this study of Latter-day Saints in Canada is the significance of dwelling (making homes) and crossing boundaries because this helps explain how Latter-day Saints negotiated their competing identities: American, Canadian, Latter-day Saint, not to mention father, husband, bishop, wife, mother, farmer, politician, activist, and so on.

Religions are "clusters of dwelling practices," explains Tweed, that "orient individuals and groups in time and space, transform the natural environment, and allow devotees to inhabit the worlds they construct."[42] Building meetinghouses and temples, joining political parties and winning elections, and making kitchen medicines and healing their neighbours are examples of initiatives and encounters that oriented Latter-day Saints to their new home in Canada and their previous homeland in the United States. These practices and experiences moved Latter-day Saints through time and space, transforming both Canadian society (by introducing Mormonism) and the Church (by causing adaption and integration), and eventually allowing Latter-day Saints to inhabit both Canadian and their own Mormon "worlds." Like transnational migrants, Latter-day Saints, while far from home, carried their distinctive religion onto Canadian soil and negotiated the tensions with their Church and the Canadian public. They selected surprising architectural styles, they practised plural marriage, and they favoured cooperative businesses, but they also, eventually, adapted to Canadian expectations and abandoned the more controversial practices. By navigating through their Canadian circumstances, Latter-day Saints oriented themselves and their Church to local expectations and environments and constructed a new home for the Church in Canada.

Understanding The Church of Jesus Christ of Latter-day Saints in Canada requires discussing transitions, adaptions, and tensions –

all aspects of negotiating religious identity. Part of Tweed's definition of religion includes the idea of "organic-cultural flows," which he describes as spatial, temporal, organic, and cultural elements and features moving through time (e.g., passing through generations) and space (e.g., missionaries carrying their religion from one land to another).[43] Mormonism flows from Utah to Alberta to eastern Canada, through generations, through mostly American, Canadian, and European hands, all the while being organically adapted to the new environment and society by Latter-day Saints. What happens when these flows meet barriers, such as law enforcement, competing theologies, or lack of worship spaces? While these organic-cultural flows move through time and space, they will likely come up against barriers, restrictions, and challenges, and how directors of these flows respond to barriers will determine its success and survival. How does the religious believer, in this case the Latter-day Saint in Alberta, move around the barrier? Do they change the barrier? Or does the barrier change them as they try to fit around it?

Tweed also discusses how humans cross boundaries and defines three categories of movement: terrestrial, corporeal, and cosmic.[44] Latter-day Saints, in addition to dwelling, or homemaking, performed all three types of crossings: They crossed natural landscapes, environments, and social spaces (terrestrial); they pushed the limits of their physical bodies when they cleared and cultivated acres of land (corporeal); and they contemplated stages after human death and the plan of salvation (cosmic). Terrestrial crossings will receive the most attention on the following pages as we examine how Latter-day Saints not only crossed natural terrain (travelling between rural communities), but also voyaged into Canadian social spaces (joining political parties, earning business contracts, participating in the war effort, building sacred spaces, etc.). Metaphors of crossing and flow create images of movement, but these movements, or transitions, were not without challenges (e.g., barriers). How the Latter-day Saints in Alberta responded and adapted to these barriers shows how they negotiated their place in Canadian society.

Lived Religion

While reading Church historical reports, mission journals, personal diaries, oral histories, correspondences, and meeting minutes, I ruminated on the everyday thinking and doing of Latter-day Saints. What did the settlers in southern Alberta think about their new home? How did it feel to be separated from Church headquarters? What did they do to embrace or distance from Canadian society? As Robert Orsi explains, everyday places, like homes and workplaces in addition to familiar sites of religious activities, are sites where people "make something of the worlds they have found themselves thrown into, and, in turn, it is through these subtle, intimate, quotidian actions on the world that meanings are made, known, and verified."[45] With this in mind, I looked beyond expected sites of religious activity, like Zion, and considered unexpected sites of religious activities, such as business transactions, political campaigns, recipe sharing, medicine making, town planning, architectural designing, and grave marking. What could these everyday sites teach me not only about Latter-day Saints, but also about Canadian and southern Albertan identity? Orsi contends,

> The interpretive challenge of the study of lived religion is to develop the practice of disciplined attention to people's signs and practices as they describe, understand, and use them, in the circumstances of their experiences, and to the structures and conditions within which these signs and practices emerge ... Lived religion cannot be separated from other practices of everyday life, from the ways that humans do other necessary and important things, or from other cultural structures and discourses (legal, political, medical, and so on).[46]

By immersing myself in primary sources and listening to Latter-day Saints describe and understand their own experiences in southern Alberta, I learned that there existed a relationship between their religious identity, Canadian identity, and the Canadian cultural structures and discourses that they chose to participate in.

Building off Orsi, Meredith B. McGuire informs my understanding of religion as lived with the suggestion to think about religion as "an ever-changing, multifaceted, often messy – even contradictory – amalgam of beliefs and practices that are not necessarily those religious institutions consider important."[47] Considering this, then, I should not expect Latter-day Saints in southern Alberta to replicate Utah Mormonism in a straight-forward manner. Yes, they transplanted their religion, and in most ways it resembled the Utah Church, but there were small differences, which we can attribute to their relationship with Canadian society. For example, the selection of a distinct architectural style for the first temple outside the United States, the continuation of plural marriage even after the Church announced the end of the practice, and the allegiance to political parties that supported social credit and cooperation indicate that Latter-day Saints in southern Alberta negotiated an identity that was both similar to and different from the identities of American Latter-day Saints. Their beliefs and practices changed and adapted and were sometimes not necessarily cohesive with the institutional Church. My study and analysis is less concerned with high-ranking Church leaders in Utah and more interested in Latter-day Saints in rural Albertan communities, farming land, organizing communities, building homes and meetinghouses, joining provincial and federal political parties, cooking kitchen medicines, and navigating Canadian society. How did these everyday actions and experiences of Church members change The Church of Jesus Christ of Latter-day Saints in southern Alberta?

Studying the lived experiences of Canadian Latter-day Saints reveals stories of transition and integration. In her analysis of the Americanization thesis and Latter-day Saints, Jan Shipps argues, that "the responsibility for boundary maintenance had to be shifted from the corporate body to the individuals within that body."[48] This book observes instances of boundary maintenance that happened at the individual level among Canadian Latter-day Saints. In order to answer my research questions, I observed the work of scholars supporting the Americanization thesis in search of a method to organize and understand my primary sources and data. While the second half of *The Angel and the Beehive* deals with Mormonism after the 1960s, the first half, in particular Mauss's account of assimilation in the early twentieth century, showed me a model method. Mauss identifies signs, like the renunciation of plural marriage and economic communitarianism, changing rhetoric in conference talks, and doctrinal and ritual developments, that communicated Church-wide assimilation.[49] I considered the categories of social programs, education, and signs at the grassroots level and realized the applicability of these concepts to my own research. For example, the Boy Scouts established troops in southern Alberta before taking the program to the United States and creating a long-term partnership with the official Church. In order to consider integration in Canadian society, then, I had to figure out what examples were local or at the grass roots (local to southern Alberta and Canada), and not Church-wide (American and top-down policy from Salt Lake City). Mauss argues that Latter-day Saints were highly assimilated by the 1960s. In this book I pay attention to whether I can say the same for Canadian Latter-day Saints.

In *Transformation of the Mormon Culture Region*, Yorgason provides a similar model for categorizing data by cultural and social processes. He examines issues such as gender authority, economic responsibility, and patriotism, and how disagreements over these issues transformed the region. Considering regionality and geopolitical boundaries, Yorgason studies certain events, like the Reed Smoot hearings, institutions, like the United Order, and issues, like women's suffrage, and how eventually Americans no longer identified the Mormon culture region as un-American.[50] Yorgason's study shows that themes like politics, economics, and gender can help organize our observations of Latter-day Saints as they transition from feared other to acceptable minority.

Canadian, Prairie, Albertan Identities

This study considers competing identities: mainly Canadian, Albertan, and Latter-day Saint. The adaption of The Church of Jesus Christ of Latter-day Saints to their Canadian environment occurred during a time of change and upheaval for Canadian society. From 1881 to 1911, the population of Canada grew by more than two-thirds, introducing new religious and ethnic identities into Canadian society including Ukrainian, Greek Orthodox, Japanese, Mennonite, Buddhist, and Confucian.[51] In his telling of these changes, Peter Beyer outlines the dominant attitude of prejudice held by Euro-Canadians against different groups of people from places such as India, China, and Japan. Beyer explains,

> Euro-Canadians ... were very aware of the range of religious and cultural diversity that existed around the world and in their own backyard; but they understood these differences in an explicitly dichotomous and hierarchical fashion. There were the white, European, Christian, and civilized peoples, some of whom were admittedly "more equal than others"; then there were the unalterable "others" who had to be kept apart or, to the extent deemed possible, "civilized."[52]

He does not mention, let alone categorize, Latter-day Saints in either of these camps, but it is fair to say that they fell under the umbrella of "white, European, [arguably] Christian, and civilized" and were likely among those classified as less equal than other white, European, civilized Christians, such as British Anglicans. However, with the influx of immigration and the introduction of diversity not seen on Canadian soil before the 1880s, Latter-day Saints were perhaps no longer the most threatening to European Canadian identity (whether it be Anglo-Protestant or French-Canadian Catholic).

Although not the most threatening to developing forms of national identity, Latter-day Saints and the Church were still perceived by Canadians as risks to certain ideals and values. N.K. Clifford illustrates the evolving vision of Canada as the Kingdom of God, or "His Dominion," through the eyes of Canadian Protestants striving for consensus and coalition in their attempts at creating an ideal society.[53] Canadian Protestants visualized a land where political democracy ruled, evangelical Protestant Christianity reigned, and immigrants conformed by Christianizing and adapting to the standards of Canadian white Anglo-Saxons.[54] Discussing the same wave of immigration mentioned by Beyer, Clifford considers what groups, such as the Ukrainians and Chinese, were perceived as most threatening to dominant society as well as other minorities, such as Latter-day Saints, Jews, and Hutterites, that morally and politically jeopardized the Protestant vision with their alternative religious, communal, or pacifist ideas.[55] Depending on the level and perception of threat, Canadians reacted differently to different groups (through exclusionary laws or attempts at deportation, etc.), but eventually Canadian Protestants accepted the realities of living in a diverse society, tolerating some minority groups over others, and welcoming those that assimilated. The Latter-day Saints found the right balance by integrating and adapting to most Canadian expectations; but what were the expectations of their Canadian neighbours in southern Alberta during this period? We must look closer at the region of western Canada, the prairie provinces, to fully understand the identity negotiation of Latter-day Saints settling in Alberta.

To accomplish this analysis, we need to find and define the dominant identity that Latter-day Saints negotiated with. Since the majority of their settlements and interactions, as covered in this book, take place in southern Alberta, the dominant identity is western Canadian, or prairie identity. In his essay for *Historical Papers/Communications historiques*, Friesen unpacks aspects of western Canadian identity to show the various beliefs supporting the myth of this regional consciousness: essentially, western Canadian identity relies on the notion of building a new society that is democratic, egalitarian, cooperative, and progressive. This myth heavily depends on the origin story that "the West itself was founded upon local expectations of growth, prosperity and power."[56] R. Douglas Francis analyses this myth of a new, ideal society and explains that "The [Canadian] West was seen as the home of democracy, the inspiration for reform, and the seed-bed of individualism, radicalism, and freedom, in contrast to the more privileged conservative and reactionary East."[57] In a later article, Francis identifies four significant parts of the prairie myth: regional identity, regional protest, social reform, and imagery. He traces the intellectual and cultural historiography of the prairies and classifies his findings under these categories to show what connects residents of the prairie provinces (e.g. regionalism, agrarianism, the social gospel movement, and creativity).[58] The metaphor of Promised Land appears in the volume *The Prairie West as Promised Land* and solidifies an image of the region the Latter-day Saints entered in the late nineteenth century. In their introduction, Francis and Kitzan argue that Canadians depicted the prairies as a Promised Land because it was seen as a paradise far away from urban and industrial eastern Canada: It was considered a place where a perfect society could flourish, and it would allow settlers to escape tradition and privilege of the homeland to embrace opportunity and destiny in the new.[59] As the westward expansion in the United States ended, Canada offered not only new but also different opportunities because settlers and immigrants recognized that the Canadian prairies were "a gentler, milder west . . . [where] the ideals of 'peace, order, and good government' would be placed above that of the 'inalienable rights of the individual,' and British culture and British law and order above American frontier culture and vigilante rule."[60] Latter-day Saints entered a place that, as a Promised Land, "would uphold values of harmony, cooperation, and the good of society as whole."[61] The District of Alberta in the North-West Territories of Canada was, at certain times and under certain circumstances, more British than American, and more peaceful than violent. However, economic depressions, world wars, religious revivals, and agrarian revolutions would change the myth and identity of the Canadian prairies. By the 1940s, the prairie provinces had evolved their regional identity. Friesen defines this "regional consciousness" as rooted in, "the sense of a unique landscape and site, the struggle of the pioneer, federal-provincial bickering, the turn-of-the-century boom and the Depression catastrophe of the 1930s, and the intense experience of nativism and ethnic acculturation."[62] The identity, or identities, of the Canadian west did evolve, but the significance of this identity remained the same and impacted incoming Latter-day Saints throughout the period.

Political scientist Roger Gibbins offers a framework for understanding the evolving prairie identity. In *Prairie Politics and Society: Regionalism in Decline*, Gibbins examines the political integration of prairie society into the Canadian mainstream and provides seven "pillars of regionalism" to understand the distinctive nature of the prairies.[63] The pillars most helpful for defining prairie identity for the purposes of this book include rural population, ethnic composition, religious composition, prairie agriculture, and political regionalism. Latter-day Saints settled in an area that fit this description: a combination of rural and small-town settlements, waves of immigration from Europe and the United States, interactions with the social gospel movement and other varieties of Protestant Christianity, wheat economy and other agricultural endeavours (e.g., sugar beets, ranching), and participation in political parties indigenous to the western provinces. If Latter-day Saints situated themselves among these "pillars" then what factors complicated the integration process?

In *Patterns of Prejudice*, historian Howard Palmer focuses on the province of Alberta and issues of prejudice, racism, and nativism. Palmer acknowledges that articulating a singular national identity is nearly impossible for most Canadians (and historians, political scientists, sociologists, etc.), but they can usually identify shared assumptions and attitudes.[64] Palmer concentrates on Alberta to show how a majority (in this case, British-born immigrants and eastern Canadians) not only founded the province's political, social, religious, and educational institutions, but also shaped public opinion and determined public policy especially regarding newcomers.[65] Palmer's assessments of the dominant group, their expectations, and the role of Latter-day Saints inform my own study. First, Palmer connects the social reform and social gospel movements to expectations that assimilation would help immigrants and therefore stop the deterioration of foundational institutions.[66] This tells me to consider how Latter-day Saints contributed to or participated in important institutions, like education, health care, and politics. Second, he observes that "most Anglo-Albertans judged minority groups on the basis of how quickly they could be assimilated," so I also need to reflect on the speed and efficiency of the Latter-day Saints' efforts of integration.[67] Last, Palmer specifically examines the Latter-day Saints and provides his own conclusions on their process of assimilation, writing that "Mormons in southern Alberta began to win gradual acceptance through their rapid adjustment to the economic, educational, and political institutions of the area. They were experienced farmers, they were English-speaking, they were predominately public school supporters."[68] Palmer's other case studies suggest that the "Anglo-Albertan" majority considered other minority groups much more problematic, especially in terms of race and religion. While Latter-day Saints did threaten the western Canadian Protestant vision with their practice of plural marriage, communal economic plans, and misunderstood theology, they also met many other crucial criteria of the prairie identity, such as cooperative, progressive, successful, individual, and democratic.

Another helpful contribution of Palmer's work on prejudice in Alberta is his concluding section summarizing various factors that have been most important in determining the rise and fall of nativism – weighing, for example, political and economic matters, such as economic depressions and world wars; social developments, such as reform movements like women's rights; and intellectual factors, such as new ideas and philosophies like the social gospel.[69] These factors appear throughout this book when I discuss Latter-day Saint involvement in politics, participation in social work and activism, design of architecture, and evolving theology.

Outline

This book argues that the integration of Latter-day Saints into the mainstream of Canadian society occurred at different sites of negotiation, mostly located in what became the province of Alberta, and at varying levels of success, across a span of approximately 60 years. Alberta is the geographic focus because Latter-day Saints permanently settled and colonized several towns (e.g., Cardston, Magrath, Raymond) and rural regions to create a "Mormon culture region" in southern Alberta. The period for this study – late nineteenth to mid-twentieth centuries – begins with the permanent settlement in what was called the District of Alberta, North-West Territories. In the year 1887 the first group of Latter-day Saints migrated from Utah to the District of Alberta in search of safe place to live outside the United States and far away from prosecution for the practice of plural marriage. Choosing a span of approximately sixty years was an attempt to match the period of Americanization. The late 1940s and early 1950s allows the inclusion of a specific case study regarding Latter-day Saint politician John H. Blackmore (1890–1971), which helps illustrate the Church's evolving policies and attitudes towards plural marriage.

The six chapters that follow come from themes, or sites of negotiation, identified while exploring the primary sources. The first chapter looks at Latter-day Saint families and the practice of plural marriage. In this chapter, I observe Canadian's reactions to non-monogamy in published, political, and legal situations as well as the impact this had on Latter-day Saints in southern Alberta. This chapter ends with two case studies that show just how far Latter-day Saints shifted in terms of marriage. The next chapter explores gendered roles with specific attention to Latter-day Saint women in southern Alberta. In this chapter, I demonstrate the diverse roles held by Latter-day Saint women, including their work as spiritual advocates, healers, and political activists. Latter-day Saint women offer another example of how Church members stepped outside the boundaries of their communities in southern Alberta and entered public, Canadian spaces. The third and fourth chapters highlight Latter-day Saints' contributions to business and politics in Canadian society. By looking at their cooperative organizations, involvement in irrigation, sugar beet farming, and ranching, we can identify additional shifts in their commitments to building connections beyond the Church. Politics offers another lens to understand their changing perspectives. As it became apparent that their time in Canada was more permanent, Latter-day Saints joined Canadian political parties, became political candidates, and won elections. Their participation in Canadian political parties, such as the United Farmers of Alberta, Social Credit, and Co-operative Commonwealth Federation, teaches us that Latter-day Saints in southern Alberta actively participated in political and social movements that looked to improve living conditions for Albertans and Canadians. They shared similar ideologies, such as a strong belief in cooperative economics, and made valuable contributions.

Mauss argues that by the mid-twentieth century The Church of Jesus Christ of Latter-day Saints lacked tension with society because they had assimilated too much.[70] If there is no tension, there is no difference, and if there is no difference from other religions, what makes the Church worth committing to? By looking at sites of lived experience such as families, business, and politics, we can see moving and changing tensions throughout Latter-day Saint experiences. The Cardston Alberta Temple offers another form of tension, which I demonstrate in the sixth chapter. After its construction, Latter-day Saints in Canada had one less reason to return to Utah – members could perform marriage ceremonies, sealings, and ordinances without travelling hundreds of miles.[71] The temple, generally a peculiar sight and a symbol of secrecy, kept the Canadian Saints distinct from their Canadian neighbours while also rooting them in the Canadian land. Similarly, cemeteries and grave markers offer a final site of negotiation to understand the Latter-day Saint experience in southern Alberta.

This book seeks to show how Latter-day Saints integrated into Canadian society by studying several sites of negotiation such as architecture, politics, business, gendered roles, and family. These

26 Thirsty Land into Springs of Water

are sites of negotiation because Latter-day Saints decided how they wanted to cross into Canadian spaces, how they wanted to maintain their "peculiar" identity, and what they were truly willing to abandon or adopt. Mainstream society forced the newcomer to make these decisions. The process of negotiation takes time, and it is multidimensional and complicated.

Chapter Two

Families

Introduction

By the time Latter-day Saints began colonizing the District of Alberta in the North-West Territories, mainstream Canadian society held specific expectations regarding marriage practices and rejected deviations from these standards. Therefore, any group known for practising non-monogamy, such as The Church of Jesus Christ of Latter-day Saints, would come under serious scrutiny from Canadians. Facing criticism and possible government intervention, Latter-day Saints built, maintained, and crossed boundaries while continuing their practice of plural marriage on Canadian soil. Eventually, changing marriage customs and family dynamics shows how this community balanced their religious distinctiveness with integration into Canadian society. Shifting away from plural marriage and towards monogamy demonstrates how Latter-day Saints oriented themselves to Canadian expectations.[1] They managed to inhabit both Canadian spaces and their own "worlds" through their willingness to eventually abandon the unique practice of plural marriage and instead emphasize different doctrine, like eternal marriage and eternal families. The transition to monogamous relationships is an example of initiatives and encounters that oriented Latter-day Saints to both their new home in Canada and their previous homeland in the United States. These new practices and experiences move communities through time and space, transforming both Canadian society (by introducing plural marriage in addition to the already known polygamous practices of some Indigenous peoples) and the community members (by causing adaption and integration), and eventually allowing minority groups to inhabit both Canadian and their own "worlds." Like transnational migrants, Latter-day Saints, while far from home, carried their distinctive religion onto Canadian soil and negotiated the tensions with their Church and Canadian public. They practised plural marriage, but they also, eventually, adapted to Canadian expectations and abandoned the controversial practice.

Latter-day Saints practised plural marriage – practices that offended Canadian mainstream society and resulted in various actions and consequences. In the chapter that follows, I will share popular reactions to plural marriage by presenting academic, political, and legal responses in Canada. Next, I will discuss the actions that followed these reactions. Specifically, an examination of changes to the Criminal Code and of the impact on the Church. Finally, I will end with an analysis of the consequences of these reactions and actions. Latter-day Saints in Canada faced a choice: resist or accept Canadian public opinion, political reactions, and legal changes. How they navigated these pressures teaches us another part of their story of integration into Canadian society. First, an explanation about the state of the family in Canadian society at the time the Latter-day Saints began immigrating to the NWT.

The Canadian Family

By the turn of the twentieth century, white Canadian society demanded Christian monogamous unions. "Through its use of law," writes historian W. Peter Ward,

> [G]overnment reinforced the stability of marriage. It defined the range of acceptable spouses, it established the terms under which men and women married, it empowered the agent authorized to perform wedding ceremonies, it frustrated the dissolution of marriage, and it punished those who transgressed its bounds. In these ways the state put its weight behind the traditional Christian concept of marriage.[2]

In 1841, when the provinces of Upper and Lower Canada united, the government defined bigamy in the Provincial Statutes of Canada as occurring "if any person, being married, shall marry any other person during the life of the former husband or wife."[3] Bigamy was a felony in the newly established United Province of Canada, and the punishment was hard labour for no less than seven years, or imprisonment no longer than two years. The Magistrate's Manual, a complete digest of the criminal law of Canada, and provincial law of Upper Canada, repeated the provincial statutes.[4] In 1859, the Consolidated Statutes of Canada reworded the definition of bigamy to be, "Any person who, being married, marries any other person during the life of the former husband or wife, whether the second marriage takes place in this Province or elsewhere, and every person who counsels, aids, or abets such offender, shall respectively be guilty of felony" with a punishment of imprisonment in a penitentiary or prison for two years.[5] While the exact wording evolved and the punishment changed, the basis of the law remained the same: Canadians could not marry more than one person at the same time. In 1867, the British Parliament passed the British North America (BNA) Act and created the Canadian federation. The BNA Act distributed legislative powers, including authority over marriage and divorce. While the exclusive legislative authority of the Parliament of Canada extended to matters concerning marriage and divorce, each province was responsible for the solemnization of marriage.[6] Regardless, monogamy, as imagined by white, Christian Canadians, was not the only way that marriages, relationships, and families existed in lands that would become known as Canada. Indigenous peoples, practising their own marriage customs, became repeat transgressors of the statutes defining bigamy, and authorities continued amending and rewording the law to further restrict deviations from their image of marriage and family. According to Cynthia R. Comacchio, the period of rapid change between 1850 and 1940 caused "a widespread public perception that 'the family' was in a state of crisis."[7] The model Canadian family was white, middle class, Anglo-Celtic Protestant, or French-Catholic, involving "masculine authority, feminine submission, and the reproduction of certain socially defined qualities."[8] Minority groups not following this model threatened Canada's stability and acceptability.

This review of Canadian statutes regarding marriage demonstrates how far Canadians were willing to go to define acceptable marriage practices, and what was acceptable to those making these laws was monogamy. In order to enforce that standard, lawmakers had to create statutes that defined deviant practices and the punishments for those who transgressed the traditional Christian concept of marriage. Fuelling these decisions was the rapid change Canada experienced in terms of immigration, expansion, and industrialization. To protect the model Canadian family as monogamous, Christian, and white, with specific gendered roles and qualities, the Canadian Government needed to put statutes and laws in place that would enforce conduct that all peoples living in Canada would have to abide by. These statutes show that non-monogamy was unacceptable, and thus, bigamy, or the act of marrying more than one person at the same time, became a punishable offence.

In her contribution to *Contact Zones: Aboriginal and Settler Women in Canada's Colonial Past*, Canadian historian Sarah Carter examines the prohibition of non-monogamy in western Canada and the government's attempts to impose monogamy on the Indigenous populations.[9] Carter followed this with her chapter in *Unsettled Pasts: Reconceiving the West Through Women's History* and added the problem of divorce to her study of the federal administration of marriage among First Nations in western Canada.[10] In her monograph *The Importance of Being Monogamous: Marriage and Nation Building in Western Canada to 1915,* Carter addresses the widespread anxiety over the state of marriage, family, and home in western Canada where the Indigenous populations initially outnumbered the white settlers. Among these Indigenous peoples, the concept of marriage was diverse and took on numerous forms such as same-sex unions or polygamous relationships.[11] While Carter's research concentrates on Indigenous communities in western Canada, she also explores the settlements in the District of Alberta that were founded by Latter-day Saints from Utah who practised plural marriage. Carter astutely identifies their reasons for immigrating to Canada and briefly discusses their leader, Charles Ora Card, but fails to consider post-Manifesto polygamy, that is, plural marriages that continued and new unions that were solemnized after the Church publicly advised against future plural marriages in what was an official Church statement and policy known as the First Manifesto in 1890.[12] Furthermore, Carter acknowledges the Canadian government's harsh treatment of the Niitsitapi population, who refused to give up polygamy, but ignores the drastically different course of treatment received by the Latter-day Saints. Instead of prosecution or punishment for practising non-monogamy, the government and officials rewarded the Canadian Latter-day Saints with lucrative business contracts and immigration assistance.

Carter's research is fundamental to understanding the context of the situation that the Latter-day Saints were entering in the late nineteenth century as immigrants to the NWT. Latter-day Saints colonized territory and settled land directly adjacent to the First Nations reserve inhabited by the Kainai Nation, members of which Carter studied, and she demonstrated that they were subject to white Canadian anxiety about non-monogamy. Therefore, Latter-day Saints were not just moving to an uninhabited land, they were colonizing and settling communities beside Indigenous peoples who, like them, practised marriage customs and established relationships that Canadians deemed deviant and threatening to the model Canadian family. This context is important because it reveals that Latter-day Saints were not alone in their practice of non-monogamy and, by moving to the NWT, alongside the Indigenous population already there, they doubled the threat to the standards expected by the Canadian authorities.[13]

Latter-day Saint Families

The Church of Jesus Christ of Latter-day Saints' public confession to plural marriage shocked North Americans and initiated a campaign to end the practice. In 1852 Brigham Young (1801–77) introduced the concept to all believers and guided Orson Pratt (1811–81) to publicly defend it. To outsiders, plural marriage threatened Victorian ideals of the family and sexuality. Next to slavery, polygamy was the next most contentious issue in the United States. The controversial practice brought unwanted attention from the United States government, which eventually passed a series of laws prohibiting polygamy. In 1862, the US Congress passed the Morrill Anti-Bigamy Act, but the Civil War, among other factors, prevented the suppression of plural marriage. The US Supreme Court tested the constitutionality of the Morrill Anti-Bigamy Act with *Reynolds v. United States* in 1878. The anti-polygamy bill stood the legal test, and the Supreme Court rejected the argument of religious freedom. The US government's next line of attack came in the form of the Edmunds Act of 1882, which deemed both polygamy and unlawful cohabitation illegal. Prison sentences, prohibition of voting, and exclusion from public service were the punishments facing those convicted of either or both crimes. In 1887, the Edmunds-Tucker Act further restricted activities of The Church of Jesus Christ of Latter-day Saints and nearly destroyed it by disincorporating both the Church and the Perpetual Emigrating Fund and seizing Church-owned property.[14] This background provides one reason why Latter-day Saints immigrated to Canada – they thought Canada was a place to hide from prosecution and continue to practise controversial customs. However, bigamy was illegal in Canada, and Canadians were just as concerned about maintaining their standard of the "ideal" family.

Charles Ora Card was one of these Latter-day Saints escaping anti-polygamy prosecution. The U.S. Marshals Service arrested him on 26 July 1886 for taking four wives (his first wife divorced him, but he remained married to three), but he escaped from the train transporting him to the jail.[15] These events forced Card into hiding, and he decided that it would be best to flee to Mexico. Instead, Church President John Taylor (1808–87) suggested that Canada would be an even better location for the fugitive. Taylor, originally from England and later Upper Canada, believed that there was more freedom and flexibility to practise their religion under British law.[16] The suggestion from his spiritual leader along with the need to leave the United States led to Card's exploration of British Columbia and the North-West Territories in search of suitable land for colonization. He finally decided to settle on an area around

Lee's Creek. By the end of March 1887, the first group of settlers arrived and camped at this spot.[17] The Woolf family, in particular, recorded their journey, which started from Utah, in April of 1887, of over 1,000 miles from Hyde Park to Lewiston and Rexburg, Idaho, to Dillon and Helena, Montana, and finally across the United States-Canada border into the North-West Territories.[18] John A. Woolf (1843–1928) practised plural marriage, like Card, and was in search of refuge. In her account of the founding of Cardston, Woolf's daughter Jane Woolf Bates (1873–1951) noted the difficult and dangerous journey: "Idaho and Montana through which we were to travel was wild, Indian infested, unsettled country for the most part, with rugged mountains and turbulent rivers to cross. The roads were poor at the best, often cut through forests, and were sometimes only narrow trails."[19] The families that endured the trek to Lee's Creek were plural families, but, while men brought only one wife into Canada, they brought children from other wives too. For example, John Theodore Brandley (1851–1928) moved to Stirling in 1899 with some of his younger children by his wife Margaret Keeler (1863–1910), while Keeler stayed in Utah and Brandley married Rosina Elisabeth Zaugg (1868–1951), who lived with him in Canada.[20]

Historian Jessie L. Embry describes the lifestyle of Latter-day Saints in Canada as "de facto monogamy."[21] Mentally and spiritually they were polygamous because they practised plural marriage and had plural wives/families, but day-to-day they lived monogamously within a larger community of monogamist polygamists in the NWT. For example, Samuel Matkin (1850–1905) had three wives when he immigrated to Canada in 1887: Sarah Ann Wiles (1853–1930), Permelia Julia Drury (1853–1936), and Sena Georgina Andersen (1860–1914). Andersen moved with Matkin to Lee's Creek and was his Canadian wife and mother of his Canadian family.[22] Thus, simultaneously Matkin had one wife in Canada and other wives remained in Utah making visit between his multiple families less frequent. But the reality was that this is how plural marriage operated for many Latter-day Saints who had families in multiple locations. In addition, Ephraim Harker (1854–1932) married Alice Jane Bennion (1856–1929) in Salt Lake City in 1876 and married his second wife, Sarah Elizabeth Carter (1869–1951), in 1889. Harker's wife Carter accompanied him to Canada while his first wife remained in Utah.[23] As well, Thomas Rowell Leavitt (1834–91), husband to more than one woman, brought his third wife, Harriet Martha Dowdle (1862–1924), to the new Canadian settlement.[24] This became a common practice. And while bringing one plural wife to Canada made it look like the Latter-day Saints were monogamous, in reality they were still wed to multiple spouses who just happened to be residing in different locations, often in a different country. At one point, Card's wife Lavinia Clark Rigby (1866–1960) lived in Idaho while Zina Young (1850–1931) split her time between Canada and Salt Lake City and Sarah Jane Painter (1858–1936) remained in Logan, Utah. As these examples demonstrate, most Latter-day Saints moved to Canada with one wife while other wives and families remained elsewhere, often in the United States and sometimes in Mexico.

The United States and Canadian governments agreed that plural marriage needed to be suppressed. Both governments established anti-bigamy statutes and bills, but it was the enforcement of these laws in the United States that sent some Latter-day Saints north to Canada. Most of the Latter-day Saint families that settled in the NWT brought only one wife, but that did not mean they stopped believing in the practice of plural marriage, nor did it mean they stopped promoting the continuation of the practice in Canada. As such, Canadians were very aware of the reputation associated with the Church and their practice of non-monogamy. As the examples below will highlight, Canadians were sceptical and cautious about the new immigrants, especially concerning their marriage customs and how these practices would influence Canadian society.

Canadians Respond to Plural Marriage

Published Reactions

The capital of Canada was over 2,000 miles away from the North-West Territories, so Canadians learned about non-monogamous marriage practices second-hand. For example, Christian missionaries recorded their interactions and observations, which were later published in manuscript format for the public to purchase and read. One such writer was John Maclean (1851–1928), a Methodist missionary among the Kainai from 1880 to 1889, who left us with numerous, although biased, accounts of his time in the NWT. In *The Indians, Their Manners and Customs*, Maclean described marriage among the Niitsitapi as he viewed it as, "simply a bargain between the suitor and the young woman's father, for a certain number of horses."[25] Maclean's one-sided, Christian perspective of the Niitsitapi revealed the type of information eastern Canadians received about both Indigenous peoples and alternative marriage customs. Maclean tried to rationalize the practice of polygamy and guessed that "the Blackfeet did not intermarry with tribes outside their confederacy."[26] In Maclean's fictional work *The Warden of the Plains*, he revealed more of his opinion of polygamy in the short story titled, "Asokoa, the Chief's Daughter." Maclean explained that the character Asokoa's "inferior position" was a result of her female sex.[27] To confirm that she was a victim of "the customs of the people," Maclean narrated that the chief traded his 14-year-old daughter to Running Deer, a 60-year-old warrior, for four horses.[28] Running Deer's three other wives confronted Asokoa when she first entered the lodge and, following convention, she "would be obliged to submit to the rule of the one who was the queen."[29] Even when Asokoa found true love and desired to leave the polygamous relationship, she could not simply request freedom; she had to run away.[30] This story reveals that Maclean saw the non-monogamous marriage practices of Indigenous people as both a way of controlling women and as an undesirable practice that some might want to flee. While not every marriage is ideal, regardless of how many partners are involved, this story specifically emphasizes the business transaction and hierarchal structures at play in such a negative light that the character has no choice but to run away. Maclean, like many white Christian missionaries, witnessed Indigenous life as completely other to their own reality and this informed how they recorded and shared these experiences with other Canadians. Unfortunately, in the case of non-monogamy, an already threatening practice to monogamous Canadians, Maclean saw the practice completely foreign to his beliefs and reproduced it in such a horrifying way that any reader would perceive such unions as dangerous and threatening.

In addition to fiction and missionary biographies, readers learned about non-monogamy through the work of anthropologists. For instance, George Bird Grinnell published his ethnographic studies of the Niitsitapi in 1892. "The Blackfeet take as many wives as they wish," he observed, "[I]f the man had proved a good, kind husband to his first wife, other men, who thought a good deal of their daughters, might propose to give them to him."[31] Additionally, representing Oxford's Pitt Rivers Museum, anthropologist Beatrice Blackwood (1889–1975) visited the Blood Reserve on the 3rd and 4th of August in 1925 during her three-year North American research trip. In her field notes, Blackwood wrote on the subject of marriage and believed, "Marriage is often 'Indian fashion': by exchange of presents, and when the man gets tired of his wife, he gives back the presents and goes to live with someone else. This is stopped by the [Indian] Agent whenever possible but is difficult to change."[32] What Blackwood and other outsiders labelled as "Indian fashion" could just as easily fall under the definition of a dowry. White Canadian women could receive a dowry, which might be a portion of their inheritance, at the beginning of a new marriage. In nineteenth century Canada, a dowry "consisted typically of cash, bed, and cow ... and was simply a contribution by the bride's kin towards the setting up of the new household."[33] Alternatively, for the Kainai, the gift, or dowry, might have been horses instead of household goods. According to Kainai community member Andy Blackwater, "[I]f you're going to marry you give presents, you don't get presents."[34] In another interview, and in contrast to Blackwood's observations of Kainai marriage, Blackwater argued, "Marriages occur through traditional ways, based on survival ... you don't want to put your daughter where she would have to struggle, where she would be abused. So, a lot of arranged marriages did occur."[35]

Esther Schiff Goldfrank (1896–1997), another anthropologist, arrived in 1939 and visited numerous Blackfoot reservations from Alberta to Montana. In *Changing Configurations in the Social Organization of a Blackfoot Tribe During the Reserve Period*, Goldfrank judged that marriage within the Kainai Nation was unstable due to "psychopathic possessiveness and aggressive behaviour" and, furthermore, that tribe members had "re-establish[ed] the polygamous past with considerable success."[36] Goldfrank offered the example of a woman joining another family "not unlike a second wife" if her husband was absent due to circumstances, such as a prison sentence.[37] She disregarded traditional customs and familial bonds that connected tribe members and caused them to assist one another, especially in times of need.

These publications from missionaries and anthropologists show a few examples of what Canadians might have read and learned about non-monogamy in western Canada. The stories of non-monogamy among Indigenous peoples in western Canada were not positive accounts. Goldfrank uses offensive language to describe Kainai marriages; Blackwood describes a custom very similar to a dowry but frames it as entirely separate and different because it is not practised by white Christians; and Grinnell overly simplifies the tradition as men simply taking as many wives as they want. Regardless of whether these reports were accurate, the subject matter, language use, and tone would have communicated to Canadian readers that non-monogamy was a very real threat, regularly occurring among the non-white, non-Christian populations in the western territories. Therefore, with the arrival of Latter-day Saints, widely known for their practice of plural marriage, it should be no surprise that Canadians reacted both politically and legally to their immigration.

Political Reactions

Representatives of the Canadian government added to the growing dialogue regarding "deviant" marriage practices. In government reports, debates, and legislation, representatives expressed fears of non-monogamous unions. These expressions of fear and mistrust for the Latter-day Saints are important because it highlights how far they had to battle to integrate into Canadian society. For example, in the House of Commons in 1882, during a debate over Bill No. 9 and marriage with a deceased wife's sister, Member of Parliament Guillaume Amyot (1843–96) moved that every marriage celebrated by competent religious authority be hereby declared valid and legal.[38] Wilfrid Laurier (1841–1919) asked if this Bill would apply to "the Mormon Church," and Amyot replied, "I am happy to reply that the Mormon Church is not accepted by the law in this country, and I hope it never will be; so it is not necessary to consider that point."[39] But Amyot was incorrect, and the Latter-day Saints arrived five years later.

Just as they could have read missionary or academic publications to learn about Indigenous peoples, Canadians might have read newspaper or magazine articles about Latter-day Saints. A monthly review of current events called *The Bystander* described the Saints as "a strange community, which has relapsed into polygamy ... Mormonism ought to perish, of course, and will perish; but it is a human aberration, with some features not unworthy of study."[40] On 27 September 1887, several months after the first Latter-day Saint settlers arrived in the North-West Territories, *The Macleod Gazette* published an article actually defending the Latter-day Saints, which stated, "It is our duty to take people as we find them, and to judge them by their lives among us. There are thousands and thousands of Mormons who have never practised polygamy, and have apparently never shown a desire to do so."[41] Positive yet naive, the article continued, "No one has a right to assert that those who have settled in this country were ever among the number who did indulge in that practice."[42] The *Edmonton Bulletin* had fewer positive statements to make about the Latter-day Saint immigrants in an article two years later. The article stated, "[Canadians] can do better without them than with them, if they introduce into our country their polygamous practices; the persistence in which has been the means of driving them from the soil of the United States."[43] Closer to the truth, the article asked, "Will a change of latitude be accompanied by a change of life and belief? Or are they coming to this country to escape, what they claim was persecution in the one they are leaving, without ceasing those practices, that were the direct cause of these so called persecutions."[44] This writer for *The Edmonton Bulletin* was more accurate than they possibly knew for indeed the "change in latitude" did not mean a change in the belief in plural marriage for the immigrating Latter-day Saints. Instead, these new arrivals expected to find a place where they could continue their religious practices, undisturbed by critics, government representatives, and law enforcement.

The articles from *The Bystander*, *The Macleod Gazette*, and *The Edmonton Bulletin* are just a small sample of the types of stories Canadians read about Latter-day Saints. These types of stories show various attitudes towards the Church, their religious beliefs, their practice of non-monogamy, and their immigration to the NWT. Canadians would likely have known about plural marriage even before the immigration due to the popular press in the United States and the ongoing prosecution of American Latter-day Saints. However, now they were reading about plural marriage happening in their land, within their borders, among other upstanding, white Christian Canadians, which made the threat of non-monogamy much more daunting. These editorials and published accounts reveal what many Canadians thought about the Church and its members, which shows us just how far they would have to adapt and change to blend in with mainstream society, if they chose to, which they did not seem keen to do at first.

Latter-day Saints had a specific plan to ask and receive permission to continue the practice of plural marriage on Canadian soil. On 30 October 1888, Charles Ora Card and Apostles Francis M. Lyman (1840–1916) and John W. Taylor travelled from the Lee's Creek settlement to Lethbridge and then by train to Winnipeg, Manitoba. The company left Winnipeg on Monday, 5 November, and arrived in Ottawa on Thursday. On Friday, 9 November, Card, Lyman, and Taylor met with the Minister of the Interior and requested to purchase land, use of timber and rock, and permission to transport their people from the borders for free.[45] The following day they met with Prime Minister Sir John A. Macdonald (1815–91) and presented the same requests. Afterwards, Lyman appealed to the prime minister on behalf of all Latter-day Saints, but especially those imprisoned and fined in the United States, asking if the Canadian government would provide "a resting place upon their Soil for they were the choicest of men and had many sons and ample means to sustain themselves and would bring wealth into the Dominion.[46] One interpretation of Lyman's plea is that he tried to demonstrate the value in allowing polygamous Latter-day Saints because plural families equalled numerous children, who were all hard workers, and would, therefore, bring prosperity to Canada. Canada received some of the more industrious and prosperous Latter-day Saints because those were the men who received permission to wed more than one woman, and men with more than one wife were running from US authorities straight into Canada.

At the same meeting, John W. Taylor continued and, "Explained the great principle of plurality of wives as viewed by the s[ain]ts and as practised in its purity for the purpose of observing God's Law in multiplying and replenishing the Earth."[47] When Prime Minister Macdonald asked them to differentiate between bigamy and polygamy Lyman responded that, "Bigamy was deception and the wives were deceived and injured, while polygamy as we viewed and practised it, it was understood and consented to by the former wife or wives and knowing by the one married."[48] This inaccurate differentiation between the two marriage types reveals Lyman's attempts to convince the Canadian government that the Latter-day Saint version of non-monogamy was less harmful than they perceived it to be. After, Card recorded in his diary that Prime Minister Macdonald "acquiesced by a gesture of the head. We thank God for thus opening up the way."[49] According to the verb usage by Card, they interpreted and believed the prime minister had reluctantly accepted their requests.

On 14 November, Card, Lyman, and Taylor met with the Minister of Customs Mackenzie Bowell (1823–1917) who rejected non-monogamy because "he felt also that polygamy was not proper and very unpopular and consequently could not be admitted."[50] Further rejection followed on 16 November when Minister of the Interior Edgar Dewdney (1835–1916) informed them that they would have to homestead like everyone else rather than be allowed to purchase the land. Card noted that Dewdney "did not refer to our request for our brethren who were in bondage which was referred to Sir John A. Macdonald."[51] The "brethren who were in bondage" were their fellow polygamists in the United States. This trip to Ottawa placed the Latter-day Saints more than ever on the Canadian government's radar after explicitly asking for permission to continue the practice of plural marriage in the NWT.

Meanwhile, immediately following this Ottawa visit, *The Canada Presbyterian*, a Toronto-based publication, called the success of The Church of Jesus Christ of Latter-day Saints "one of the religious puzzles of the time." The journalist, who called Mormonism fraudulent and absurd, promised:

> So long as the Mormons in Canada choose to conform to the laws of the country and make industrious citizens, they will be left unmolested by the State. In a land where religious liberty prevails, they need not expect

special privileges. The time for giving exemptions is past. One thing is certain, that Canadians will not tolerate in their midst a community that practises polygamy.[52]

A few months later, during the third session of the 6th Parliament, Member of Parliament Cyrille Doyon (1842–1918) voiced similar concerns regarding the Latter-day Saints and read from the Montreal newspaper *La Minerve*:

> Some hundreds of Mormons have crossed the frontier and are grouped near Fort McLeod. The dispatches say that they are now importing a large number of cattle for stock-raising, and that they are preparing for a large colony. This is very bad seed grain, and we do not want to see any corner of the North-West poisoned with it. Polygamy is forbidden by our laws, and whosoever practises it infringes them.[53]

Doyon proceeded to ask what steps the Canadian government intended to take, but Conservative MP Hector-Louis Langevin (1826–1906) replied that the government had no information before them to assist with any decision making regarding the Latter-day Saints in the NWT.

As the articles in *The Canada Presbyterian* and *La Minerve* demonstrate, Canadians perceived the Church as strange and even fraudulent and poisonous. From what they could understand about the Church, the practice of plural marriage stood out, and they were not comfortable or happy about this happening within Canadian borders. However, it seems that Canadians, according to these articles, were willing to accept the Latter-day Saints if they obeyed the laws, practised monogamy, and contributed to Canadian industry and society. Journalists and politicians made it clear that Canadians would not tolerate any deviations from monogamous unions.

However, thus far in Canadian legal history, Canadian criminal law only mentioned bigamy, the act of marrying one person while still legally married to another, and did not include polygamy, the act of marrying multiple spouses. On 7 February 1890 (three years after the Latter-day Saints began permanently settling in Canada) Sir John Thompson (1845–94) introduced Bill No. 65 to further amend criminal law by creating "effectual provisions for the suppression of polygamy."[54] On 21 February, while in Logan, Utah, Charles Ora Card received a forwarded letter from the Deputy Minister of the Interior Alexander Mackinnon Burgess (1850–98) who relayed a report that Card and his people on Lee's Creek were practising polygamy and cohabitation. The next day Card responded, including a copy of his reply in his personal diary, in which he denied the allegations of "Polygamy and Cohabitation," promised that Latter-day Saints in the NWT did not practise either, and swore they had assured Ottawa of this, stating that "Our people understand too well the laws of the Dominion of Canada to infringe upon them."[55] However, previous to writing this letter, Card had taken his breakfast with one of his plural wives, Sarah Painter. Yes, this was a bit of a fib, and Latter-day Saints did indeed engaged in plural marriage in the NWT, but their plural families were likely not permanently residing there altogether. Card's diary entry highlights two important points. First, he acknowledges that the Canadian representatives with whom the Latter-day Saint envoy met in Ottawa did not grant permission to continue plural marriage in Canada. This is a different interpretation from his earlier entry that records the prime minster as "acquiescing by a gesture of the head" regarding their requests. Second, Card reveals the specific strategy of the Latter-day Saints in the NWT. By keeping plural families separate (e.g., one in Utah, one in Idaho, one in Mexico, and one in Alberta), Latter-day Saints were technically not breaking or infringing on any Canadian laws.

Back in Parliament, discussion of Bill No. 65 continued several months later. On 10 April Members of Parliament examined Section 8, extending the prohibition of bigamy, and Section 9, dealing with polygamy. After a recess, Thompson revealed his lack of knowledge and reported that it was "the Mormon practice" to marry more than one person at a time, but by this he meant a man married two women on the same day, which was not the case in most Mormon plural marriages. Edward Blake (1833–1912) spoke in support of the amendment, claiming that Latter-day Saints are seeking a "more congenial place, wherein they hope to be able to carry on these practices [of plural marriage]" and thus approved the Minister of Justice's efforts to establish severe restrictions against such practices.[56] Blake proceeded to quote clause 34 from Brigham Young's will, which was published after his death in 1877: "To avoid any question, the words married, or marriage, in this will shall be taken to have become consummate between man and woman, either by ceremony before a lawful magistrate or according to the order of The Church of Jesus Christ of Latter-day Saints, or by their cohabitation in conformity to our customs."[57] Then Edgar Dewdney, who was Minister of the Interior when the Latter-day Saints visited Ottawa, referred to the Mormon delegation of December 1888 and incorrectly reported, "[A]t the time they stated most distinctly that those coming into the Territories did not propose to practise polygamy."[58] Not only did Latter-day Saints request permission to practise plural marriage and bring their families into the country, but also, only two months prior, authorities accused the Latter-day Saints in the NWT of practising polygamy and cohabitation. In addition, Liberal MP John Charlton (1829–1910) did not want the Canadian government to encourage Latter-day Saint immigration because he perceived the Saints as an undesirable class of immigrants.[59] While the MP for Northumberland in New Brunswick, Peter Mitchell (1824–99), disagreed with Charlton and argued that the Latter-day Saint immigrants were "first-rate settlers, that they are industrious and frugal; and all we should do is to see that they obey the laws which compel them to live as other people do in a Christian community.[60] Blake stated his impression was that Latter-day Saints "were coming here in the hope that they would be able to re-establish in our country a condition of things which they had found it difficult to continue in the United States."[61] Meaning, of course, the practice of plural marriage.

A few weeks following this discussion in the House of Commons, the Senate read Bill No. 65 and opened the criminal law amendment for debate. John Abbott (1821–93) summarized the third chapter as "mainly devoted to the prevention of an evil which seems likely to encroach upon us, that of Mormon polygamy, and it is devoted largely to provision against that practice."[62] Prime Minister Macdonald clarified that the Bill had a specific section regarding Mormonism that prohibited Latter-day Saints who had been convicted of polygamy from serving on juries or voting in elections. Relieved, Senator Patrick Power (1841–1921) responded, "It is desirable that no one holding views which Mormons do should be allowed to vote or serve as jurors."[63]

Debates over the details of Bill No. 65 reveal that some members of Parliament did not really know or understand the Church, their religion, or their practice of plural marriage, while other members of Parliament did in fact support the Latter-day Saints. Those against were convinced that Latter-day Saints were undesirable immigrants, seeking a place to practise plural marriage, while their supporters saw them as industrious, ideal settlers. This conflict between an industrious settler and non-monogamy would eventually be resolved, but not before the Canadian government introduced new laws specifically naming and targeting the Latter-day Saints.

Legal Reactions

While some members of Parliament voiced their support for the Latter-day Saint settlers, no one supported the practice of plural marriage, and the Canadian government amended Canadian Criminal Law and repealed Chapter 161 of the Revised Statutes related to the laws of marriage. They reworded the section regarding bigamy, making it clear that regardless of location, marrying more than one person was a felony with a punishment of up to seven years' imprisonment.[64] Furthermore, a section on polygamy followed and included mention of religious rites and ceremonies as it relates to marriage concerning polygamy, conjugal unions, and cohabitation; but most importantly it specifically named the Latter-day Saint practice: "What among the persons commonly called Mormons is known as spiritual or plural marriage.[65] Most importantly, this new law specifically targeted polygamy connected to both secular and religious reasons and named the Latter-day Saint practice of "spiritual or plural marriage" as illegal. Thus, plural marriage was now officially illegal in Canada. Even so, the Church in the United States had already been dealing with legal pressures for several years, which makes it hard to determine how closely the Canadian Criminal Law Amendments influenced the Church's decision and Church President Wilford Woodruff's revelation regarding plural marriage in September of 1890.

Church President Woodruff (1807–98) publicly released the Official Declaration, or First Manifesto, on 6 October 1890, which stated,

> We are not teaching polygamy or plural marriage, not permitting any person to enter into its practice.... Inasmuch as laws have been enacted by Congress forbidding plural marriages, which laws have been pronounced constitutional by the court of last resort, I hereby declare my intention to submit to those laws, and to use my influence with the members of the Church over which I preside to have them do likewise.... I now publicly declare that my advice to the Latter-day Saints is to refrain from contracting any marriage forbidden by the law of the land.[66]

This statement marked the beginning of the end of the official practice of plural marriage for the mainstream Church. However, it did not mean plural marriage would discontinue in Latter-day Saint communities. It did not even mean the prohibition of new plural marriages. One might interpret the Manifesto as not necessarily a lie but not the truth either. When Woodruff said the Church would not teach polygamy or plural marriage, what he really could have said was that they were not publicly, or obviously, teaching the doctrine. Woodruff may have "advised" the Latter-day Saints to stop plural marriage, but the strength of this encouragement is up for debate.

Charles Ora Card kept suspiciously quiet on the issue, even having attended the October conference in person. For his diary entry dated Monday, 6 October 1890 he wrote, "To day I attended meeting at 10 & 2 P.M. at the Latter meeting ... the noted Manifesto by Prest. Wilford

Woodruff presented & unanimously sustained by the S[ain]ts assembled."[67] He adds no personal commentary to the stated events. Three years after the Manifesto, on 26 December 1893, Card met with John W. Taylor, John A. Woolf, Henry L. Hinman, and other Canadian polygamists "to consider further the advisability of planting Settlements in British Columbia & Montana" and recalled that Taylor announced, "[W]e have called you together to consult upon the subject to aid us in keeping the Commandments of God & relieve [retrieve] other families."[68] Taylor, referencing "the Commandments of God," means the doctrine of plural marriage because he mentions their "other families" which can only be a reference to their plural families located in different places such as Idaho and Utah.

Similarly, Thomas Archibald Hendry (1857–1929) commented that Latter-day Saints in Canada were "comfortable here with our families but we need to provide for our other families … it is not safe in the U.S. with more families than one … The Lord has Commanded this principle & it will go on & on … I propose to bring my families into the North Country."[69] Hendry and his wife Jane Elizabeth Stuart (1863–1936) immigrated to Canada in 1888 and left Hendry's other wife, Jennett Agnes Glenn (1860–1952), in Utah. Hendry's situation demonstrates that the First Manifesto of 1890 did little to solve the issues facing already existing plural families, especially families separated by long distances and borders.

At the stake conference in Cardston on 28 November 1897, Zina D. H. Young (1821–1901), a plural wife of Brigham Young, preached, "The principle of Celestial Marriage [another term for plural marriage in the 19th century] is a grand principle and will revolutionize the whole Earth."[70] Likewise, during a meeting of the Cardston Relief Society in 1905, Nellie Taylor (1869–1945) encouraged her audience to be "loyal to every principle and hold them sacred and teach our children the same. The gospel will never be changed to suit the government … [L]et us quietly, modestly live for the holy principle that gave many of our dead ones birth and is assailed by our enemies and is very unpopular."[71] As these two examples highlight, even though the Church publicly denounced plural marriage in 1890, it seemed to continue at the local level, especially in the NWT and later Alberta.

Latter-day Saints in Canada were concerned about all their families, not just the ones they brought to settle in the NWT, and these concerns did not disappear after the First Manifesto in 1890. As the discussions in 1893 demonstrates, leaders contemplated establishing new communities in locations closer to the settlements in the District of Alberta to bring their plural families to more manageable distances. All these conversations and sermons show that the belief in and practice of plural marriage persisted after the First Manifesto, and Latter-day Saints in the NWT, facing new Canadian laws and new announcements from their Church leaders in Utah, faced new challenges involving their relationships, families, church, and state.

Laws prohibiting bigamy and polygamy remained when the Parliament of Canada passed the Criminal Code in 1892. Once again, authorities reworded and redefined the crimes. Section 275 defined bigamy as "the act of a person who, being married, goes through a form of marriage with any other person in any part of the world."[72] The bigamy section stated that marriage was "any form either recognized as a valid form by the law of the place where it is gone through or, though not so recognized, is such that a marriage celebrated there in that form is recognized as binding by the law of the place where the offender is tried."[73] Section 278 on polygamy repeated the 1890 amendments of Chapter 161, Section 5, of the Revised Statutes of Canada and maintained the specific wording targeting Latter-day Saints.[74]

By the twentieth century, Canadian authorities were very aware of the Latter-day Saint colonization and settlement efforts in the District of Alberta in the North-West Territories. Journalists and politicians openly discussed the Church, their religion, and especially their marriage practices. Plural marriage by Latter-day Saints impacted Canadian policy and law, as we saw with the prohibition against polygamy in the Revised Statutes and eventually in the Criminal Code, in addition to the specific wording, "What among the persons commonly called Mormons is known as spiritual or plural marriage." The Latter-day Saint response to both Canadian law and their Church's First Manifesto shows that they were not yet ready to give up plural marriage, especially by those who had plural families in both Canada and other places, and most importantly, because this was still a religious belief and one of the main reasons they came to the NWT in the first place. However, the new laws and the 1890 Manifesto put them in a complicated position. They wanted to establish new homes and communities in Canada, and they still wanted to remain faithful Latter-day Saints, which included the practice of plural marriage. They had many moving parts to negotiate at this time of change.

Monogamy?

Despite the introduction of the Criminal Code, Latter-day Saints continued to practise plural marriage in the North-West Territories. Coincidentally, to outsiders, Latter-day Saints appeared to be assimilating. In his annual report of 1893, North-West Mounted Police Commissioner Lawrence W. Herchmer (1840–1915) reported that the approximately 650 immigrants were "doing well, improving their places and attending to business" by digging an irrigation ditch and flume to power their mill.[75] In fact, "they are a well-behaved people," continued Herchmer. "[They] give no trouble in any way, and have greatly reduced the cost of living in the district."[76] A similarly positive report composed a year later by Frederick W. Wilkins (1854–1944) to the surveyor general of the Department of the Interior named the Latter-day Saints an honest and fair group of people to deal with.[77] According to Wilkins, they were "the best settlers in the North-West, and they will undoubtedly succeed in making their part of the country prosperous and valuable."[78] In his 1899 report to the Superintendent of Immigration, Charles W. Speers (1856–1920), the general colonization agent, wrote that the 1,700 Latter-day Saints in the District of Alberta were a "very progressive people, with good schools and churches" albeit "a socialistic people, but observe Canadian laws and usages. They are first class settlers" who farmed bushels of grain, opened cheese factories, and constructed irrigation canals.[79] As these reports demonstrate, some attitudes to the new settlers had shifted, almost to the point of glorifying the Latter-day Saint colonization efforts as exemplar for other settlers moving west, even despite their non-monogamy. However, indeed some of these "first class settlers" had multiple wives, just like their neighbours the Kainai. Just as the Department of Indian Affairs was aware of Indigenous polygamy, so was the North-West Mounted Police (NWMP) informed of the Latter-day Saint practice of plural marriage. As such, the NWMP sent Corporal E.H. Bolderson to Cardston with the purpose of surveiling the Latter-day Saint community and their "polygamous practices."[80] In a letter dated 10 February 1899, Corporal E.H. Bolderson presented evidence that Charles McCarty (1850–1926) lived with two women. Bolderson wrote that he observed two women living with McCarty and even met one of them whom McCarty introduced as his wife, and the other woman he later met who was introduced to him as "Mrs. McCarty" too, which confirmed his suspcions that both women residing with McCarty were in fact his plural wives.[81] Bolderson referenced an article from Salt Lake City, reprinted in the Cardston Record on 8 February 1899, which stated, "American Fork, Jan. 26. – Charles and Maud McCarty from Cardston, Alberta, Canada, are visiting here at present."[82] The two sisters mentioned in Bolderson's letter would have been Mary Mercer (1855–1943) and

Margery Mercer (1860–1934), and McCarty was in fact married to both. Bolderson was convinced that Charles McCarty was guilty of polygamy under Sec. 278 of the 1892 Criminal Code.[83]

The example of Charles McCarty is significant because the NWMP never laid any charges against him or his wives even though they had ample evidence. One explanation for the absence of criminal charges is the fact that McCarty was an industrious, hard-working businessman. As the chapter on business will show more carefully, McCarty was one of several practicioners of plural marriage that also worked hard to colonize, farm, and irrigate southern Alberta. Therefore, one might wonder if his influence in other realms, especially those that extended outside Latter-day Saint boundaries and into Canadian business and political spheres, helped him avoid further legal hassle regarding his plural marriages.

Suspicion did not end there. In an article titled "A Big Family," the writer warned readers of deceptive Latter-day Saint missionaries in Canada and the colony in the NWT whose members "claim that they have given up one part of their system, polygamy, but it is feared that this profession is in many cases not a fact."[84] Ultimately, this accusation was accurate. It was really not until Church President Joseph F. Smith (1838–1918) issued the Second Manifesto in 1904 that explicitly laid out a prohibition on plural marriage and a re-branding of marriage in terms of longevity rather than multiplicity. The Church's stance on marriage evolved as such most members replaced plural marriage with monogamy and a greater emphasis on eternal marriage and family. However, not all Latter-day Saints agreed with the end of plural marriage, but most conceded that the practice was indeed over and focused their attention on raising monogamist, nuclear families with members actively participating in the Church and adapting to mainstream society's expectations of the ideal modern family.

Despite accusations against them, no Latter-day Saint faced prosecution from Canadian authorities. However, eventually the Church began punishing disobedient members for ignoring the Church's Manifestos and for continuing the practice of plural marriage. The separate cases of John H. Blackmore and Zola Brown demonstrate how far the Latter-day Saints of the 1940s differed from early Latter-day Saint attitudes regarding marriage and family. By the 1940s, 40 years since the Church announced explicit consequences and disciplinary measures for members that continued the practice of plural marriage and also 40 years of assimilating the Latter-day Saint family structure to society's expectations, monogamist Latter-day Saints by this point held strong opinions and attitudes towards deviations from their current expectations on marriage and family. This shift to actively policing their own marriage practices demonstrates the extent of their integration.

John H. Blackmore

The rise and fall of John H. Blackmore demonstrates the enduring conflict plural marriage had on the Latter-day Saint community in southern Alberta. His parents, William Blackmore (1862–1918), a native of England, and Mary Christina Ada Horn (1874–1966), married in 1889 in Idaho. In 1892, William was "greatly disgusted with the enforcement of the laws in Idaho ... [and left] for the great unknowns of Canada, blessed by the British flag."[85] William became a citizen soon after and raised all his children, including the eldest, born in Idaho, John H. Blackmore (1890–1971), as "good Canadians."[86] John H. Blackmore went on to earn his teaching certificate, taught at schools in the region as well as the Knight Academic in Raymond, and eventually became the principal of Raymond High School.[87] He married Emily Woolley (1894–1976) in 1915 in Salt Lake City and remained regularly active in the Church, even serving president of the Taylor Stake Mutual Improvement Association.[88]

Elected as Member of Parliament for the Lethbridge Constituency in 1935 and selected as party leader for the Social Credit Party of Canada, Blackmore became the first member of The Church of Jesus Christ of Latter-day Saints elected to the House of Commons. In a newspaper interview, Blackmore stated, "[W]e will be missionaries both in the house and out of it. We will champion Social Credit views on money and credit."[89] By this point, part of Blackmore's life was now situated in Ottawa, and he and his wife Emily joined the Ottawa Branch of the Church. But, back in Alberta, spiritual concerns haunted his eldest son, Harold Woolly Blackmore (1916–2000).

Writing to his other son, Winston Blackmore (1920–43), in 1939, John revealed Harold's spiritual dilemma: "Harold is contemplating very important decisions. In the last analysis all I can do is to endeavour to lay before him all the correct principles, as far as my intelligence and experience can show me what they are, and then let him depend upon the inspiration in his heart to decide what is the correct course to follow."[90] The pamphlet "Reverence for God" appeared in the John Horn Blackmore Fonds of the Glenbow Archives and hinted at what might have troubled the minds of John and Harold Blackmore. The pamphlet stated, "And the so-called Fundamentalists are the only people on the earth who are able to live these laws and are doing it successfully and worthily. And they are braving the persecutions that are waged against them...."[91] Fundamentalist Mormons denied the Manifestos ending the practice of plural marriage and believed that God endowed John Taylor (1808–87), the third Church president (who refused to eliminate plural marriage even when pressured from the government), with the power to continue the practice of plural marriage. As such, an underground movement developed, and plural marriage continued. Lorin C. Woolley (1856–1934) believed he inherited the authority from John Taylor to perform plural marriages and formed the polygamist organization called the Council of Friends. Doctrines of communalism and plural marriage united the Council, but also isolated them from the Church and forced them to move from Salt Lake City to Short Creek, Arizona, to avoid persecution.[92] In 1935, the Church asked the polygamist residents of Short Creek to sign an oath denouncing plural marriage, which they refused and, consequently, the Church excommunicated them. The US government raided Short Creek in 1944 during the time of John Y. Barlow's (1874–1949) leadership. In total, authorities charged 46 adults with unlawful cohabitation and conspiracy to commit polygamy. The Church of Jesus Christ of Latter-day Saints publicly endorsed the efforts made by the government to extinguish polygamous marriages and, once more, re-emphasized their rejection of plural marriage and, therefore, Mormon fundamentalism.[93]

Fundamentalist Mormons continued to perform plural marriages because they considered it an essential religious practice. It was a religious duty connected to their belief that Joseph Smith received a revelation from God that defined eternal marriage and justified man taking another wife.[94] As a defence against opponents and critics, they used this divine commandment and biblical precedents, such as Abraham and Jacob, to argue that plural marriage was a religious principle. Another religious belief of fundamentalist Mormons was that Jesus Christ and Joseph Smith visited the Church's third president and prophet John Taylor on the night of 26 September 1887 and instructed him to continue plural marriage despite pressure to end the practice. Not only did God and the prophets sanction plural marriage, argued the fundamentalists, but also it was a requirement to enter the highest level of heaven, the Celestial Kingdom.[95]

Canadian Latter-day Saints were not immune to this fundamentalist movement. In 2010, Lorna Blackmore told the B.C. Supreme Court that her father, Harold Blackmore, "became interested in [fundamentalism] after attending a meeting in Rosemary at the home of Eldon Palmer, at which an American fundamentalist by the name of Owen LeBaron talked about plural marriage. [Her] father subsequently decided to practise polygamy."[96] Harold Blackmore (1916–2000), son of John H.

Blackmore, moved his family to property near Lister, B.C., in 1946 and married his second wife, Florence Williams (1916–98), the sister of his first wife, Gwendolyn Williams (1914–2002), thereby entering into plural marriage. Eldon Palmer (1914–2004) and Joseph "Ray" Blackmore (1915–74), Harold's uncle and John's brother, joined them in what became the closed community of Bountiful in Creston Valley, British Columbia. Ray's wives included Anna Mae Johnson (married in 1941), Nesta Kay Boehmer (married about 1952), and Aloha Bohmer (1921–2016). Writing about his brothers, Harold "Pete" Blackmore (1906–94) recalled that before Ray's marriage to his third plural wife he confided in his brother that he did not want to marry her but felt pressured to do so.[97] Regardless of his conflicted feelings about his third marriage, Ray ended up marrying a total of five women and was eventually excommunicated from the Church.

The fact that Harold, Eldon, Ray, their families, and other so-called fundamentalists could not remain in the Albertan enclaves originally established to preserve Latter-day Saint distinctiveness, which included plural marriage, signalled the effective completion of the initial integration process for the new Latter-day Saint mainstream in Canada. The majority of Latter-day Saints in southern Alberta, aligned with the mainstream Church, had completely accepted that monogamy was the only acceptable type of marriage and rejected deviation from it, just like Canadians had rejected earlier generations' practice of plural marriage, too. But as the fundamentalist movement shows, the desire to continue the practice of plural marriage continued and united a small group of dissidents, who chose to relocate and continue the practice, even with serious consequences from both their governments and Church leaders.

Regardless of the unsanctioned practices of Latter-day Saints in Creston Valley, John and Emily Blackmore visited Camp Lester, B.C., in the summer of 1947 to visit their daughter, Fayila Williams, and their now polygamous son, Harold.[98] John would soon reap the consequences. Back in Ottawa that fall, Easter Woods (1904–96) received a letter from branch president Frank A. Cook (1901–85), who was acting under direct orders from the Canadian Mission Headquarters, requesting her presence at an Elders' Court Meeting on 28 September 1947 for the investigation of alleged "Teaching, and endeavouring to put into effect doctrines contrary to the established practice of The Church of Jesus Christ of Latter-day Saints."[99] Part of the evidence presented at this meeting was Hilda Crawshaw's witness statement summarizing a conversation between herself, Easter Woods, and John H. Blackmore. Crawshaw reported that during this conversation she learned that "Brother Frank Cook and I were to be the first in Ottawa to begin polygamy, and Brother Blackmore and Sister Woods were to be the first to begin living polygamy in the Dominion of Canada."[100] During the same discussion, Blackmore informed Crawshaw that they "would not be married in the temple, but that there was a man in Salt Lake who holds the keys of temple marriage ... [Blackmore] insisted that the Manifesto was illegal; that it had been forced upon Wilford Woodruff under the threat of refusing to take Utah into the Union. Also, that President John Taylor had successfully held out against this during his time was president of the Church."[101] Easter Woods did not appear at the Elders Court Meeting but those present heard the evidence and voted unanimously that she was guilty and "disfellowshipped" her, the Church's term for a temporary suspension of membership privileges.[102]

In Alberta, on 14 October 1947, John H. Blackmore, Lethbridge Stake President Octave W. Ursenbach (1893–1981), Alberta Stake President Willard L. Smith (1891–1955), and Bishop of Cardston Third Ward Forest Wood (1903–95) met to discuss "certain matters pertaining to [Blackmore's] conduct while residing at Ottawa, Ontario, ... teaching and promoting of Fundamentalist doctrines and practices."[103] The leaders informed Blackmore that elders of the Ottawa branch had disfellowshipped Easter Woods and that witnesses associated his name with hers. The record showed that "Brother Blackmore was asked to state his position relative to Fundamentalist doctrines which he did not do in a straightforward manner but did considerable 'hedging,' and questioning of terms used in the discussion. There were some admissions made which confirmed, in part, the report and evidence formerly received." Blackmore admitted that he had taught the doctrine of plural marriage as a part of the Gospel of Jesus Christ, had referred people who had inquired to written statements of Joseph Smith, Brigham Young, John Taylor, and others, but evaded references to whether he always taught what President Wilford Woodruff had announced in the First Manifesto. He stated that he had, at the request of two sisters in Ottawa, consented for them to be sealed to him in the hereafter. Furthermore, Blackmore admitted having paid attention to purported reports of messages received by Sister Woods from some "personage," to the effect that he and Sister Wood were to be the first couple in Canada to engage in plural marriage, and that Frank Cook and Hilda Crawshaw were to be the first couple in Ottawa to enter into that relationship. He denied that the "personage" had been reported as having made the statement that "the Manifesto was illegal." Ursenbach wrote that "Blackmore presented a rather strong defence of his position and activities, seemingly feeling fully justified in his actions and beliefs [because] he had done only that which he had been taught by great men in the early days of settlement in Alberta." Blackmore argued that Latter-day Saints cannot avoid plural marriage when discussing the Gospel. Ursenbach reported that Blackmore denied having done anything wrong and as a result

> President Smith very plainly informed him that he was "playing with fire"; that if he insisted in advocating Fundamentalist doctrines "his die would be cast"; that while he now represented the Mormon people in the Dominion Parliament he would not do so in the future; that he would lose his membership in the church; that his family would suffer humiliation, and that his economic position would become seriously affected.[104]

Less than two weeks after that, Ezra Taft Benson (1899–1994) wrote to Willard L. Smith instructing him to hold a formal Bishop's Court for Blackmore on the charge of teaching and advocating the doctrine (not the practice) of plural marriage.[105] Blackmore briefly returned to Ottawa after his trial but returned to Cardston for the Christmas holidays.[106] Newspaper articles from 29 December 1947 informed the public that the Church had excommunicated John H. Blackmore; David O. McKay (1873–1970), second counsellor in the First Presidency, confirmed the report.[107] A statement from Blackmore in the *Toronto Daily Star* read, "I deny the charge. I definitely declare I have done no wrong ... that I am the husband of only one wife, and that to her I have always been scrupulously faithful."[108] Blackmore claimed shock and surprise in an interview published on 30 December: "As regards the whole situation pertaining to my excommunication from the L.D.S. Church on Nov. 28, 1947, one aspect which I find bewildering to me is this: In August 1947, there began to be spread in my constituency of Lethbridge various falsehoods reflecting on my moral integrity. Such slanderous stories were industriously circulated all through the latter part of August, all through the months of September, October, and November."[109] The fact that fundamentalist Mormons from the United States converted his son Harold to plural marriage, with whom he remained close, and the existence of witness accounts of his conversations with Church members in Ottawa heavily suggested that Blackmore was probably guilty of advocating for the doctrine of plural marriage, even if he never entered into a plural marriage himself.

The case of John H. Blackmore shows that no matter how prominent the Church member (e.g., a Member of Parliament, former schoolteacher, and principal, etc.), at this point in the Church's integration and evolution, Church leaders deemed any discussion of plural marriage as extremely problematic and threatening. Interestingly, Blackmore was not saying anything that Canadian Latter-day Saints in the nineteenth century were not previously discussing, even after the First Manifesto. Recall Zina D.H. Young's 1897 talk in Cardston where she argued that plural marriage was a grand principle, or when Nellie Taylor told the Relief Society in 1905 that they would never give up the principle to suit the government, or Thomas Archibald Hendry's plea in 1893 to make a new home for all their plural families. These public professions in support of plural marriage did not result in discipline, disfellowship, or excommunication, even though they occurred after the First Manifesto, and in the case of Nellie Taylor, after the Second. But by the late 1940s, circumstances for the Church had significantly changed, and non-monogamy was a thing of the past, something they wanted to bury. If people brought up plural marriage, then the Church was willing to dole out serious consequences.

An example of how far the Church was willing to go comes from the summer of 1953. Following the second Short Creek Raid, The Church of Jesus Christ of Latter-day Saints investigated more than ten people of the Creston Valley in connection with polygamy.[110] President of the Church's Western Canadian Mission R. Scott Zimmerman (1887–1960) completed the investigations by 5 August and announced he had not excommunicated anyone, at that time.[111] However, less than a month later, the Church excommunicated 10 members from the Lister, B.C., area for apostasy.[112] These actions emphasize the fact that the Church had now established a strong message of zero tolerance for fundamentalism and the persistence of plural marriage.

Zola Brown Jeffs Hodson

The marriage of Zola Brown Jeffs Hodson (1911–2005) offers a second case study involving plural marriage and Canadian Latter-day Saints. In 1934, Zola Brown, the daughter of Canadian, and future apostle, Hugh B. Brown (1883–1975), married Rulon Jeffs (1909–2002) in Salt Lake City. Within five years, claimed Zola, according to court documents, Rulon firmly believed he should marry another woman or women and intended to follow through with the practice of plural marriage.[113] Rulon denied that he intended to marry another without the consent of his wife, stating that if Zola did consent "that he might, under proper conditions, enter the law known as the law of celestial marriage" and that together they attended meetings where other Latter-day Saints taught the law of celestial marriage.[114]

Born in Cardston, Alberta, Zola's parents were Zina Young Card (1888–1974) and Hugh B. Brown (1883–1975). Her grandfather Charles Ora Card had three wives, and one of his wives, Zina Young, was the daughter of Brigham Young. Her great-grandfather on Hugh's side of the family had three wives: Sarah Woolf (1834–1911), Hannah Woolf (1838–1927), and Bertha Nielson (1842–66). Consequently, she was not unfamiliar with the doctrine and practice of plural marriage in the history of her family. Similarly, Rulon Jeffs' father was also a polygamist. David Jeffs (1873–53) married Phebe Woolley (1873–1948) in 1900, and Nettie Timpson, Rulon's mother, in 1909.

Zola and Rulon ended up getting divorced in 1941. After, Rulon went on to marry other women and fathered the now convicted Warren Jeffs, former leader of the Fundamentalist Church of Jesus Christ of Latter-day Saints (FLDS). However, before their separation, all seemed well with Rulon and Zola's marriage. For example, in 1938, her mother, Zina, wrote, "all is sweet and lovely at Zola's" in a letter to her daughter Mary.[115] In another letter, Zina claimed that Mary's father-in-law would be pleased with Rulon's work because he "excels at his accountant's work. He's a splendid man and just the one for Zola."[116] Later that month, Zina wrote that there was "no nobler [man]" than Rulon.[117] The next winter, in 1939, a letter from Zola's father, Hugh, to his wife in California revealed that Rulon and Zola might have experienced difficulties: "[S]o glad [Zola] is better in every way. Hope their affairs will work out satisfactorily and think they will as time is a great healer of ills and fads and idiosyncrasies."[118] But by November of the following year, Hugh's patience with his son-in-law ran out and he wrote, "[Rulon] is adamant and impossible, more fanatical all the time.... After my last talk with him I am more than ever sure his case is hopeless and that [Zola] has only one course."[119] Rulon revealed further fundamentalist leanings in a letter to Zola at the beginning of 1941, which Hugh described as proof of "how far he is from the Rulon she used to know and how baneful is the effect of constant association with law breakers and apostates."[120] Zola's mother, Zina, was "so utterly disgusted" with Rulon and greatly desired her daughter to remarry soon after the divorce trial ended.[121] Indeed, by 1945 Zola was happily married to Waldo Hodson. The Brown family could not entirely separate themselves from Rulon Jeffs and Mormon fundamentalism since Zola's two sons, Hugh and Zina's grandsons, remained in contact with their father. Their reactions to Rulon's conversion to Mormon fundamentalism and decision to practise plural marriage provide another example of how much Canadian Latter-day Saints had changed since their immigration to the NWT. Zina Brown's own grandfather was a polygamist, but by the 1940s the Latter-day Saint mindset was trained to reject this not-so-distant practice.

Conclusion

The examples of Zola Brown Hodson and John H. Blackmore demonstrate the very different attitudes that developed regarding the practice of plural marriage among Latter-day Saints in Canada. These two cases show how members adapted to Canadian circumstances due to both the criminalization of the practice and evolving Church doctrine. To inhabit both Canadian society and their own communities, they had to eventually abandon plural marriage, but it took time. Academics, politicians, and legal professionals all commented on the non-monogamous marriage customs of minority groups in Canada, include the Latter-day Saints. Mainstream Canadian society made it very clear that the ideal Canadian family looked and acted a certain way. The shift away from plural marriage and the transition to not only monogamy but also punishment of members that did not obey new policies demonstrates how family and marriage reveal how a minority religion in Canada crosses and maintains a balance of integration and distinctiveness.

Chapter Three

Women

Introduction

Delivering Hannah Gibb's (1855–1941) patriarchal blessing, John A. Woolf, communicating an inspired message of counsel and guidance from God, told Latter-day Saint midwife that "Thou shalt have faith to heal the sick and to rebuke the adversary and to be a comfort and a blessing to thousands, for your labours are great."[1] Gibb was one of several midwives working to deliver babies, care for mothers, and heal the sick in the developing Latter-day Saint communities in what became southern Alberta. In addition to healing, this blessing also emphasizes Gibb's role in comforting and blessing many in their community, responsibilities that went beyond the sickroom for many Latter-day Saint women. This example demonstrates some of the roles and responsibilities Latter-day Saint women shouldered during their colonization and settlement efforts in the North-West Territories. As spiritual advocates, healers and midwives, family members, social activists, and political participants, Latter-day Saint women helped guide their communities from isolated settlements to active participants in Canadian society.

The lives of Latter-day Saint women offer another site of negotiation for understanding the process of integration into Canadian society. Latter-day Saint women made homes, or helped orient themselves and their community members to a new place in the North-West Territories, on land that would become the province of Alberta, by advocating for their leaders, their new homeland, and the practice of plural marriage, often through the experiences of spiritual gifts, or special abilities believed to have been given by God, such as prophecy. They also worked as healers for family and community members by practising folk medicine, midwifery, and faith healing throughout their new settlements. Latter-day Saint women were members of the Church's women's organization called the Relief Society, mothers, and wives, (and, of course, sisters, aunts, etc.) and these roles also required special responsibilities that contributed to their homemaking as new Canadians. Eventually, external factors and internal conditions changed the roles and responsibilities of Latter-day Saint women, which led to a crossing over into more public, non-Latter-day Saint spaces. Thus, as a result of Latter-day Saint women leaving the private, domestic spaces and entering public Canadian spaces, they helped navigate their community further into mainstream society.

The Church of Jesus Christ of Latter-day Saints uses the "separate but equal" principle to differentiate between women's roles within the "sphere" of motherhood from men's authority within the Latter-day Saint Priesthood. In this chapter, I complicate and challenge the metaphor of separate spheres by showing how the ever evolving spheres in which Canadian Latter-day Saint women operated, from domestic to public, from the late nineteenth century to the mid-twentieth century, demonstrate another site of negotiation that teaches us about how religious minorities establish new homes and cross into unfamiliar territories. Analysing the thesis of anthropologist Michelle Rosaldo, historian Estelle Freedman summarizes, "[T]he greater the social distance between women in the home and men in the public sphere, the greater the devaluation of women ... Thus, to achieve an egalitarian future, with less separation of female and male, we should strive not only for the entrance of women into the male-dominated public sphere, but also for men's entry into the female-dominated domestic world."[2] For Latter-day Saints in Canada, sometimes this overlapping of spheres occurred organically, and at other times men and women remained in their "complementary" roles as dictated by Church authorities. It is one of the arguments of this chapter that, while Church authorities removed significant duties from the hands of its women, the same women then (re)created roles within both the private and public spheres that ultimately affected their interactions with the larger Canadian society.[3]

Nineteenth century Latter-day Saint women believed their religion and the practice of plural marriage provided greater opportunities for personal improvement, social development, and community involvement. One example of these opportunities was their successful efforts to secure woman suffrage in Utah in 1870.[4] In *Transformation of the Mormon Culture Region*, Ethan Y. Yorgason explains that until the 1890s, "Mormon feminists questioned the authority women held in America compared with that held by men. They argued that the ideal of romantic love and the dominance of monogamous marital relations left women too emotionally and socially dependent on (usually unreliable) men."[5]

Latter-day Saint women who supported plural marriage saw mainstream society's practice of monogamy as inferior, problematic, and limiting, especially to women's authority. Nevertheless, with the relocation of non-Latter-day Saints to Utah, the secularization of the territory, and the eventual loss of plural marriage, "Mormon women throughout this period consistently maintained that women's greatest influence resided in the home," and Latter-day Saint men reasserted their privilege, retreated to Victorian ideals of love, and codified family gender roles.[6] Similarly, at the same time in Canada, women "were the mainstay of the domestic production that sustained the family economy" by performing unpaid labour within the domestic sphere and making that sphere, or home, "increasingly a haven and source of nurture rather than a production, at least for those urban middle-class families that could in some measure embrace the Victorian "cult of domesticity" that depicted women as "angels of the hearth."[7] The so-called women's work within the domestic sphere performed by Latter-day Saint women in southern Alberta included gardening, cooking, cleaning, and child-rearing in addition to healing sick community members.

The Church argued that women belonged in the home undertaking the most important role as nurturing mothers and supportive wives while men shouldered the responsibilities of the priesthood.[8] However, the categories of motherhood and priesthood are problematic because priesthood corresponds to priestess and motherhood to fatherhood. By matching motherhood to priesthood, The Church of Jesus Christ of Latter-day Saints neglected the roles of men within the home under the category of fatherhood and removed women from religious authority as priestesses. Considering the work of traditional Church theologians justifying the "separate but equal" doctrine, Mary Farrell Bednarowski clarifies that Latter-day Saints believed that God determined these "ontological categories of parallel function," that both roles are complementary, and during the stage of pre-existence (pre-mortal life) women selected the role of mothers instead of priests.[9]

During the first half of the twentieth century, Latter-day Saints shared with most Canadians the belief that maternalism was central to women's lives. Especially after the First World War, Canadian society saw "women-as-mothers" as the key to social renewal, and the "angel of the hearth" received guidance from family experts to help make them more scientific and efficient at this new mission to manage both home and family.[10] The Great Depression and Second World War only enhanced society's expectations on women's duties inside and outside the family home. Up until the 1940s, in addition to their duties inside the home, Latter-day Saint women exercised spiritual gifts, such as publicly prophesying, speaking in tongues, or healing by anointing, While they maintained membership in Relief Society, their increasingly restricted roles took them more inside the family home as wives and mothers responsible for social reconstruction and maintaining home and family. However, even as their roles shifted, they remained concerned about the welfare of their communities, health care, education, and other social issues, which led them to join non-Latter-day Saint organizations such as the Alberta Women's Institute and the United Farm Women of Alberta. They refused to stay within the specific sphere as designated by their church. By crossing into the public, they helped show outsiders that their Church was just another respectable Canadian minority religion willing to participate in circles outside their own community in order to improve the province and country.

Latter-day Saint Women's Diverse Roles

Spiritual Advocates

In the late nineteenth century, Latter-day Saint women were spiritual advocates during a very difficult time of diaspora. After leaving their homes in the United States and moving to the remote District of Alberta in the North-West Territories, they faced the need to construct new homes, organize churches, and establish communities, all while remaining separated from their plural families and the majority of their Church community. Latter-day Saints in southern Alberta felt isolated, afraid, unsure, and worried about their future. Through their supernatural experiences and reception of spiritual gifts, Latter-day Saint women offered encouragement and reassurance to their husbands, families, and fellow Latter-day Saints. Through the manifestations of spiritual gifts, such as speaking in tongues and prophecy, Latter-day Saint women specifically provided confidence and reassurance to their communities regarding their purpose in Canada. As many of them were in plural marriages or members of plural families, they also maintained support for the doctrine of plural marriage during conflict with outsiders.

In the December 1890 issue of *The Woman's Exponent*, a couple of months after the First Manifesto announcing the end of plural marriage, reflecting on Canada, Zina Young Card wrote, "What Jerusalem is to the Jew, – so is Utah to the hearts of her mountain boys and girls, yet I would not, *could* not live there now. Why? Because the holy priesthood has said my place was here [in Canada]. So my wings are folded, content in my nest, I sing, no I mean chirp to my little brood, try to be content with all the changes that find me."[11] In this passage, Card emphasizes a message of obedience to the priesthood since Church leaders were the ones telling her, and other Latter-day Saints, to stay in the NWT. However, her bird metaphor, stating her "wings are folded" suggest that the Church had not clipped her wings; she chose to fold them, in obedience, and be content with her life and situation on the prairies. Contemplating the Church's announcement to end the practice of plural marriage, Card wrote that, "it took my breath away, but it gradually narrowed down from what at first seemed a strange pill to the very draught that was needed in our present state, religiously and politically."[12] Card admits the Manifesto shocked her and, at first, seemed wrong and difficult. Despite these initial reactions, she believed the Church needed the Manifesto to remain healthy, or return to full health, signalled with the phrase "the very draught that was needed." Card notes that "it has caused some comment here from various stand points, but we feel our true position is known and appreciated now as it could not be before the issuing of the Manifesto, and the saints here as a whole all feel our leaders are carrying on Christ's work to victory and are *one* with the saints in the land of Zion."[13]

Unsurprisingly, the announcement that the Church planned to end plural marriage would cause "some comment here from various stand points" because many families first moved to the NWT so they could escape the charges against them for having more than one spouse. Card confuses the contemporary reader when she says, "We feel our true position is known and appreciated now as it could not be before the issuing of the Manifesto." This raises the question of how strongly Latter-day Saints in Canada supported plural marriage. Were they actually pleased, or maybe relieved, by the Manifesto because now they could be "true" instead of promoting or defending a doctrine they disapproved of? This is unlikely since many records include words of encouragement for the practice, but Card's statement here does cause one to wonder if there was some dissent. In addition, Card states that the Albertan Latter-day Saints "are one with the saints in the land of Zion," which suggests they felt alienated before 1890. Were the Latter-day Saints feeling close to the brethren in Utah because they had plural families there, or because they supported discontinuing the practice of plural marriage? Card is writing in *The Women's Exponent*, the publication for Latter-day Saint women, so her known audience would have been women, like her.

Openly discussing the internal conflict brought by the Manifesto in addition to the struggles associated with living far from Utah would have been very relatable content for Latter-day Saint women reading from various locations beyond Salt Lake City. Card's editorial demonstrates the thought process of one Latter-day Saint woman as she is faced with diaspora in addition to changing Church doctrine. She acts as both a role model and advocate for Latter-day Saint women in the evolving Church, admitting it was okay to have conflicted feelings especially during such challenging times. We will see the use of spiritual gifts in a similar manner that provide opportunities for Latter-day Saint women to lead and also support other Church members by emphasizing difficult subject matter such as navigating the challenges of their new home in Canada.

Writing and speaking in public were two ways in which Latter-day Saint women advocated for themselves, their Church, and their beliefs and practices. They also claimed to receive spiritual gifts, such as prophecy and speaking in tongues, and through these powerful mediums they communicated specific messages to their own membership, following a long tradition of spiritual manifestations in the Church. Starting with Paul, in his letter to the new converts at Corinth, around 54 C.E., he wrote, "Now there are diversities of gifts, but the same Spirit," a verse we now read in First Corinthians Chapter 12. Similarly, the last Nephite prophet, Moroni, wrote about spiritual gifts in the conclusion of the Book of Mormon: "Ye deny not the gifts of God, for there are many; and they come from the same God."[14] In Kirtland, Ohio, Joseph Smith received a revelation that is now recorded in *The Doctrine and Covenants*: "For there are many gifts, and to every man is given a gift by the Spirit of God."[15] In 1842, Smith composed the Articles of Faith and included the statement "We believe in the gift of tongues, prophecy, revelation, visions, healing, interpretation of tongues, and so forth."[16] The gift of tongues is the ability to speak languages by inspiration; prophecy is the ability to foretell future events; healing is healing the sick by laying on of hands or with prayer; interpretation of tongues is the ability to render foreign languages readily and properly into their own. Latter-day Saints in southern Alberta experienced many of these spiritual gifts. These experiences helped orient them to their new home in Canada by communicating messages that reinforced their connections to the Utah Church, their reasons for migrating, and their ability to colonize the region.

Concerns and fears about their settlement in southern Alberta strengthened as the temporary nature of the Church's Canadian mission ended in May 1895 when the First Presidency decided to organize an Alberta stake, a unit of organization comprised of several wards, and named Charles Ora Card as its president. Card delivered the news to the Latter-day Saints in the District of Alberta and began organizing the new stake in June. The experience and exhibition of spiritual gifts began to function as ways to reassure Latter-day Saints feeling worried or doubtful about their changing residency. For example, at "a very spirited meeting" on 6 June, Card recorded that a "Sister L. Hinman" spoke in tongues and Zina Young Card interpreted the message: "The angels are watching over us. Some of you think you are exiled from the Church, not so. You are part of the Church ... The Lord is watching over us."[17] The members in Canada felt exiled because their temporary stay away from their homes, families, and Church in Utah had become more permanent, and not necessarily by their own choice, but by the authority and decision making of Church leaders. The organization of a stake and the transformation of branches to wards, the basic units of the Church, changed the lives of those in Alberta who were one day living in a temporary mission, planning to return to Utah, and the next day living in a permanent stake of Zion.[18] This change might have been a catalyst as most experiences of spiritual gifts occurred between 1895 and 1903. As historian Maureen Beecher explains, "On the outskirts of Mormondom, there seemed to be a need for a more potent expression of God's approval, and the women created the circumstances that would foster it."[19] The role of Latter-day Saint women, while experiencing and sharing these spiritual gifts, became communicators, or advocates, for the Church's mission and existence in Canada.

Many of the messages communicated by Latter-day Saint women experiencing spiritual gifts confirmed their place in the Church's master plan, boosted their community's morale, and encouraged their leaders. For example, on 20 November 1895, Sarah Hyde (1857–1946) approached merchant and future stake president Heber S. Allen (1864–1944) and counsellor in the stake presidency Sterling Williams (1870–1965) stating, "They had a great work to perform."[20] She ended with Card, telling him he "should be better known in the future than in the past" and blessed him.[21] As well, depicting the testimony meeting of 6 February 1896, Card recalled Elizabeth Hammer's (1858–1919) expression of the Spirit and wrote in his diary that she stood up, threw off her shawl and hat, and "burst out in tongues which was accompanied by the spirit of prophecy blessed all about her especially the leading Priesthood," telling Card that he was "the right man in the right place" doing everything he could for the Latter-day Saints in the NWT.[22] At Samuel Matkin's house two days later, Elizabeth Hammer once again experienced the gift of prophecy and told Matkin that he would feel better if he visited Utah, returned to Canada, and his children turned to the Lord.[23] The manifestation of spiritual gifts in this context shows how these special experiences functioned to reassure community members feeling doubtful about their new, permanent residency in Canada.

Accepting that their once temporary home was now their permanent residence was part of the homemaking, or dwelling, strategy of the Latter-day Saints in the NWT. Before they could make any attempts to integrate with Canadian society, they needed to accept and embrace their new homes and settlements. The messages communicated through these spiritual gifts helped the process of acceptance, especially for Church leaders. Because these gifts were given to them by the "Spirit of God," the authority was coming from God, who members saw as their Heavenly Father, not the women who were experiencing the gifts. As such, the messages, such as being watched over, acknowledgement of exile and hardship, confirmation of acting in the best interests of the community, recognition for the great work to be done in Canada, and so on, helped facilitate both crossing and dwelling. Latter-day Saints mentally crossed over from Zion (or Utah) into Canada, further accepting their place physically apart from Church headquarters and the greater Church community. In addition, it allowed them to focus on the new settlements and communities throughout the District of Alberta that they were colonizing and establishing. Reassurance, through spiritual gifts, allowed Latter-day Saints to progress towards acceptance that their time in Canada was only just the beginning of a longer settlement plan.

Like spiritual gifts and published editorials, Latter-day Saint women also publicly spoke out in support of their experiences and communities. For example, reports from the April 1897 general conference note that Cardston resident Mary Woolf told the Salt Lake City audience, "I am living a long way from here but possibly it seems farther off to you than it does to me. I am glad we have been called to this land in the north; there will be a good chance for our sons to make a start and understand the Gospel in its true light. Our children will go on and carry on this work. It must be so."[24] Similar to Zina Young Card's editorial in *The Women's Exponent*, Woolf's speech communicates the hardship and pain of living far away from the greater Church membership, but also touches on the positive aspects of settling in Canada. Her fellow Canadian settlers would have heard or later read this speech and felt similar conflicted emotions about their relocation and settlement plan. However, hearing or reading the speech of one of the earliest settlers and one of their leaders, Mary Woolf would have reassured others that they were doing the right thing – obeying Church leaders and embarking on a new adventure that could lead to many exciting opportunities for their Church in the new land of Canada.

Concerns endured, however, and Latter-day Saint women in southern Alberta continued to receive spiritual gifts. On 28 May 1897, Sarah Hyde addressed those who "were fretting about schools & going away," promising they "would have good schools & [their] sons would be taught in the things of God & take the Gospel to this nation for there were many honest souls here & [members] should be humble & respect the local priesthood men."[25] In this instance, Hyde works to convince her fellow community members that Canada offers opportunities to both attend good schools and share the message of their Church. Similarly, in June of 1898, Rachel Archibald (1876–1936) spoke in tongues and instructed the brethren "to be faithful [and] also plow and sow & raise wheat for the time would come that we would have to raise grain for the United States would need wheat for bread."[26] Archibald predicted that southern Alberta would become a place of valuable resources. On 7 May of the following year, Archibald spoke in tongues at a fast meeting and Zina Young Card provided the interpretation that the Latter-day Saints must remain faithful because "the angels are watching over [them] and [they] should be grateful for this goodly land."[27]

In addition to convincing their fellow Church members about the positive aspects of living in Alberta, the women of The Church of Jesus Christ of Latter-day Saints helped change the negative public perception of their position and religion. In 1898 Charles Ora Card said goodbye to his wife Zina Young Card as she left for a trip to the eastern states on a mission that he wrote was to "allay prejudice."[28] The Church sent a delegation to the Triennial National Council of Women in Washington, and Zina Young Card represented the Relief Society, the Church's women's organization.[29] Card addressed a large audience at the Council on the topic of "The Mother and the Child." The report stated, "She referred to the tender solicitude felt by all classes of women for noble Miss [Susan B.] Anthony, and she felt that the work done by this heroine was due to the deep womanliness of her character."[30] Later, members of the Council debated the Edmunds Bill, arguing whether or not a person should be allowed to hold a place in any law-making body who is not a law-abiding citizen. During the discussion of monogamy and polygamy, "there were so many good and glorious words said in [their] behalf," and women's rights activist Susan B. Anthony said that Congress was full of men who violate laws of monogamous marriage so there was no need to go to Utah to punish the men there.[31] Zina's presence at the Triennial National Council of Women and her advocacy for the Church, not just the practice of plural marriage, helped remove some negative perceptions of the Church and reassure some non-Latter-day Saints that Latter-day Saint women were active, happy participants in both their religion and marital relationships. This example illustrates how a resident of Canada and Latter-day Saint represented her Church to a largely non-Latter-day Saint audience. Later, Canadian Latter-day Saints will similarly represent themselves by joining, leading, and participating in women's organizations such as the Alberta Women's Institute and United Farm Women of Alberta. These interactions and memberships acted as vehicles for crossing over into mainstream society and contributed to the Church's integration.

Latter-day Saint women worked hard to convince both insiders and outsiders of certain messages. To outsiders, such as those at the National Council of Women, Zina Young Card represented the Church and the controversial practice of plural marriage, even winning over some acceptance and understanding from the likes of Susan B. Anthony. Latter-day Saint women used speaking, writing, and spiritual gifts to convince insiders, like their community members in southern Alberta, but also those living in other diasporic communities, such as Mexico, that they were still very much a part of the Utah Church, contributing to both the overall mission of the Church and the local causes keeping them there. The spiritual gifts that they received, such as prophecy, meant that their messages held a certain power and authority to persuade others of certain themes, including the creation and establishment of new homes and communities in the NWT. The role of Latter-day Saint women in the case of dwelling and homemaking in the District of Alberta (soon to be the province of Alberta) was to advocate for their cause, well-being, status, and purpose.

The Church leadership did not uniformly appreciate women experiencing spiritual gifts, or, in particular, the gift of tongues. For example, at the general conference in April 1900, warning Church members of the dangers of sign seeking, second counsellor in the First Presidency Joseph F. Smith (1838–1918) stated, "The devil himself can appear like an angel of light. False prophets and false teachers have arisen in the world. There is perhaps no gift of the spirit of God more easily imitated by the devil than the gift of tongues ... I do not ask you to be very hungry for the gift of tongues, for if you are not careful the devil will deceive you in it."[32] However, during the next several decades, women in Alberta continued to claim to be receiving gifts of prophecy, tongues, and interpretation.[33] Yet, the content being communicated, and the location of the experiences changed. Latter-day Saint women became less likely to receive and perform spiritual gifts independent of Latter-day Saint men and Church leaders. The spiritual gifts were not always witnessed inside a meetinghouse at a sacrament, testimony, or fast meeting, and the recipients of the gifts did not reveal prophecies affecting or impacting Church leaders (men). In addition, unlike earlier records that depicted women exercising spiritual gifts independently of priesthood bearers (men), a diary entry from Joseph Y. Card (1885–1956) revealed a different perspective. Recalling the events of the Cardston Second Ward meeting on 12 April 1921, Joseph wrote that Nellie Pitcher prophesied that "the 10 scribes shall come down to us from the North. That the people were not ready to go into the temple."[34] After, Bishop Thomas Duce (1871–1947) "rejoiced that Sister Nellie Hinman Pitcher was blessed by Patriarch Hinman in [his] presence with the Spirit of Prophesy."[35] Joseph's wording indicated that the presence of Patriarch Hinman facilitated the gift of prophecy, and that Pitcher would not have received the spiritual gift without the presence of the priesthood. Women went from independently performing these gifts in their own right to needing prominent (men) priesthood holders' attendance to enable or legitimize such gifts. In addition to shifting gendered roles both within the Latter-day Saint community and broader Canadian society, their role as advocate for their mission and cause in Canada was no longer needed by this point. By the 1920s, they had lived in Canada for over 30 years, so doubts regarding their purpose there or connection to the Utah Church were long faded.

Healers

Latter-day Saints began their life in Alberta as exiles from their Church in the United States, fleeing from legal prosecution, but always remaining connected to their homeland, Utah, but isolated from the

Figure 3.1 Early view of Cardston, looking north.

Source: Peel's Prairie Provinces, (peel.library.ualberta.ca), a digital initiative of the University of Alberta Libraries.

conveniences of large cities. Comparatively, Utah seemed decades ahead of the District of Alberta in terms of urbanization and growth. For example, census data showed that Salt Lake City had a population of over 50,000 by 1900. Latter-day Saints moved from populated areas in Utah to the District of Alberta in the North-West Territories where the two closest towns, Fort Macleod and Lethbridge, each had under 4,000 residents. The success of the Latter-day Saints in Alberta depended on their creative responses to the challenges of isolation and diaspora. One of these challenges was health care, and women were suitable healthcare providers because they were already responsible for nurturing and caregiving while many had been trained in herbal medicines and midwifery, too.

In 1886, seven medical practitioners registered in the entire North-West Territories.[36] Two of the 14 doctors registered by 1889 lived in Lethbridge, 70 kilometres away from Cardston, and another two lived 79 kilometres away in Macleod.[37] Researchers estimated a rough ratio of one doctor per 1,000 residents in the territories at this time, but these residents were separated by great distances that needed to be crossed using horses or on foot and without a modern transportation system that includes maintained roads and highways.[38] In 1899, 95 certified members of The College of Physicians and Surgeons, N.W.T., practised in the North-West Territories.[39] Even as the region became an official province of Canada, Alberta had under 150 physicians for a population of over 100,000.[40] Latter-day Saints living in the south handled the absence of trained physicians with creativity and resourcefulness. "Much of the nursing, prior to the opening of the hospital, was done by the members of the Women's Relief Society of the Mormon church."[41] Latter-day Saint women were midwives and practical (unlicensed) nurses using herbal remedies and faith healing to care for their families and community members.

The use of traditional medicines, herbal remedies, midwifery, and faith healing were not new to the Church. On 9 February 1831, part of the revelation that Joseph Smith promised "embraced the law of the Church" stated, "And whosoever among you are sick, and have not faith to be healed, but believe, shall be nourished with all tenderness, with herbs and mild food, and that not by the hand of an enemy."[42] Historian Thomas Alexander notes that during the lives of Joseph Smith and Brigham Young many church members "shunned medical doctors and opted for priesthood healing, home remedies, or Thomsonian medicine [a democratic, egalitarian medical movement combining North American Indigenous herbal and medical botanical lore]. By the late nineteenth century, orthodox medicine was more widely accepted, but some antagonism still persisted."[43] In Smith's journal, Willard Richards (1804–54) recorded Joseph Smith's praise for Thomsonian doctor Levi Richards (1799–1876) and wrote, "[P]eople will seldom die with disease provided we know it seasonably, & treat it mildly, patiently, & perseveringly, & do not use harsh means ... we should persevere in the use of simple remedies."[44] Preference for herbs and botanical cures continued after Smith's death. Generally, before 1900, 80 per cent of all medicines generally were from roots, barks, and leaves.[45] The meeting minutes of the 1873 Cooperative Retrenchment Association (CRA) in Salt Lake City offered home recipes to battle yellow fever and dysentery. For consumption they suggested one ounce of flax seed and one ounce of bone set boiled in one quart of water, strained, and added one pint of molasses and one quarter of a pound of sugar; to take one tablespoon three times a day.[46] At the next CRA meeting, Amanda Smith (1809–86) said, "She regretted that there was so much sickness among them, and that sending for doctors had become so prevalent. It was best to send for the elders first ... washing and anointing, administration and simple medicines, such as the Lord will reveal to those who trust Him, are preferable to the treatment of doctors."[47] Women shared their remedies, and many recipes appeared on the pages of *The Woman's Exponent*. For example, one such recipe advised homemakers to treat burns and flesh wounds by melting together two quarts of raw linseed oil, three pounds of good fresh resin, and three pounds of beeswax.[48] The tradition of sharing remedies and recipes and treating your own family and community members followed the Latter-day Saints into Canada.

Latter-day Saints brought traditional medicine and herbalism with them from their Utah homeland, but settlers and Indigenous peoples already practised herbalism in the North-West Territories.[49] Alberta historian Anne Woywitka writes, "In the first days of homesteading in Alberta, the settlers had no choice but to depend on themselves in tending their sick … Not only was there a lack of money to pay the doctor but distance and mode of travel often kept the sick at home."[50] Sociologist Sandra Rollings-Magnusson agrees that "Self-help and home remedies that had been passed down in families from generation to generation were the sole, or at least the most important, aspects of medical care available."[51] Like *The Women's Exponent*, the Cardston newspaper published home remedies for ringworms and irritable stomach in its 17 September 1898 edition. For instance, to cure an irritable stomach, the article suggested mixing a slightly sweetened, well-beaten egg white with a few drops of vanilla and serving to the patient.[52] The similarities between Latter-day Saints and other settlers in the region is notable for two reasons. First, it shows how the Latter-day Saint community shared some similarities with other settler communities, which made them less peculiar and more like their white settler neighbours. As well, it highlights a common strategy of survival on the prairies that would not have been unique to Latter-day Saint women. While healing practices worked to establish borders around their settlements since it helped maintain the health of its members without seeking outside, medical assistance (when possible), various communities performed similar healing methods and recipe sharing too.

Midwife Zina D.H. Young (1821–1901) most likely passed down her medicinal recipes to her daughter, Zina Young Card (1850–1931), one of the founders of the Cardston community. For example, Young's treatment for rheumatism consisted of combining one ounce each of ether, spirits turpentine, ammonia, and spirits camphor, blended with four ounces consecrated oil.[53] Latter-day Saint women in Alberta relied on similar, if not identical, recipes. Local historians of Magrath remarked that "In the home the mother did most of the nursing, out of sheer necessity and used many home remedies such as wild peppermint tea, a salve made of a drop of carbolic acid in olive oil, egg membrane for covering scalds and burns, spice and bread poultices, pepper and mustard teas ... they made special efforts to stock up on those delightful and delicious items, epsom salts, castor oil, and good old cod liver oil extracted from over-ripe cod livers."[54] Similarly, Rojanea Bingham (1917–2011) remembered her mother, Dora Jacobs (1880–1953), as "a wonderful nurse. In the summer months she would gather herbs from the banks of the creek and dry them in the sun. They were stored in cans, and when the need for them arose, she steeped them, and we were given the natural herb tea, rather than a patent medicine from the drug store."[55] By 1905, there were at least three reported herbalists in the Church community and recipes like these can be found throughout the records of meeting minutes and newspaper articles.[56]

Medicinal remedies and herbal recipes shared throughout the Latter-day Saint communities teaches us two things about integration into Canadian society. First, it shows a resistance to integration by maintaining and feeding their connection to both the Utah Church and early Church leaders' preference for home remedies and Thomsonian medicine. This connection to Utah and Church leaders is important because it was a way to metaphorically cross back to the homeland and remind themselves of where they came from and who they descended from. Second, the herbal and medicinal remedies demonstrate the Latter-day Saint commitment to survival, independent from other Canadians due to their isolation in southern Alberta. The lack of trained doctors was not necessarily their choice, but in the face of this challenge they drew on known methods, such as herbalism, and cared for their own as needed. Health and healing practices inform us of part of the Latter-day Saint integration strategy at this early stage in their dwelling in the NWT and what would later become the province of Alberta because it required them to establish networks between community members in need rather than seek help outside the boundaries of their own communities.

Also common in the new settlements were midwifes who combined their knowledge of women's health with natural remedies. Many women that moved to the North-West Territories were midwives and practical nurses who offered their services to neighbours and friends such that "In the isolated Mormon settlements, the midwife was an obstetrician, surgeon, dentist and a homebrewed folk heroine."[57] Writer Chris Rigby-Arrington describes Mormon midwifery as the "paradoxical milieu of mystical beliefs, folklore, natural remedies, and faith in divine intervention."[58] Latter-day Saint women in southern Alberta often combined midwifery, folk medicine, and faith healing.

Most Latter-day Saint communities eventually had their own midwife. Writing for *Cardston News*, Vernon Shaw (1872–1960) remembered when the closest doctor lived in Macleod and one of Cardston's first midwives was Elizabeth Hammer (1857–1919), who handled all calls for medical assistance "with prompt response, with no thought of remuneration except the gratitude of those she helped."[59] Similarly, Ella Nelson (1859–1941), who came to Cardston in 1890, practised obstetrics in the District of Alberta from 1892, and at her funeral Nellie Pitcher (1877–1950) recalled that Nelson trained in Utah, learned the art of obstetrics, returned to Alberta, and "faithfully answered every call from 1892 to the time when the district was supplied with medical men, and after that time when there was more work than one doctor could do, she was often called to assist."[60] In the story of Nelson's life, Dorothy Merrill remembered that, "she not only helped women who gave birth to babies, but she learned to cope with the various diseases: small pox, typhoid fever, and the diseases common to that time. She had a home remedy for everything."[61] Nelson herself admitted that, in addition to her training and supplies, she also regularly relied on faith, sharing "many experiences of how she felt hands stronger than her own helping to turn babies and aiding her in difficult deliveries."[62] She said, "Whenever I had a difficult case beyond my skill I simply told the Lord I could do no more and he must help me, and he never failed me, not once."[63] Often, a form of faith healing and midwifery went hand-in-hand in the isolated communities of southern Alberta.

To the east of Cardston, Sarah Ella Milner (1857–1943) cared for the sick in the newly settled town of Raymond, which she and her family came to in 1903. At her funeral in 1943, President Heber F. Allen (1894–1968) said, "In the days when doctors were scarce and nurses fewer, the deceased spent much of her time ministering to the sick, where she displayed a rare skill and understanding in easing pain and distress."[64] He continued, comparing Milner to Florence Nightingale, claiming she had special, magical gifts and powers in the sick rooms that she travelled through blizzards to reach, delivering approximately 65 babies over her career.[65]

Midwifery is significant to the story of Latter-day Saints in Canada. It was a very important role within the community, performed by Latter-day Saint women, requiring a combination of special skills, training, and faith. For Latter-day Saints at this time and in this place, health care almost always coincided with spiritual gifts. In addition, the practice of midwifery contributed to the settlement and success of Latter-day Saint communities because it facilitated the birth, and therefore growth, of these communities. Midwives played a special role in bringing new life into the new homes in southern Alberta. These were future members of the Church and future contributors to society. Healing and midwifery allowed Latter-day Saint women to remain in their separate, domestic spheres while helping to heal and grow the new communities in the new territory.

In addition to midwifery and herbalism, the Saints relied on faith healing – what they specifically referred to as laying on of hands and administering to the sick. The contemporary church dictated that only Melchizedek Priesthood bearers exercised the gift of healing, but that was not always the case.[66] Women cannot hold the Melchizidek Priesthood and therefore cannot technically administer to the sick in the same way as male Church members. However, according to historical records, both men and women in the Church received gifts of healing.

Hannah Russell (1858–1944), a midwife sent to Stirling, Canada, with her husband Adam Russell in 1899, delivered many babies with both skill and faith. Sharing a miracle of healing with her granddaughter, Russell recalled her husband getting very ill, so she "administered to him" (the Latter-day Saint terminology for faith healing), explaining, "Where there [aren't] any Elders close, a woman may administer in the name of Jesus. I always kept a bottle of consecrated oil in my house and taught my children that it was the best medicine that could be given. So I got the oil and administered to him with all faith the Lord would make him better. I hardly had my hands from his head till he opened his eyes and wanted to get up."[67] As such, Russell always asked for guidance from her Heavenly Father before attending to the sick.[68] According to historian Claudia Bushman, "The women of the early Church were as involved in spiritual experiences as men. The spirit did not come through priesthood leaders alone ... women tended to be more receptive to the spirit. They were particularly blessed in the 'woman's sphere': their children were healed, their husbands blessed, their families provided for."[69] First counsellor in the first presidency to Brigham Young, Heber C. Kimball (1801–68) argued that women "might administer by the authority given to their husbands in as much as they were one with their husband."[70] There are numerous accounts of both men and women Latter-day Saints administering to the sick; all relied on faith when healing one of their community. According to her granddaughter Dorothy Merrill, Ella Nelson performed a special, personal prayer with the family before delivering each baby and attributed her success as a midwife to the fact that "I was called by the Lord to do his work, and when I had done all that I could I left the rest up to him and he never let me down."[71] Another Latter-day Saint midwife in southern Alberta named Sarah Kinsman (1857–1943) was reported to have "great faith in the healing of the sick ... great faith in prayer and in the power of God to alleviate suffering and save lives of mothers and babes."[72] Around 1916, Allie Jensen's (1871–1944) daughter Cleo (1904–81) suffered from a goitre next to her jugular vein, and doctors said it was too dangerous to operate, so the two women "prayed for healing power and Allie rubbed Cleo's throat with consecrated olive oil many times the next few weeks. She was cured."[73]

The inclusion of these examples of Latter-day Saint women performing miracles of faith healing show their continued, active role within the Latter-day Saint community. Faith healing was another spiritual gift, similar to speaking in tongues and prophecy, that was exercised by both men and women. Including the examples of Latter-day Saint women shows how their roles as healers and midwives involved a religious element. Prayer, miracles, and laying of hands were just as important as the training, skills, and tools of the nurses and midwives. The ongoing, active role of Latter-day Saint women is key to understanding the overall integration process for the Church and its members because women played a central part in creating home, family, and community, including healing and delivering babies. Faith and health were tied together, and keeping community members healthy meant using both faith and skills in tandem to heal the sick, comfort the grieving, and deliver the newborns. All these things worked together to establish home, or facilitate dwelling, in southern Alberta.

Even when orthodox medicine, clinics, hospitals, and physicians were available to those living in southern Alberta, faith healing continued in the Latter-day Saint communities, but with an increasing absence of women healers. In her diary during the month of October in 1910, Cynthia Wight (1860–1943) recorded the illness of her two sons, Charles Ora (1904–78) and Francis (1899–1947), and demonstrated how Latter-day Saints relied on both medical doctors and church leaders: "Next day the [Church] Elders administered to [Charles Ora], and for days thereafter. Dr. Lynn said he had bronchitis in one lung, pneumonia in the other ... Francis took sick ... tuberculosis, incurable ... We depended wholly on the Lord. Pres. E.J. Wood asked the high priests to fast and pray for him, which they did, holding Prayer circle for him. They also gave me a blessing. Francis steadily improved."[74] In the 1920s, five doctors at the Galt Hospital in Lethbridge told Ida Fossey (1898–1989) she would not live through the night, so her husband called Bishop Levi Harker, and he administered to her, and she lived many more years.[75] Similarly, Beth Johnson (1908–2002) remembered her time in the hospital when she suffered from back injuries and received a visit from John Green, who was known for his gift of healing. Thinking of this hospital stay in the 1930s, Johnson recalled, "He laid his hands upon my head and started to talk to the Lord. In a few seconds the pain was forgotten, and I seemed to be off somewhere in space ... I was quite without pain, and my mind was at rest ... To me it was a manifestation of faith, the Power of the Priesthood, and the goodness of the Lord."[76] With time, Church leaders (men) were more often entering the sickroom and attending to ailing members who wanted prayer and healing.

As Church leaders removed healing from the realm of women's authority, the community also faced the transition to the accessible modern medicine in their towns and region. Therefore, the movement of medically trained doctors and registered nurses to Latter-day Saint towns as well as the construction of clinics, maternity homes, and hospitals diminished the need for herbal remedies and midwifery over time. This highlights a crossing over into Canadian society because the Latter-day Saint community became less isolated and less self-reliant. They welcomed trained medical practitioners and also followed the trends of Canadian society, which included removing authority and power from the hands of women, as demonstrated by their removal from health care and spiritual gifts such as faith healing.

The First World War brought many crises to North America, including the threat of "the new woman" and her challenges to "the family." In the 1920s, argues historian Cynthia Comacchio, the concept of maternalism became a central strategy to uplift not only the nation but also the family by explicitly connecting motherhood to the health of the nation.[77] Society placed an emphasis on maintaining the "ideal modern family" where, as Comacchio explains, fathers were heads of households and breadwinners while mothers were responsible for homemaking, such as cleaning, cooking, and caregiving, with a new authority figure, in the form of the external expert (i.e., social worker) infiltrating the family unit.[78] While Canadian society was in flux after the war and attempting to maintain patriarchy and the ideal family, the Church saw one solution being the redefinition of male authority, which they accomplished by removing rituals from the hands of women. Yorgason, investigating shifting moral orders relating to gender authority, explained, "Domestic self-sacrifice more completely dominated women's roles. By 1920, Latter-day Saint culture told women that motherhood and home duties not only should take top priority but also should, except for a few exceptional women, become virtually the only priority."[79] Surprisingly, health care no longer qualified as a "home duty," but, instead, became an institutionalized religious rite known as administering to the sick now exclusively practised by men. While male Church leaders tried to define motherhood and home duties, Latter-day Saint women in Canada stepped outside the family homes and organized together to better their communities.

Relief Society Members

Adult women in The Church of Jesus Christ of Latter-day Saints are members of the Church's auxiliary organization called Relief Society. Today the Church defines the objective of this organization as follows: "Relief Society prepares women for the blessings of eternal life by helping them increase their faith and personal righteousness, strengthen families and homes, and help those in need. Relief Society accomplishes these purposes through Sunday gospel instruction, other Relief Society meetings, visiting teaching, and welfare and compassionate service."[80] In the nineteenth century, at the time when some Church members colonized the North-West Territories, Relief Society members were responsible for the care of those suffering and needing assistance and for the organization of economic self-sufficiency in the form of homemade products and grain storage.[81] One of the first Latter-day Saint women to arrive on Lee's Creek was Mary Woolf (1848–1915), and she became president of Lee's Creek Relief Society in 1887. Latter-day Saints spread out from Cardston as more members arrived from Utah and established communities in the surrounding areas they called Mountain View, Beazer, Aetna, and Leavitt. All organized their own Relief Society that fell under the umbrella of the Alberta Stake. Latter-day Saints in the NWT wasted no time organizing the Relief Society as this was an important step in dwelling and making home in this new foreign place. The Relief Society created a network among women to keep them spiritually and socially connected. These networks were vitally important during settlement to alleviate feelings of distance, isolation, neglect, and separation from their families and friends in Utah and the Utah Church. Relief Society also provided a place to discuss important issues facing the settlers.

In the first several years of settlement, Relief Society members repeatedly discussed motherhood, their children and husbands, and the challenges of their new home. At a Relief Society meeting in the home of Mary Woolf, Annie Layne "spoke of the necessity of Mothers controlling themselves and of the power Satan gained over us if we yield to our tempers and passions. [She] spoke of a dream she had on the way [to Cardston] of our blessings here, our freedom and how much better [it will be] for us and our husbands."[82] Another speaker at a Relief Society meeting in 1890 stated, "We as mothers have a responsible frontier to fill. We must guard against the evils that may creep in our midst."[83] These women looked to each other for ways to manage their families, especially the children, in this new place. At the October Relief Society Conference in 1895, Sarah Daines (1841–1929) instructed the audience on rearing children and the necessity of teaching them strict obedience.[84] The following year Sterling Williams asked Relief Society members "to look after their daughters, know where they are at night and with whom they associate."[85] Latter-day Saint women decided the best defence against outside interference was patience with and education of their children, to raise pure, obedient Latter-day Saints.

The Saints in southern Alberta were geographically isolated, which helped them remain in close-knit communities for some time. On 4 August 1899 an Elder spoke to the Alberta Stake Relief Society and hoped that "this should be a select society separate from all the evils of the world, chaste, virtuous and holy." The Elder asked the women to encourage the younger members to join Relief Society and not outside clubs because, he argued, "we cannot afford to lose our girls, and these clubs will tend to draw them away."[86] The Alberta Relief Societies fulfilled this request for several decades and focused their efforts on their own people. One example of how Latter-day Saint women cared for their fellow Church members was the practice of burial and funeral preparations by sewing clothing, preparing bodies, trimming caskets, and comforting the grieving.[87]

Membership in Relief Society remained a constant for Latter-day Saint women, but between 1908 and 1920, Joseph F. Smith implemented a reform that turned the Church's women's organizations into "auxiliaries" that fell under the supervision of the priesthood.[88] Communications expert Tina Hatch summarizes, "In reaction to outside cultural forces that both demanded and gave women more authority and credibility, the LDS Church reacted by emphasizing men's authoritative role in both Church administration and home."[89] By the 1960s, the Relief Society had lost most of its autonomy. Similarly, Relief Societies throughout southern Alberta, once operating as independent organizations, now fell under the control of Church leaders – an unsurprising change considering the discourse around motherhood, women, and the ideal family in North America, especially after the First World War.

The role of Latter-day Saint women as member of the Relief Society was a significant part of the integration process in Canada. By establishing and building these insular networks and organizations, Latter-day Saint women established a stable foundation of women they could rely on for motherly advice, homemaking tips, gardening help, burial preparations, charity work, and so on, in addition to sharing herbal recipes and knowing who to call on for assistance during childbirth or healing. The Relief Society, from the outside, looked like a strategy of building borders around their own communities of Latter-day Saints. However, establishing the Relief Society in southern Alberta was an important step that allowed them to build a stable foundation in their new home, that kept them self-reliant and surviving, until they were able to flourish and expand outward, or until the time the Church pushed them outward, looking for new ways to make a difference and support both their own people and Canadian society.

Mothers and Wives

In *The Mormon Experience: A History of the Latter-day Saints*, historians Arrington and Bitton observe a "renewed emphasis on the woman in the home [as] not only a restatement of a dominant American theme" but also the case for "worldwide applicability" of the Church.[90] As Comacchio demonstrates, Canadians held a similar attitude, and by the conclusion of the Second World War, Canadians "would reinstitute a version of the cult of domesticity that prevailed a century earlier, actually setting off a 'baby boom' in their renewed commitment to 'the family.'"[91] Despite industrialization, world wars, and economic crisis, Canadians believed "that the best solution was adherence to a family model based on a gender-defined male-breadwinner ideal ... the power relations governing the family dynamic remained essentially unchanged ... Familial power relations – the internal subordination imposed by gender and age – likewise persisted."[92] Latter-day Saints in southern Alberta followed this pattern. In particular, Cardston resident Winnifred Newton Thomas (1911–2001) described her father, a general contractor and builder, Samuel Smith Newton (1858–1954) as "king of the castle. We loved and respected him."[93] Her mother, Amy Newton (1869–1963), "kept a good house, and she was always there. She never worked; she never went out of the home. We always knew that when we went home Mother was there."[94] Similarly, J. Harris Walker (1912–97), eldest child of Mary "Fannye" Walker (1887–1969), wrote, "Mom's life centred around her family and helping Dad with his church jobs ... Mom's life was wrapped up with these positions."[95] The roles of mother and wife, like participation in Relief Society, remained a constant part of Church and community life. Latter-day Saint women maintained some cultural authority by influencing their children and spouses with rituals of family prayer and family home evening. These roles within the Latter-day Saint family unit connected to integration because it illustrates both dwelling and crossing – helping the family to inhabit a new place with specific Latter-day Saint practices, such as family prayer and family home evening, and crossing over into mainstream society by following Canadian patterns and expectations for how a family should operate, as we learned in chapter 2.

Family prayer was not strictly a Latter-day Saint ritual, nor was it a unique Canadian Latter-day Saint practice, but kneeling at the table, the "family altar," made it distinct to the Church, and it was common for Latter-day Saint families to engage in some sort of daily group prayer. Speaking to an audience at the annual conference in 1881, Joseph F. Smith said, "It [family prayer] is a duty, it is the word of the Lord to the Saints, that they should meet with their families morning and evening, and call upon God in His name ... it is absolutely necessary that the Latter-day Saints should come together in the family capacity, and kneeling around the family altar, call upon God for His blessings morning and evening."[96] According to Wilford Woodruff (1807–98), Brigham Young confirmed that "the family altar was the same as an altar in the prayer circle. It is for parents and children to join hands over the altar and pray."[97] However, to keep temple rituals well-defined and separated from day-to-day activities, the family altar became more symbolic of rather than similar to the altars in the temple. Therefore, families gathered around other objects such as the dining table, coffee table, or kitchen table, which they happened to keep in the women's sphere.

Reviewing family histories, many Latter-day Saints associated prayer and faith in the family home with their mothers. Ralph Leavitt (1902–89), whose family immigrated to Alberta in 1890, claimed, "The first thing I can remember was kneeling with my mother [Mary Alice Leavitt (1866–1929)] night and morning for family prayer."[98] Similarly, in his autobiography, Cardston resident Frank H. Pitcher (1903–89) offered a sentimental description of his mother: "[S]he [Nellie Hinman Pitcher (1877–1950)] always looked so well in a housedress, she prepared such good meals, she brought spirituality into our home. It was upon her suggestion that at breakfast the chairs were always turned around at the table and we knelt in family prayer before eating."[99] The Paxman family moved to Taber, Alberta, in 1903 and one of the sons, Ezra Paxman (1893–1959), remembered,

> My mother [plural wife of William Paxman (1835–97) named Katherine Ann Love (1860–1931)] had unbounded faith in the Lord. Her missionary and pioneer experiences had taught her to pray often and with great faith. I remember the prayers we had together as a little group in our humble farm home. Mother would talk to the Lord so plain and natural like that I felt like looking up to see if He was there in the room.[100]

Willard M. Brooks (1903–2005), whose family moved to Alberta in 1913, named his mother, Hattie, the "spiritual force in our family."[101]

Stories and recollections about family prayer reveal how Latter-day Saints remembered their mothers and the roles they played in strengthening families and homes in southern Alberta. Latter-day Saint women were performing labour that included cleaning, cooking, and child-rearing, in addition to leading the family spiritually through both family prayer and her own demonstrated attitudes and commitments. From the late nineteenth century to the early twentieth century, Latter-day Saints remembered their mothers has bearers of spirituality in the home, examples of spiritual forces, and models of Latter-day Saint faith, often associated with the connection between family prayer, the family altar, and commitment to the Church.

Church authorities back in Salt Lake City announced an innovative practice that would help maintain "their heritage as a truly distinctive people with a unique message."[102] On 27 April 1915, the First Presidency addressed a letter to the stake presidents, bishops, and parents concerning the family. Editors published this letter in the June issue of *The Improvement Era* for all to read: "[W]e advise and urge the inauguration of a 'Home Evening' throughout the Church, at which time fathers and mothers may gather their boys and girls about them in the home and teach them the word of the Lord."[103] This was the formal introduction of the Family Home Evening. Xarissa Merkley Clarke (1909–86), daughter of Magrath, Alberta, residents Alva and Jehzell Merkley, claimed that they practised a regular family evening even before the Church officially mandated Family Home Evening.[104] Eva Dahl Salmon (1903–95) reported the same occurrence in her family home in Raymond. They also had a weekly time where the family met in the home, even before the Church stressed the importance of such a practice.[105] Winnifred Newton Thomas (1911–2001), born in Cardston to Amy and Samuel Newton, in her 1982 oral history interview, reported, "Family home evening is something that was almost every night in our home. We had no radio; we had no T.V.; we had nothing else."[106] The tradition of family home evening facilitated a weekly ritual within the domain of the mother, rather than under the bishop, a male Church leader, in the meetinghouse.

Later, Church manuals in the early 1960s presented a resistance to feminism and a re-emphasis on patriarchy.[107] These particular values are often cited as "important distinguishing traits" of Latter-day Saints.[108] Latter-day Saints were like their Canadian neighbours in some ways (emphasis on the family) and unique in others (family prayer and Family Home Evening). The patriarchal family became more and more a symbol of the Church. In a published family history from the 1940s, authors Bennion and Richards described the daughter of Ernest and Olive Graham Bennion, Deloise Bennion Hill (1906–81), as "An efficient wife and mother, [who] has always kept her children well in hand, her home immaculate, and is a perfect hostess."[109] This characterization of Deloise coincided with an account of her church activities – the two consistent pillars of Latter-day Saint women's identity.

Family Home Evening illustrates both a resistance to and an acceptance of Canadian expectations. The specific Latter-day Saint weekly ritual was unique in that it was specifically mandated by Church leaders. At least once a week, Latter-day Saint families would come together to receive lessons and perform activities with their family members. There was a specific connection to the Church, but also an emphasis on their family unit. This kept Latter-day Saints tied together and was another unique practice tied to their Church that kept them alike fellow Church members in their new home. However, most Canadian families, regardless of their religious affiliation, would have spent time together – maybe not mandated by their religious leaders, but family time would have been a feature of domestic life found in many other Canadian homes in mainstream society, especially those looking to recreate the ideal modern family unit. Therefore, by emphasizing the importance of both their family and religion, Latter-day Saints picked the perfect time to introduce Family Home Evening, and this allowed another step crossing into Canadian spaces of acceptance. Family Home Evening, if outsiders were even aware of it, was a non-threatening Latter-day Saint custom that actually made them more like other white, Christian Canadians by placing great weight on family dynamics, the importance of domesticity, and the role of motherhood.

Canadian Latter-day Saint Women as Political and Social Activists

By the 1940s Latter-day Saint women found their roles changing within their homes and Church. Their private spheres changed and pushed them out from some of the familiar responsibilities, such as receiving spiritual gifts and healing. At the same time, some Latter-day Saint women moved further into the public sphere, engaged with non-Latter-day Saint women, and participated socially and politically outside their immediate communities. Latter-day Saint women joined both the Women's Institute (WI) and the United Farm Women of Alberta (UFWA) and contributed to discourse around social and political issues including immigration, citizenship, and health care. By adopting the language of these Canadian organizations, Latter-day Saints used these conversations and debates to separate themselves from people the WI and UFWA labelled as "foreign" and "unsuitable." This strategy, whether intentional or not, helped the Latter-day Saint program of integration into Canadian society.

Community-based organizations, like the Women's Institute and United Farm Women of Alberta, provided an entry-way for Latter-day Saint women to join and participate in Canadian society. The Women's Institute, which began in Ontario in 1897, as anthropologist John William Bennett summarizes, aimed to promote home economics to the highest standards so that "each home [ran] smoothly, then the collection of homes – the community – [would] also function well."[110] In her dissertation on feminism in the prairie provinces, Barbara Nicholson explains the organization's goal was to encourage learning about household science because it would lead to the improvement of home sanitation, economics, hygiene, nutrition, and child-rearing.[111] As historians Catherine Cole and Ann Milovic clarify in their chapter on Alberta Women's Institutes (AWI), the AWI was important to rural women in particular because

> It enabled them to face the loneliness of farm life in the early years by providing a social outlet, an opportunity to meet women from surrounding farms and share common concerns.... The community work in which AWI branches became involved, particularly during the two world wars, was widely seen as an acceptable means to broader public participation for women.[112]

The AWI connected women with various backgrounds because it was non-sectarian and non-partisan. It was also an acceptable organization for women to join and an acceptable reason to leave the domestic bubble.

The AWI arrived in Cardston in the summer of 1912 and elected Lydia Brown (1855–1935) the first president.[113] At some of their first meetings, which members hosted in their own homes, members of the Cardston branch discussed domestic problems such as how to make bread, how to lighten the burdens of wash day, and how to make the home more beautiful.[114] By the next year, the AWI spread to surrounding towns such as Spring Coulee, Magrath, and Raymond. During her visit to Cardston in March of 1926, provincial President Mable Huyck (1880–1961) explained their goals in regard to health: "[T]he W.I. plan is most ambitious. A free doctor and nurse for rural Alberta supplied by the W.I. to all districts lying more remote than 20 miles from an established office of a doctor."[115] In October 1928, public health nurse Amy Conroy presented lectures on infectious diseases, diets, obstetrics and child care. In 1934, branches of Alberta Women's Institutes at Raymond, Cardston, and Spring Coulee organized a travelling baby clinic.[116] According to the *Raymond Recorder*, this was not the first baby clinic sponsored by the AWI, which had started as early as 1926.[117] The baby clinic in 1931 was not only sponsored by the Cardston Women's Institute but also by the Department of Health.[118] In 1939, focusing on the problems of child welfare, the Cardston WI listened to two trained nurses present on First Aid work in bleeding and artificial respiration and other topics such as burns, bruises, broken bones, and common diseases.[119] These examples show how Latter-day Saint women still cared about the health and well-being of their families and community members even though they no longer administered to the sick in the same ways as before. Public health clinics, doctors, and nurses replaced midwifery, folk medicines, and faith healing, but these changes provided a bridge, or crossing, to broader Canadian society.

Participating in these organizations and contributing to the war effort became another way Latter-day Saint women crossed into more public, non-Latter-day Saint spaces. For example, the AWI worked with the Red Cross during the First and Second World Wars, and branches in Raymond and Cardston were particularly active. In a report for the Raymond Red Cross Society, under the direction of President Mary Rouse, the Raymond Women's Institute, comprising mainly of Latter-day Saint members, made 12 pairs of pyjamas, seven bed jackets, 18 many-tailed bandages, 36 T-bandages, 11 wash cloths, 18 straight bandages, 12 bedside bags, 39 personal property bags, eight pairs of socks, nine bed pads, 43 triangular bandages, and 19 pillow cases.[120] At the end of 1916, the AWI reported that they "had been most zealous in the raising of funds and generous in its disbursements for charity, Red Cross and patriotic purposes."[121] In addition, the Raymond WI's contribution of $32.50 for the War Services Fund in 1941 and the donation of an Afghan blanket to the Red Cross offers another example of the Latter-day Saint's contribution to the war effort.[122]

Another Albertan institution that attracted Latter-day Saints' attention was the United Farmers of Alberta (UFA). The Alberta Farmers Association and the Alberta Society of Equity merged in 1909, established the UFA, and worked to achieve goals related to the economic and social conditions of Alberta farmers. From 1913 to 1914, members amended the UFA constitution and admitted wives and daughters of farmers to the association. Women members of the UFA established the Women's Auxiliary in 1915 and changed the name to United Farm Women of Alberta (UFWA) in 1916. The rural perspectives of the United Farm Women of Alberta made members stand out among the various women's groups, such as the Women's Institute, in the province. In particular, the physical location of their homes and farms and the distances from resources made rural women more concerned with issues related to health care and education. In *The Rise of Agrarian Democracy*, Rennie writes, "[T]he UFWA was more agrarian, class conscious, and independent than the government-funded Institutes, which included both town and country women."[123] Having developed during the First World War, the UFA and UFWA worried "that the soldiers' sacrifices might be in vain, [and] farmers concluded that governments must create a new society through prohibition, health care, eugenics, social welfare, and progressive taxation."[124] Many of the Latter-day Saint farmers in southern Alberta shared these concerns, and many Latter-day Saint women living in areas around Cardston, Magrath, Raymond, and Taber joined the UFWA. A history of the UFWA from the 1920s called the organization "a great Provincial training school for citizenship, where women stood on their feet and expressed opinions."[125] But they also acted on those opinions and some of their early achievements included securing legislation instituting municipal hospitals, increasing support for Public Health Nurses, and reforming several Acts that benefited women and children.[126]

Talitha Carlson (1870–1939) moved to Cardston with her husband and children in 1902 and in 1921 became the first president of the first organization of the UFWA in Cardston.[127] During a visit to Taber in 1926, Carlson spoke at the Convention and stated, "The Farmers' movement had grown out of the desire of people on the farms to attain a decent standard of living and to live in peace. A farmer might work by himself like a slave and attain to neither. Only by organized and cooperative effort could these things be gained."[128] That same year she reorganized the Cardston Local UFWA, and the next year she became director of the entire Lethbridge district.[129] During her time as director, the executive committee appointed Carlson convenor of social service, a position she held for two years, and in July she spoke at a board meeting on social services and its close relation to the welfare of children.[130] In April 1927, *The U.F.A.* newspaper published a series of programs created by Carlson for local branches of the UFWA, revealing some of the organization's focus. The final program submitted by Carlson was for 15 April called "Civic Pride." She linked civic pride to good fellowship, following the law, and maintaining clean public spaces, initiating a community clean-up of roads and schools.[131] This selection of program topics for UFWA Locals suggests that women in southern Alberta cared about bettering their private and public spaces by sharing experiences and doing what worked best for others. The theme of civic pride demonstrates that the UFWA operated in a way that allowed Latter-day Saint members to cross into Canadian mainstream spaces and demonstrate their commitments to the broader community in terms of public spaces, cleanliness, following the law, and building community.

The Lethbridge constituency of the UFWA held its first conference on 7 November 1930 at the Masonic Hall in Lethbridge. According to the UFA newspaper, about 100 women attended the conference, where the Raymond UFWA President and Latter-day Saint Relva Ross (1891–1971) presented a paper on the District Health Units.[132] Dr. Fitzpatrick of the mental health department addressed the conference on the subject of mental hygiene and praised the UFWA "as being the most forward organization in the province in connection with the establishment of [mental health] clinics.[133] Earlier in January at the annual convention Dr. Fitzpatrick spoke about the Sex Sterilization Act and the marriages of "unsuitable people."[134] Messages of this nature appealed to some Latter-day Saints because it moved attention away from themselves and towards other marginalized groups. In the nineteenth century, non-Latter-day Saints argued that Latter-day Saints belonged to a new race with physiological, degenerate characteristics, as a result of plural marriage.[135] If Albertan Latter-day Saints did not want the label of "unsuitable" then deflecting attention from themselves and helping define exactly what "unsuitable" meant ensured that it did not include themselves, their community, or their Church.

At a meeting on 24 July 1931, Latter-day Saint Matilda Boyson (1889–1982) lectured on immigration policies and argued in favour of the ban on immigration.[136] The group then turned to the subject of "Socialization, Education, and Canadianization of the strangers already within our gates." During a reading, "listeners were made to visualize themselves as foreigners, and thus was developed a greater sympathy for the strangers among us," but these Latter-day Saints were once foreigners in this land, too. Had they forgotten? Many of the Latter-day Saint women involved with the UFWA were not Canadian born. For example, Jehzell Merkley was born in Wales, immigrated to the United States when she was still an infant, and moved to Alberta with her parents and siblings in 1899. Her father, John Lye Gibb (1848–1920), had two plural wives, named Sarah Gibb (1845–1923) and Hannah Simmons Gibb (1855–1941), and they all came to Canada. Similarly, Talitha Carlson also descended from polygamists. Her maternal grandfather, William Taylor Dennis (1810–94), was originally from Tennessee and migrated to Utah Territory in the 1850s where he took his second wife and eventually married four women. Allie Jensen's father, Ruel Rogers (1833–1903), had three wives by the time she was born in 1871 in Draper, Utah. Allie and her husband, Christian Jensen (1868–1958), immigrated to Magrath in the year 1903. In addition, Matilda Boyson was born in Schofield, Utah, and came to Alberta as a teenager with her mother and siblings in 1902. Many active Latter-day Saint members of the UFWA were not born in Canada, but perhaps coming from the United States,

United Kingdom, or Europe made them more desirable and suitable to Canadian expectations.

By 1930, the president of the Glenwood UFWA was England-born Rachel Archibald (1876–1936), and the group re-elected her for the fourth year.[137] In fact, during this time period, very few UFWA Latter-day Saints were born in Canada. One of these Canadian Latter-day Saints was the granddaughter of Talitha Carlson, Delia Woolf (1906–76), who was born in Cardston. Woolf became vice president of the Raymond UFWA in 1931 and was elected president the next year, remaining as such until 1936.[138] Delia's father, Orson Bigelow (1884–1935), moved to Canada in 1893 and her mother, Eva Carlson (1888–1929), probably moved about 1902, when her parents Talitha and Isaac moved. These Latter-day Saint women were members of an organization that might have campaigned to prevent their settlement of southern Alberta in the late 1880s. But now they were not only active members of said organizations, but leaders paving the way, speaking in public, and guiding policy.

When they discussed immigration, the UFA and UFWA encouraged assimilation. The UFA magazine reported plans for improving conditions for immigrant women in 1923 and stated that there should be "greater care in the selection of girls who will adapt themselves to Canadian conditions."[139] At their annual convention the following year, the UFWA appealed for "better assimilation of the foreign born," even though immigration regulations already barred "idiots, imbiciles, feeble minded, epileptics, insane ... persons suffering from chronic alcoholism or the drug habit; and anarchists."[140] The United Farm Women of Alberta defined their Immigration Committee with "the purpose of helping the newcomer, and making them feel that they are welcome to the new country." However, helping seemed to mean assimilating, but sometimes even integration was not enough to satisfy everyone. UFA member, Latter-day Saint, and solicitor Hjaldermar Ostlund (1878–1942) (whose parents were born in Sweden) called for the cessation of "the flooding of Canada with immigrants," and, later, connected unemployment rates to immigration.[141] Latter-day Saints, as members of the UFWA, contributed to the discourse around assimilation and immigration, which is ironic since, up to this point, their own status of assimilation might have come under fire by the very people they were now cooperating with through these women's organizations. But it shows that they had significantly crossed over into Canadian public spaces that they not only blended in with other white, Christian Canadians, but they also agreed with their anti-immigration, pro-assimilationist messaging.

Adapting and adopting these opinions and messages was a productive strategy of integration for the Latter-day Saints because it further aligned them with the mainstream, as shown through the UFWA topics of discussion.

Local Latter-day Saint constituencies of the Women's Institute discussed similar subjects and appointed various convenors for committees on Canadianization and immigration. At a meeting of the Cardston constituency in 1926, Sadie Taylor stressed the importance of immigration, and by the 1930s they were still discussing Canadian customs regulations and how to help "Canadianise" immigrants.[142] Reporting on a meeting in July of 1932, the *Cardston News* wrote that American-born Clara Stutz (1885–1950) talked about how Canada needs "the right type" of immigration: "[Canada must] allow only those immigrants to enter who are adaptable and who can establish themselves in this land without Government help …The Stranger within our gates," she argued, "need[s] but to be known and understood to be appreciated and even loved."[143] At times Latter-day Saint women were tolerant of newcomers but, as members of these provincial and community-based organizations, they debated whether or not to allow immigrants into Canada, and interfered in the sex lives of others and reproduction rates (i.e., Sterilization Act). These Latter-day Saints women were either immigrants themselves or daughters of immigrants but had reached such a point of comfort, integration, and familiarity in Canadian society that they considered immigrants as potentially dangerous "others," unlike themselves who had worked hard to blend in in various ways, such as by abandoning the practice of plural marriage.

Conclusion

Historian Brian T. Thorn, writing about Canadian women after the Second World War, reveals that, "Postwar political women used a maternalist viewpoint to argue for an increased female role, and their maternalism had specific elements" such as a value system based on care and nurturance, a collective responsibility to protect children and families, and an emphasis on motherhood being a unique qualification that enabled them to lead specific types of reform and campaigns.[144] In a similar vein, Canadian Latter-day Saint women, by the 1940s, were mothers, wives, Relief Society members, and seekers of social and political change in local women's movements. These gendered roles replaced their once diverse repertoire of spiritual gifts, including faith healing and prophecy, activism in support of plural marriage, and medical care of their fellow Latter-day Saint settlers. Both internal and external factors facilitated these changes and negotiations of identity.

Examining the lives of Latter-day Saint women in southern Alberta shows us how religious minorities make homes in new places and cross into new spaces. Latter-day Saints established a new home in southern Alberta by using spiritual gifts, such as prophecy, to confirm and reassure members why they had to leave their homes in Utah and why they were settled in Canada. In this case, Latter-day Saint women, using their spiritual gifts, were not only making a new home, but convincing their fellow community members that Alberta was their home. Women also made homes by supporting the well-being and health of their family and community members. Curing and treating the sick and delivering babies were part of the health care infrastructure of their settlements. Maintaining the health of their community in a new home contributed to the Latter-day Saint settlement strategy. Women's organizations, like the Relief Society, also demonstrate instances of dwelling and homemaking by building networks between women and providing relief when needed, like burial preparation for the deceased. Latter-day Saint mothers and wives provided connections within their own families too. They organized family home evenings and family prayer as purposeful practices that maintained and nurtured family and spiritual relationships.

While Latter-day Saint women initiated and followed through on these various strategies of dwelling as newcomers in Canada, they also navigated barriers that challenged their integration process. For example, they joined the Alberta Women's Institute and United Farm Women of Alberta and participated directly in improving Canadian society through these community-based organizations. Working alongside non-Latter-day Saints, Latter-day Saint women in southern Alberta helped organize health classes teaching proper sanitation methods, raised funds to build a municipal hospital, collected supplies for the Red Cross, and debated policies of immigration. They placed themselves within organizations determining and defining what it meant to be "Canadian," which was a significant and smart strategy of integration.

Observing the changing roles of Latter-day Saint women helps us answer the three research questions guiding this study of Canadian Mormonism. First, by joining the AWI and UFWA, Latter-day Saint women embedded themselves in a significant structure of Canadian society: local, community-based, women's auxiliary organizations. Second, the Church adapted to Canadian circumstances by removing certain responsibilities from the hands of women (i.e., administering

88 Thirsty Land into Springs of Water

to the sick) and emphasizing the importance of motherhood, maternalism, and family. Lastly, Latter-day Saints in southern Alberta maintained some distinctive beliefs and practices that drew boundaries around themselves to maintain their identity of harmless, peculiarity. This included membership in the women's Relief Society, ties to plural marriage, and the weekly ritual of family home evening.

Chapter Four

Business

Introduction

Canadian authorities, such as the North-West Mounted Police, were cautious about the arrival of the first Latter-day Saints. Comissioner L. W. Herchmer reported,

> They are, so far as progress and enterprise go, the very best settlers in our country, but any attempt to introduce the practice of polygamy under any guise must be promptly dealt with. They are, so far, if straight on this point, law-abiding citizens.[1]

"Progress" and "enterprise" were two values critical to the success of Latter-day Saints in the North-West Territories. Therefore, business provides another site of negotiation to observe how Latter-day Saints integrated into Canadian society. An emphasis on economic cooperation shows how Latter-day Saints drew boundaries around themselves in order to maintain an identity of peculiarity and self-sufficiency. They can attribute their initial economic and social successes, at least partially, to their self-sufficiency. They were creative, hardworking, and dedicated to a cause (their Church) larger than themselves. Furthermore, their self-sufficiency did not stall progress and adaptation to their surroundings. Their willingness to give up some of this self-sufficiency and reach outside their community, with more long-term financial plans and broader goals, required interaction and cooperation with non-Latter-day Saints, and enabled them to take another step towards integration into Canadian society. Before they accepted their permanency in Canada, Latter-day Saints remained tied to the ways of their homeland in the nineteenth century. They settled communities following the farm village plan and developed businesses with community benefits in mind. The Mormon Farm Village and cooperative interests were products of strategies, intentional or not, that kept Latter-day Saints isolated and self-reliant. Eventually, though, they began to embed themselves in the social, economic, and political structures of Alberta, which lead to large-scale irrigation projects that impacted not only the Latter-day Saints but also their Albertan neighbours. While they were willing to cross into public Canadian spaces to do business, they still organized cooperative ventures, such as sugar beet farming and ranching, to improve the lives of their members and communities.

The Mormon Farm Village

Latter-day Saints physically left their homes in Utah behind when they migrated to the North-West Territories and established a new homeland by constructing houses, farms, businesses, and communities. They brought with them the designs of their former homeland to transform their new land into something familiar. This style of settlement, the Mormom village or farm village, was one way that Latter-day Saints established visible boundaries between themselves and non-Latter-day Saints. This pattern of occupying land, argues sociologist Lowry Nelson, contributed to their achievement as community builders. He continues, "The manner in which rural people arrange their habitations upon the land constitutes one of the important factors determining the nature of the social organization."[2]

The Mormon farm village settlement plan consisted of keeping family homes separate from the farms. They established homes in villages or towns with wide streets and yards large enough for smaller livestock, chicken coops, pig pens, and vegetable gardens.[3] Planners designed the wide streets following a cardinally oriented grid system, and today sights of past small farming activity within the settlement centre and large lots occupied by a single dwelling are all evidence of this settlement plan.[4] Therefore, farmers were expected to travel to their homestead and raise crops or livestock while their families, merchants, and businessmen stayed within the village, having the conveniences of nearby school, butcher, market, and church. Open field landscape surrounded the Mormon farm village as land for farming.

The creation of the Mormon village, or farm village, came from the creation of the Plat of the City of Zion, "an invention of the Mormons ... resulting from the ideologies of millennialism, communism, and nationalism which they derived from the social environment of the early nineteenth century, and the Old and New Testaments."[5] There was an urgency motivating the preparation of a dwelling for Jesus Christ at the Second Coming. Canadian geographer John C. Lehr writes, "[T]he origins of the Mormon village lie rooted in the millennialist eschatology of Mormonism, its perpetuation was solely pragmatic."[6] The Plat of the City of Zion required that all people lived in the city: The city was a mile square; blocks contained 10 acres cut into half-acre lots to allow 20 houses per block; the middle tier of blocks was 50 per cent wider than the others so it could be used for schools, churches, and public buildings; all houses set back 25 feet from the street, with farmlands outside the city.[7] Examples from early Latter-day Saint history are found in Kirtland, Ohio (1834), and Nauvoo, Illinois (1837).

Plans for the town of Cardston come from various sources. Nelson claims that Charles Ora Card designated 16 blocks to the quarter section, each block (containing four lots of equal size) was to be 34 rods square (0.2125 acres), with streets 99 feet wide, intersecting at right angles.[8] Rosenvall writes that the grid pattern for Cardston contained square blocks 8.4 acres each, to be subdivided into eight equal lots.[9] But the town plan evolved with time. First, they surveyed and laid out 12 city blocks for the town site with four lots on each block, 17 rods square (4,628 square feet, or 0.10625 acres), with streets 99 feet wide and laid at right angles. Later, the Latter-day Saints expanded the town to 16 blocks to the quarter section, 34 rods square, as described by Nelson.

Admittedly, not all Latter-day Saint settlements in Alberta followed this exact plan. Between 1887 and 1910, 13 out of 19 settlements were farm villages with only a "superficial resemblance to the Plat of Zion."[10] One of these towns resembling the Plat of Zion was Magrath, which was designed with blocks of ten acres each subdivided into eight lots with streets 100 feet wide. In total, they planned 92 blocks with four business blocks in the middle, west of main street, laid off in 30 by 150-foot lots.[11] Likewise, the Village of Stirling, over 30 kilometres east of Magrath, also followed the farm village strategy when settled by Latter-day Saints in 1899.

> The town was made up on one square mile, 640 acres. It was then divided into lots of 10 acres. Each 10 acres had a surveyed road around the entire area with a lane running north and south dividing it into two parcels. These were again divided, east and west, making four lots, 2½ acres each. This would give the residents room to build their homes, barns, and shelters for their animals and leave room for a large garden.[12]

Subsequently, whether the Alberta settlements followed every detail of the Plat of Zion is unimportant. The significance of the settlement plan can be explained by Joseph Smith's goal when devising the Plat of

Zion, which was "to design communities that enhanced the cooperation and religious unity envisioned in the revelation about Zion."[13] The key here is the enhancement of cooperation and religious unity. The success of these communities in southern Alberta can be attributed in part to the use of the farm village plan. Rather than having women and children isolated on the homesteads, the plan had them gather together in the village or town. Consequently, this allowed full participation in church and auxiliary activities, less inaccessible to those living miles outside of town.[14] In the late nineteenth and early twentieth centuries, the Latter-day Saint way of life required various commitments that occurred on different days of the week. For example, priesthood meetings were held on Saturdays and sacrament meetings on Sundays.[15] Organizing settlements so that most members lived within close distance to meetinghouses guaranteed a higher level of participation in Church activities, which ultimately helped keep the settlers connected to their fellow community members and shared commitments.

The United Order and Irrigation

Town planning was not the only way Latter-day Saints encouraged cooperation. The phase in Latter-day Saint economic history labelled "the cooperative movement" lasted, according to Latter-day Saint Church historian Leonard J. Arrington, from 1868 to 1884.[16] However, his description of the Latter-day Saint colonies in Alberta and Mexico (Sonora and Chihuahua) present situations typical of the supposedly obsolete movement. Arrington writes,

> Each of the new settlements was designated as a gathering place, and nearly all were founded in the same spirit, and with the same type of organization and institutions, as those founded in the 1850s and '60s. Colonizing companies moved as a group, with church approval; the village form of settlement prevailed; canals were built by cooperative labor; and the small holdings of farm land and village lots were parceled out in community drawings.[17]

Furthermore, ecclesiastical corporations in the 1880s held church property, and mercantile and industrial cooperatives became incorporated as joint-stock concerns.[18] As a result, one of these corporations in the North-West Territories was the Alberta Land and Colonization Company, incorporated in 1896.

As those first Latter-day Saints remembered it, there was no official practice of the United Order (a cooperative and communal economic plan) in Cardston but, as William L. Woolf (1890–1982) explained in an interview, "the people were very cooperative."[19] They were so cooperative that they formed a "joint-stock corporation, organized under the sponsorship of the Church, with a broad basis of public ownership and support ... motivated principally by welfare rather than profit; patronage was an act of religious loyalty."[20] Arrington further explains,

> Cooperation was deliberately promoted by the Church as a solution to its problems, both spiritual and material. Cooperation, it was believed, would increase production, cut down costs, and make possible a superior organization of resources. It was also calculated to heighten the spirit of unity and "temporal oneness" of the Saints and promote the kind of brotherhood without which the Kingdom would not be built.[21]

However, before the cooperative efforts in southern Alberta were established, the Church in Utah faced many financial challenges, including the panic from the financial depression of 1873 that initiated the extension of "the cooperative principle to every form of labour and investment, and to cut the ties which bound them to the outside world."[22] That year the United Order Movement began, the Church asked each member of the community to donate their property to "the Order" and receive in return the equivalent capital stock.[23] Some united orders required members to share the net income of the enterprise rather than work for fixed wages; others required members to donate all their property and share everything equally. The united order functioned like a joint-stock company with the aim of helping already existing cooperatives (no one was required to give up their property).[24] Latter-day Saint communities established about 200 orders, but this official system mostly ended around 1877, according to Arrington, with different types continuing in various settlements until the 1890s, according to the Encyclopedia of Mormonism.[25] In the District of Alberta in the North-West Territories, the third type of united order existed where

> Such orders did not require consecration of all one's property and labor but operated much like a profit-sharing capitalist enterprise, issuing dividends on stock and hiring labor ... Brigham Young believed that pooling capital and labor would not only promote unity and self-sufficiency but would also provide increased production, investment, and consumption through specialization, division of labor, and economies of scale.[26]

By their second summer in the North-West Territories, the Latter-day Saints considered implementing a type of united order. At the Card residence, Zina Y. Card (1850–1931) advised members of the Cardston Relief Society that they should prepare "to live in the United Order."[27] That winter, Charles Ora Card opened the first general store as the sole owner.[28] However, less than a year later, the Latter-day Saints in Cardston hoped "to incorporate for rearing stock, Cooperative Stores, Dairy, Saw mill and Grist mill purposes," and so Card met with a lawyer named Haultain to begin the paperwork.[29] At a priesthood meeting in May of 1890, Card

> spoke to them upon the necessity of unity among [the Latter-day Saints] in all things temporal and spiritual. [He] advised cooperation in our business operations. Advised the brethren to herd out stock and save our grain. Advised the brethren to take the Oath of Allegiance to the Canadian Government. Also to pay their tithes and offerings.[30]

Card wanted to accomplish two goals: group cooperation among Latter-day Saints themselves and, at the very least, the appearance of loyalty to the Canadian government. Latter-day Saints must work together to prosper but, at the same time, they must not alienate themselves from help extended to them from government officials.

As the Latter-day Saints united in matters of secular and sacred natures, non-Latter-day Saints petitioned against the incorporation of the Cardston Company Limited. Citizens of nearby Macleod worried about the incorporation of a joint-stock company, fearing it will "become a very powerful association, wielding an enormous influence." An editor of the *Lethbridge News* advised readers to "take steps to avert the danger that threatens this district – namely, that of becoming a Mormon country." Furthermore,

> The principles of Mormonism – namely a blind submission to the revelations of their prophets – make them a great source of danger to a country where the Christian population is small. Mormonism soon becomes a great political machine in which all the component parts act as one man for furthering, by their votes and otherwise, the objects of their religion, or the orders of their prophets as expressed in revelations.[31]

Previously, those opposed to Mormonism in the United States feared Latter-day Saint political power because of the perception that Latter-day Saint leaders held limitless influence over the Church's membership. David T. Smith summarizes, "the early persecution of Mormons in the United States occurred mainly because of the political challenge of their charismatic and theocratic leadership … Opponents of

Mormonism always constructed this threat in terms of the control they exercised over their followers."[32] Thus, it is unsurprising that similar attitudes existed in the North-West Territories towards the Latter-day Saint settlers.

Despite these public protests, Charles Ora Card, John Anthony Woolf, Neils Hansen, Simeon Franklin Allen, and Ephriam Harker together applied for the incorporation of a body corporate under the name "The Cardston Company, Limited," with the goals of milling, manufacturing, dairying, farming, stock raising, ranching, and general merchandising.[33] The official petition to refuse this request said, "We believe that concentrated and corporate wealth acquires an influence and wields a power over civil affairs that is a menace to the civil power and becomes dangerous to the liberty of the people and to the peace and good order of Society."[34] The Moose Jaw *Herald Times* reported that "there is in it [the Cardston Company, Ltd.] the element of religion, which destroys individualism and compels men to engage in enterprises as a duty to a human leader."[35] The newspaper further predicted that "By uniting as a religious community, they have seriously injured the labour market of southern Alberta ... The whole of the trade in Southern Alberta will be controlled by the Cardston Company if it is incorporated."[36] But rather than control all of southern Alberta, Latter-day Saints began with their first cooperative irrigation project and diverted water from Lee's Creek to run a grist mill and irrigate gardens.[37]

Board meetings and preparations for a cooperative store began in the first months of 1891.[38] The Latter-day Saints, operating as the Cardston Company, built a cheese factory to be run by Robert Ibey (1874–1943), and a saw mill.[39] The Cardston Company received incorporation the following year.[40] Superintendent Steele reported that "the Mormons have purchased about 700,000 acres of land between Lee's Creek, St. Mary's River, and Pot Hole Creek: 116,000 acres of this was purchased by the Cardston Co. (Limited) and since transferred to individuals ... About 25 new buildings have been erected in the village of Cardston this year, including a large general store and post office."[41] The board elected Card as the first director and then president. In his diary, Card wrote,

> [President] the same position I have held for the last 4 years although we have only organized fully as a charter Co[mpany] for 9 months but in order to lead the people in cooperation I have managed their means over my private name previously and our institution has grown from $700.00 to $7,000.00 during that time & we have managed our business successfully under the blessings of the Lord and these last 2 years had a Dairy

added and run without loss & made about 90,000 lbs. of first class cheese, 53,000 of it made the last season and for all of my labor I have received less than $500.00 but left part of my reward for the great hereafter.[42]

Several weeks later, Card equated the Latter-day Saints of Cardston with the cooperative Cardston Company Limited, feeling he had accomplished enough for their future welfare.[43] This feeling lasted less than a year when two of Card's own people left the cooperative to start their own business, perhaps inspired by the free market capitalism of their non-Latter-day Saint neighbours.[44] In his diary on 30 January 1894, Card noted that Simeon F. Allen (1839–1901) and Heber S. Allen, father and son team, opened their own store in direct competition with the Cardston Company. They did this "without advice or counsel," claimed Card.[45] The Lethbridge *News* reported that "Mr. H.S. Allen has resigned as sec'y and treasurer of the Cardstone [sic] Co. Limited. We understand another firm will soon make its appearance with Mr. Allen as its head."[46] Perhaps the Allen father and son duo saw merit in the mixed economic approaches of their non-Latter-day Saint neighbours.[47] Before Heber went into business with his father, he managed the Cardston Co., but gave his notice in June 1893.[48] "He had saved $1,800 and borrowed $1,000 from his father, who had been farming in the Mountain View area ... The Allens built a store room in the end of their house, and opened for business in August. The new business prospered from the start."[49]

Meanwhile, Card nurtured his developing relationships with former land surveyor and the mayor of Lethbridge, Charles Alexander Magrath (1860–1949), and businessman Elliott T. Galt (1850–1928). Card met Magrath back at the beginning of settlement in the NWT when they negotiated "land business," which indicates an ongoing business relationship concerning land development in southern Alberta.[50] As such, Card called Magrath "a very staunch friend of our people in refuting falsehoods and staving off persecution here."[51] Card recognized that the Latter-day Saint settlements could not remain insular if they wanted to establish themselves more permanently in the territory. They needed powerful allies, like Magrath and Galt, in order to advance both their own needs and contribute to the improvement of the territory. Galt had formed the Alberta Irrigation Company in 1893 with hopes of purchasing lands from the Alberta Railway and Coal Company (ARCC) to build irrigation canals and resell the land for agriculture. Magrath, an expert in land, and Card, a leader of a group of people capable of building canals, joined forces with Galt to start this new venture. Card and Magrath met with

Church leaders in Salt Lake City in January of 1895 to discuss "land business" and the organization of a large corporation to handle stock and land (600,000 acres) previously purchased by Taylor and Card.[52] On 17 January, Card bought 591,000 acres of land from the ARCC with the intention of signing it over to the newly formed Alberta Land and Colonization Company, a Latter-day Saint cooperative.[53]

According to the superintendent of the Macleod District, in 1895, the year the Church designated the region as the Alberta Stake, Cardston, with a population approaching 1,000, had 752,150 acres under cultivation that harvested 33,000 bushels of oats, 17,000 of wheat, and 6,000 of barley. Steele reported that the village had 1,508 horses, 4,060 cattle, and 3,550 sheep. He counted the construction of 12 new buildings that year, and the private school (still without government assistance) had 50 pupils. The Cardston cheese factory outputted 48,659 pounds of product, most of which they shipped to the Pacific Coast; the grist mill ran six months of the year at a capacity of 180 bushels per diem; and the saw mill produced 187,560 feet of lumber and 39,000 shingles.[54] It was the aftermath of this prosperity when Card issued scrip to the citizens of Cardston to use at the cooperative store or cheese factory. In his diary, Card wrote, "I signed my name to 700 Pieces of scrip or mdse [merchandise] Orders for the Cardston Co. Ltd our cooperative store & cheese factory. This is our first Issue of printed issues of which we have $500.00 printed. I signed up $890.00, being 100 pieces each denomination 5, 10, 25 & 50 cents, 100 each of $1.00, $2.00 & $5.00."[55] But by February 1896, three years into the depression of 1893–97, the high number of people failing to pay their accounts placed the Cardston Company in trouble, and Card spent the month of March looking to borrow $4,000 to aid the business.[56] In his diary at the end of the year, Card summarized his job as "supervising all points of business of the Cardston Co[mpan]y Ltd., which is our cooperative store company which includes the cheese factory & the Hog industry of our Company."[57]

In June of 1896, the Alberta Land and Stock Company filed articles of incorporation in Utah. "The stock is represented in a contract with the Alberta Railway and Coal company for the transferring of 16,145 acres of land in the North-West territory, Canada, and which will be used for stock raising purposes."[58] Charles McCarty (1850–1926) spearheaded the company's incorporation, investing $300, 20,000 sheep, and 300 head of cattle.[59] On 11 March 1897, Magrath, escorted by Card, met with the Church presidency, probably Second Counsellor in the First Presidency Joseph F. Smith (1838–1918), First Counsellor George Q. Cannon (1827–1901), and President Wilford Woodruff (1807–98), and expressed, according to Card, that he was "well satisfied with [the]

Mormon settlers ... the Mormons were the only people that could & would settle southern Alberta and make a success of it."[60]

The year 1897 was significant for the Latter-day Saints in Canada. The population of Cardston reached 1,000, the Alberta Stake of Zion received incorporation in the NWT, Chauncy E. Snow (1870–1940) established a private bank, and the government appointed the first Latter-day Saint justice of the peace, Henry L. Hinman (1837–1921).[61] But many were still unable to pay their debt to the cooperative store. On 14 April, Card reached out to Simeon F. Allen at his home in Hyrum, Utah, and asked him to rejoin the Cardston Company:

> And making it a strong firm to carry on business for [on] behalf of our people to give greater stability to our settlement there. Talked over matters and gave him my mind freely in for that we might maintain things temporally and spirituality and be able to use our talents to better advantage in preaching the gospel to the strangers in that land and not weakening our foothold.[62]

Card's attempt to cooperate with the Allens, or eliminate the competition, failed, and Allen & Co. continued operation until 1911, even after Heber moved to Raymond. The next year the board once again elected Card director, manager, and president of the Cardston Company Limited. He recorded in his diary that he had "managed the business for 10 y[ea]rs & it ha[d] grown from $700 capitol put in at first 5 or 600 Later to at Least $15000 capitol."[63] He "advise[d] the brethren to not go outside of our organizations to settle for we have abundance of land near at hand."[64]

That autumn Card recorded in his diary the immigration and irrigation plans proposed by Magrath. Magrath instructed Card to gather able Latter-day Saints and promised they would receive land and labour for constructing the proposed canal from St. Mary's River eastward along the base of the Milk River towards Lethbridge.[65] Negotiations continued through September and October and into November. In an entry dated 3 November 1897, Card wrote, "The Presidency made the proposition to Mr. E.T. Galt to form 2 settlements on 2 Blocks of land within a radius of 20 & 30 miles of Lethbridge & place [in] them 50 families each, [to] total 250 souls each within 2 years from Apr. First 1898 & take pay in Labour & land & water [rights] at $3.00 per acre."[66] They reached an agreement that afternoon. As a result, Latter-day Saints would labour to build the irrigation canal and receive payment half in land and half in cash. However, the agreement was not finalized until April of the following year. The Alberta Stake of Zion needed incorporation before both sides could sign contracts, and on 15 December 1897 the North-West Territories passed an ordinance to incorporate the president and high council of the Alberta Stake of Zion, thus allowing the Church in Canada to "acquire and possess real and personal estate within the North-West Territories of Canada." Consequently, section six gave them the "power to sell, convey, exchange, alienate, mortgage, lease or demise any lands, tenements and hereditaments held by said corporation."[67] Two days after the government passed the ordinance, Card thanked Magrath "for the great interest he had taken in getting the bill through the North-West Council to incorporate the Alberta Stake of Zion."[68] In addition to granting the Church such rights, the Canadian government appointed Card sub agent for Dominion lands in January 1898, authorizing him to grant homestead entries and aid immigration.[69] With the help of Magrath, Card now held significant power as someone in charge of immigration, homesteads, and business involving the incorporated Stake, like the irrigation canal. On 26 April, Card "met with Pres[iden]ts Cannon & Woodruff & talked Canal matters over about Alberta & the construction of the Canal the Church had engaged to do $100,000.00 worth of Labour upon the 14 Inst and papers were executed about 5:30."[70] Card also recorded that the presidency emphasized the Church's dependence on him to see that they complete the work required and carry out the contract. A big task had been placed on not only Card's shoulders, but also the entire Church's.

Work commenced that summer. At a priesthood meeting on 21 August, Card "layed before the brethren the construction of the Alberta Irrigation Co Canal as that which has been inaugurated by our leaders for our good & the good of the kingdom in this part of the Land and as such we should support it with our works & words."[71] But they needed more workers so, in January of 1899, Card spoke to Latter-day Saint audiences throughout Utah on "the advantages of southern Alberta" in order to recruit new settlers.[72] John Theodore Brandley answered this call to Canada, left his wife Margaret Keeler (1863–1910) in Utah, and arrived in Stirling, one of the new settlements at the end of the canal, in May 1899. Apostle John W. Taylor sustained Brandley as bishop of Stirling the following month, and he became a leader in the developing community.[73] According to Anna Brandley Ostlund, after they completed the construction of the canal, Galt and Magrath hired Brandley to construct a railroad from Stirling to Cardston.[74] Not only were Latter-day Saints given better transportation between their settlements, but also a Church member received the contract to build it.

With new business contracts and more colonists from Utah, some Latter-day Saints moved east and established the hamlets of Magrath and Stirling. By 1899 the population of Magrath was 270 and Stirling was 230.[75] Levi Harker (1865–1939) and Jasper J. Head (1861–1924) opened the Magrath Mercantile Company in 1899, which became Harker-Head Company Store in 1900. The same year Cardston became a village and Josiah A. Hammer (1855–1922) elected overseer. Cardston also witnessed the construction of the Cardston Roller Mills (later called Cardston Milling Company), a company destined to merge with Ellison Milling.[76] H.S. Allen & Company became more focused on the promotion of agricultural interests.[77] Finally, by the end of that year, the Cardston Company decided to lessen all credit, and any new credit required the approval of the manager James P. Low (1960–18) or assistant manager Robert Ibey.[78]

Ultimately, "The first large-scale corporate irrigation project, that of the Alberta Railway and Irrigation Company," explains Lawrence B. Less, "proved a success primarily because of the cooperation of American-based Mormon enterprise."[79] The completed canal ran approximately "86 miles along the course of the St. Mary's River between Cardston and Lethbridge and provided irrigation water for such Mormon settlements as Magrath and Stirling which were colonized in the process of fulfilling the Church's contract with the irrigation company."[80] In 1902, the success and stability of the Latter-day Saint projects and settlements convinced the First Presidency to deed over all church-owned lands to the Alberta Stake, signalling confidence and permanence in the North-West Territories.[81] Lee summarizes some of the successes: "New town sites were laid out, a quarter of a million acres were brought under irrigation, irrigable crops were introduced, and a sugar factory erected."[82] The Latter-day Saints could not have accomplished this huge project without the support from non-members, such as Magrath and Galt. In this case, the act of cooperation meant working with outsiders in order to advance the needs of the community. By crossing over into non-Latter-day Saint realms, like land business in the North-West Territories, Latter-day Saints developed relationships that benefited them in two ways. First, by gaining strong allies in the broader non-Latter-day Saint communities, they showed their opponents that they could cooperate with outsiders in order to advance the needs of the territory. Irrigation would benefit everyone, not just the Latter-day Saints. In addition, by working with non-Latter-day Saints, they gained these projects and contracts that ultimately benefited the Latter-day Saint community by providing immigration assistance for new settlers from Utah, by bringing water to their farmlands, and by establishing new town sites for Latter-day Saint settlers. As plural marriage remained a barrier for acceptance into Canadian society, Latter-day Saints found a partial solution to this barrier with their irrigation projects because financial development, contributing to progress and enterprise, proved much more important to their non-Latter-day Saint neighbours than offensive marriage practices. Demonstrating progress and success with irrigation projects helped Latter-day Saints cross into public Canadian spaces.

The year 1901 saw the incorporation of the Town of Cardston. Citizens elected Card mayor and Martin Woolf (1858–1928) secretary. To recap, Charles O. Card served simultaneously as the political leader (mayor of Cardston), spiritual leader (Alberta Stake president), and business leader (president of the Cardston Company).[83] By the end of January, Card expressed his exhaustion by writing: "Set[t]ling Biz of the Cardston Co Ltd, Cardston Implement Co Ltd & private matters etc. Am always very busy. Spend over ½ my time with Brethren in church matters, have many callers every day of the week, which requires much of my time without remuneration."[84] To relieve some of the stress, Card sought out new ownership for the business and, in October, Card's stepson Sterling Williams, Robert Ibey, Edward J. Wood, and John A. Woolf's son John W. Woolf (1869–1950) entered an agreement to purchase all the interests of the Cardston Company Limited.[85] Directors of the Cardston Company met on 24 October 1901 and agreed to the sale of the company, the four buyers taking one quarter each equally.[86]

In 1902, Cardston earned the spot of a territorial electoral district of the Legislative Assembly of the North-West Territories.[87] This symbolized a significant step into public life in the North-West Territories for the community, but maybe this success communicated that the settlements were ready to move on without their leader, Card, and in September of 1902, The Church of Jesus Christ of Latter-day Saints released Charles Ora Card as Stake president, ordained him to the office of patriarch, and allowed him to return home to Utah.[88] In a letter to his people of Cardston before he returned to Utah, Card wrote,

> I would like to say a word to those who may feel disheartened and discouraged with their lot and surroundings in Alberta. The Canadian Government has done everything to make it easy and comfortable for the new settler. They have arranged for cheap rates and transportation in every way and treat their immigrants as dutiful parent her child. But oh, how different when we get on the other side of the fence in that land where the boasted "stars and stripes" waves over the "land of the free and the home of the brave."[89]

Card alludes to a significant difference between Canada and the United States. In Canada, the Latter-day Saints received great support from the government in terms of settlement assistance (such as irrigation contracts). The United States, on the other hand, put the same men in prison for cohabitation and polygamy. Before prosecution, the Latter-day Saints fled several states due to violence and discrimination against their Church and members until establishing a safe haven in the territory of Utah. Thus, Card tried to stress the benefits of staying in Alberta; even with challenging climate and economic hardships, it was still better than the United States in many ways.

Edward J. Wood became the new president of the newly divided Alberta Stake. The Church called Heber S. Allen to preside over the new Taylor Stake, which contained the Raymond, Stirling, and Magrath wards. With his move to Raymond, Allen purchased the Raymond Mercantile from Charles McCarty. Despite this reorganization, evidence of a united order appeared in various locations. For example, in 1903, the Magrath Ward Young Women's Mutual Improvement Association listened to Doctrine and Covenants lessons throughout the year that included the topic of the United Order.[90] Many years later, in 1916, the First Quorum of Elders for the Magrath Ward discussed the United Order along with the concept of mutual support.[91] Latter-day Saint Sarah Mercer Taylor (1894–1969) visited her mother on 3 August 1924 and recorded in her diary, "I am worrying and I want to get away from this impossible United Order anyway but my Hyde [farmer Hyrum/Hyde Taylor (1891–1971)] needs me and I don't know what to do."[92] Over in Leavitt, the ward's Relief Society received a lesson on the United Order and its establishment in the Alberta settlements.[93] Although a detailed description of the type of united order present in Alberta is unavailable, the venture into sugar beets and the purchase of the Cochrane Ranch are two examples of the Latter-day Saints' continued cooperative efforts on Canadian soil.

Cooperation Continued: Sugar Beets and the Cochrane Ranch

Communal efforts among Church members to solidify the Latter-day Saint presence in the North-West Territories continued after the beginning of canal construction with two large-scale cooperative projects: sugar beet farming and ranching. On 13 July 1901, Charles Ora Card met with John W. Taylor, Charles McCarty, and Jesse Knight to discuss their desire to build a sugar factory near the newly formed hamlet of Magrath.[94] Like the canal projects, the establishment of a factory would create jobs for more Latter-day Saints in the District of Alberta. Knight

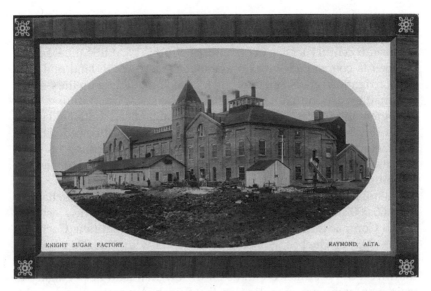

Figure 4.1 Knight Sugar Factory in Raymond, postcard published by Rumsey & Co., ca. 1910.

Source: Peel's Prairie Provinces, (peel.library.ualberta.ca), a digital initiative of the University of Alberta Libraries.

saw potential in the land of southern Alberta, and he made an agreement with the North-West Irrigation Company and the Alberta Railway and Coal Company (the companies that owned the land) to start a sugar beet factory.[95] He purchased 256,000 acres and agreed to build and operate a sugar factory for at least 12 years.[96] In August, Church leaders dedicated a site for the sugar factory in Township 16, Section 21.[97] This was the main reason the Latter-day Saints founded the town of Raymond, named after Jesse's son Oscar Raymond Knight (1872–1947). The Knight Sugar Company Limited opened the factory, and Jesse Knight acted as president and principal stockholder (Figure 4.1).[98]

By 1903, 2,000 Latter-day Saint immigrants arrived to help grow beets, develop the town, and work in the factory, although the factory only employed about 130 people.[99] At this time, E.P. Ellison (1850–1939) remained general manager; his factory superintendent and chemist was A.H. Williams, chief agriculturist T.J. O'Brien (1866–1938), and accountant J.W. Evans (1875–1945). The year 1903 also saw the creation of Ellison's flour mill, called Raymond Flour Mill and Elevator, another sign of progress for the community.[100] In his essay on sugar beets in Alberta,

William G. Hartley argues that, "The Raymond enterprise [of sugar beets] was an honorable twentieth century successor to Mormonism's nineteenth century legacy of communal efforts."[101] At this time, Latter-day Saints cooperated with non-members to purchase land and construct irrigation canals, but they still focused on building up the Church in Canada with Church-focused projects like sugar beet farming. New settlements, a new factory, and the need for sugar beets motivated many Latter-day Saints to relocate to the NWT to help grow the needed beets. The factory required beets, beets required farming, farming required labourers (the Latter-day Saints), and the labourers required homes and communities.

A similar communal effort occurred in 1905 with the purchase of over 60,000 acres from the Cochrane Ranch. In 1881, the Cochrane Ranch Company, under the leadership of Senator Matthew Cochrane (1823–1903) of Quebec, gained incorporation with $500,000 capital.[102] Two years later, directors of the Cochrane Ranch Company bought land southwest of Fort Macleod and sold the original land near Calgary to their new company operating as the British American Ranch Company.[103] In *Cattle Kingdom: Early Ranching in Alberta*, journalist Edward Brado reports that "The Cochrane Ranch now had about one hundred and seventy thousand acres of prime grazing land in the south, lying in a tract between Fort Macleod, the Peigan Reserve, and Waterton and Belly rivers."[104] Brado continues, "By 1891 there were almost thirteen thousand head of cattle on the Cochrane lease along the Belly River."[105] After Senator Cochrane died, the Corporation of the Alberta Stake of Zion purchased 67,000 acres of this lease at six dollars per acre [$402,000 total] in 1905.[106] "The cattle on the ranch were not then sold, the Church giving permission for them to be kept another year on the land. But before that year had passed by, a considerable number of Latter-day Saint farmers were already on the range preparing it for the farms, which sprang up with miraculous rapidity, fenced, ploughed and seeded."[107] In 1906, president of the Alberta Stake Edward J. Wood and his family moved to the ranch land and founded a new town site.[108] Eventually the Church divided the land into three: land for homesteading, land for farms and villages, and land for the Cochrane Ranch Company.[109] By then, the Church had instructed Wood to purchase the remaining herd of cows owned by the original Cochrane Ranch Company.[110] The Edmonton *Bulletin*, demonstrating the continued suspicion of Latter-day Saint business activity, called this acquisition a "further invasion of Mormons in the Canadian west."[111] Edward J. Wood oversaw this "invasion" and had charge of all the affairs related to the Cochrane Ranch.[112] The purchase of the Cochrane Ranch provided another path for Latter-day Saints to move to Canada, acquire cheap, fertile land, establish new settlements, and ultimately work together to create a new home for their community. It was also another way that the Latter-day Saints mixed church and business, as Wood was simultaneously responsible for the ranch and the Church in Canada as stake president. Latter-day Saints moved onto the newly acquired land and settled a hamlet near the Cochrane Ranch, naming it for Edward J. Wood's son Glen, originally called Glenwoodville (name changed to Glenwood in 1979).[113] Benjamin James Wood (1883–1959) worked for his brother Edward J. Wood on the Cochrane Ranch and eventually mixed business and Church when he also became first counsellor to V. I. Stewart of the Glenwood Ward in 1910.[114] Latter-day Saints formed another community called Hill Spring about 15 kilometres southwest of Glenwood.[115]

Conclusion

Eventually, exclusive Latter-day Saint endeavours ended, explains Arrington. "Secular government and secular industry have come to exert greater influence than the Church on the development and regulation of the local Mormon economy."[116] The 1930s brought the Great Depression and The Church of Jesus Christ of Latter-day Saints laid out assistance plans, such as welfare farms, to guide its members through the economic difficulties. However, by the 1940s, many feared that the United Order and Communism were one and the same, so the American Church needed distance from its theocratic, cooperative origins.[117] Canadians experienced a less severe fear of communism and, as political participation and ideology will show in the next chapter, actively contributed to a political ethos developing out of cooperation.

Business teaches us about Latter-day Saint decision making and how this impacted both their own community members and non-Latter-day Saints. An emphasis on cooperation drew boundaries around themslves in order to maintain an identity of peculiarity and provided enough tension with Canadian society to keep Latter-day Saints both distinctive, but also relatively harmless in the eyes of the public. However, their commitment to cooperation did not prevent them from embedding themselves in the economic structures of Canada, and they were willing to partner with non-Latter-day Saints on large-scale irrigation projects that would improve conditions for both Latter-day Saints and non-members living in southern Alberta. If we consider the dwelling practices of Mormonism and how Latter-day Saints orient themselves in time and space, then establishing cooperative businesses and completing irrigation projects are initiatives and encounters that oriented

Latter-day Saints to both their new home in southern Alberta and previous home in Utah. Business decisions and practices, heavily influenced by theology and cooperation, moved Latter-day Saints through time and space, transforming both Canadian society (by the settlement of new towns and construction of irrigation canals) and the Church (by causing Canadian Latter-day Saints to adapt to the needs of the province), and eventually allowing Latter-day Saints to inhabit both Canadian and their own Mormon worlds. While far from home, Latter-day Saints brought their passion for cooperation onto Albertan soil and remained committed to financially supporting their own members, but at the same time showed an openness to work with outsiders, like the Galts and Magrath, to complete beneficial projects for all citizens.

Latter-day Saints in southern Alberta cleared and cultivated acres of land and crossed natural landscapes, environments, and social spaces in order to develop their cooperative businesses and irrigation projects. By participating in these crossing, they voyaged into Canadian social spaces and earned business contracts that helped both Church members and Albertans.

Why study business? Orsi suggests looking at everyday places, like the workplace, as sites where people make something of the worlds in which they have found themselves. Maintaining a cooperative ethic allowed Latter-day Saints to remain connected as a community, helping one another financially and emotionally. Their business also caught the attention of government officials when making their annual reports, and they were labelled as good, productive settlers. Yet Latter-day Saints were not isolated or unwilling to cooperate with non-Latter-day Saints, and this a key step in their integration into Canadian society. Developing relationships with prominanent figures like the Galts and Magrath and then successfully completing large-scale irrigation projects that brought water to all farmers, not just Latter-day Saints, shows how lived practices are ever-changing and even contradictory. And as we will see in the next chapter, Canadian Latter-day Saints continued emphasis on cooperation and political participation will bring them closer to their fellow Albertans and Canadians, but further away from American Latter-day Saints.

Chapter Five

Politics

Introduction

Political participation signalled at least some desire to contribute to and improve their new home, and Latter-day Saints successfully entered politics at all levels: municipal, provincial, and federal. The ideologies central to three significant political parties in the province of Alberta from the early twentieth century to the end of the 1940s demonstrate how Canadian Latter-day Saints may have created barriers between themselves and their American brethren, but ultimately showed another step towards integration into Canadian society. As they became more involved in Canadian politics, many Saints joined organizations in Alberta, such as the United Farmers of Alberta, the Social Credit Party, and the Cooperative Commonwealth Federation. These distinctly Canadian associations promoted platforms that criticized capitalism and justified cooperation. In his introduction to the Mardons's book on Latter-day Saint contributions to politics in Alberta, Brigham Y. Card (1914–2006) argues that "When a person stands for nomination for the Alberta legislature or the House of Commons, it is a signal. First, that the person is a Canadian citizen, and second, that the person is willing to serve the local and larger good of the province and country."[1] Political participation symbolized another step of integration for Latter-day Saints in Canada. The following section examines political participation and the roles of Latter-day Saints as they transitioned from outsiders to active citizens, while still balancing Church responsibilities. As part of their negotiation between distinctive Latter-day Saint and active Canadian citizen, Latter-day Saints often navigated between public service as a political representative and private life as a Church leader.

Early Days

In the District of Alberta in the North-West Territories, Cardston became an electoral district in the year 1902 (16 years after Latter-day Saints began settling in the area). The constituents elected Latter-day Saint John W. Woolf (1869–1950), son of polygamist John A. Woolf, as a non-partisan Member of the Legislative Assembly (MLA) of the North-West Territories.[2] Alberta became a province in 1905, and Woolf, this time running as a Liberal candidate, was elected to the Legislative Assembly of Alberta, where he remained until 1912. John's cousin, Martin Woolf (1858–1928), son of polygamist Absalom Woolf (1832–1910), was also elected as a Liberal to the Legislative Assembly. Martin moved to Alberta in 1898 and became secretary and treasurer of the town of Cardston from 1902, the year the town was incorporated, to 1909.[3] He worked as a collector of customs and a land titles agent until 1912, when he entered politics under the Liberal party.[4] The Alberta Liberal Party embraced the ideology of classical liberalism, promoting individual liberty and free markets. From 1905 to 1921, Alberta's Liberal government established the provincial infrastructure (railroad expansion, telephone system, schools) and dealt with rapid population growth.[5] Immigrants favoured the Liberal Party because the federal Liberals handled the mass immigration to the west, and farmers agreed with their policy of free trade, disapproving of high tariffs.[6] Voters re-elected Martin in 1913 and 1917, but the election of 1921 saw the rise of the United Farmers of Alberta (UFA), and they replaced Martin with his competition.

The municipal level of government provides examples of the overlap of church and politics in Latter-day Saint communities in Alberta. When Charles O. Card became the first mayor of Cardston he was also president of the Alberta Stake. Card is an example of the economic, political, and spiritual overlap in these Latter-day Saint settlements. The second mayor of Cardston, John A. Woolf, entered the office while still serving as first counsellor in the Alberta Stake. Josiah Hammer (1855–1922) ended his term as bishop of the Cardston ward in 1908, four years before the community elected him the third mayor of the town.

Other Latter-day Saints that balanced leadership roles in their Church with political responsibilities were James T. Brown (1863–1942), Walter E. Pitcher (1871–1946), and Charles W. Burt (1877–1954). The residents of Cardston elected Brown in 1909, and he served as mayor for one term. Perhaps thinking his political career had ended, Brown accepted the role as bishop of Cardston First Ward in 1911, which he kept until 1918. Two years into his time as spiritual leader for the Cardston First Ward, Brown re-entered local politics and once again became mayor until 1916. Another example of this overlap is Walter E. Pitcher, who journeyed for one month in 1895 to reach the growing community of Cardston.[7] He started life in the North-West Territories by homesteading 160 acres, then became vice president of the Cardston Creamery Company, and later organized the Cardston Farming Company, which owned 1800 acres for sowing wheat.[8] Pitcher's leadership roles in the Church included second counsellor in the Cardston Second Ward (1914–18), first counsellor in the same ward (1918–24), and bishop (1924–32). Besides all these spiritual responsibilities, Pitcher also served three terms as mayor of Cardston from 1917 to 1920.[9] In another case, the Church called Charles W. Burt, originally from St. George, Utah, and son of a polygamist, to the role of counsellor in the Cardston First Ward in 1910. He transitioned to bishop of that ward in 1918 and remained as such until 1928 when he moved to the Alberta Stake High Council. The people of Cardston elected Burt as their mayor in 1929, and he remained in office until 1934. As these cases demonstrate, Latter-day Saint men served their Church members and broader communities often at the same time, balancing public life and private commitments.

Cardston was not an anomaly. If we turn our attention towards Magrath and Raymond, similar patterns appear. Heber S. Allen, merchant, polygamist, and president of the Taylor Stake sat on the Raymond Town Council throughout his 33 years as leader of the stake. Levi Harker, brother and son of polygamists, arrived in Cardston in 1892 and moved to Magrath in 1899. The Church appointed him bishop of the new Magrath Ward, and he remained in that position of leadership until 1931, during which time the town elected him the first mayor of Magrath in 1907, and he ran for provincial office in the Cardston riding as an independent conservative in 1909.[10] Local politician, ward bishop, sheep farmer, merchant, and irrigator were all roles adopted by Harker in the newly developing town of Magrath. Latter-day Saints demonstrated a pattern of encouraging Church leaders to cross into public spaces and serve as political leaders, too.

United Farmers of Alberta

In the introduction to the section on economics and government, editors of *The Mormon Presence in Canada* claim,

> Although Alberta Mormons have not been innovators of economic or political ideas, they have regularly adapted ideas that appear to offer solutions to the problems facing a hinterland economy. Mormons in Alberta have in the past been able to reconcile their religious beliefs with political ideas ranging from the moderate left to the extreme right.[11]

An examination of the various political parties in Alberta and the involvement of Latter-day Saints provides insight into the growing distance from the American membership. Political scientist Clark Banack explains the United Farmers of Alberta (UFA) as "an extensive network of highly participatory 'locals,' community-level groupings of farmers that sought to protect their economic interests by lobbying government and by pooling both their purchasing power and their agricultural produce in an effort to leverage their way to better financial outcomes."[12] Before the farmers of Alberta turned their lobby group into a political party, they evolved from a larger North American agrarian movement where farmers tried to protect themselves against the impact of the growing commercial-capitalist economy. Farmers developed "a sense of opposition to corporations that denied them their land's wealth, which prompted them to establish the early farm associations for protection."[13] Although American populism never officially gained a foothold in Canada, it influenced the Alberta farmers movement with the promotion of farmer cooperation, establishment of agrarian ideals in farm culture, advancement of equal rights, producerism, and anti-monopolism. Mix these ideals with British cooperative, labour, and socialist thought, and you have the situation in the province of Alberta motivating the organization of farmers.

Struggling against the dominance of the Canadian Pacific Railway (CPR) and the abuse from grain companies, farmers formed the Territorial Grain Growers' Association (TGGA) in 1902. In 1905, when Alberta became a province, the Alberta branch of the TGGA became the Alberta Farmers' Association (AFA). which aimed to forward the interests of grain and livestock businesses, to encourage superior production and breeding, to obtain by united effort profitable and equitable prices for farm produce, to watch legislation relating to the farmers' interests (particularly that affecting the marketing and transportation of farm produce).[14] Latter-day Saint communities with branches of the AFA included Cardston, Raymond, Magrath, and Stirling.[15] For example, named "one of the most progressive and enterprising farmers of Southern Alberta," Latter-day Saint Thomas H. Woolford (1856–1944) joined the AFA and served as president of the Cardston AFA branch.[16] Woolford moved to Canada from Utah in April of 1899 and settled on land that is now known as Woolford Provincial Park. In 1903, Woolford reported threshing a total of 7,700 bushels of grain (oats, barley, and wheat).[17] In 1907, he joined the executive committee of the AFA as vice president. Another prominent Latter-day Saint farmer was Richard W. Bradshaw (1868–1948) of Magrath. Bradshaw moved his family from Lehi to Alberta in 1901 and eventually acquired Rosedale Farms, initially producing fine cattle and award-winning wheat, and later expanding into the importing and breeding of Percheron draft horses.[18] In 1909, Bradshaw reported bumper wheat yields over his large acreage of winter wheat, averaging 50 bushels to the acre.[19]

That same year, the Alberta Farmers' Association merged with the Canadian Society of Equity to create the United Farmers of Alberta (UFA).[20] The UFA started as a non-partisan organization/lobby group to promote the interests of farmers in the province. According to Rennie, "At the heart of this movement culture were feelings of community; a sense of class opposition; assumptions about gender roles and traits; commitment to organization, cooperation, democracy, citizenship, and education; a social ethic; religious convictions; agrarian ideology; and collective self-confidence."[21] Collective and local projects created a sense of community, which, in addition to experience with state and business powers, fostered a sense of solidarity and class opposition to corporate economic and political control. Male farmers wanted to defend their families, class, and country. Rural women protected the home, worked for equal rights, and contributed to farm work. The root of this ideology stemmed from the UFA's most influential leader Henry Wise Wood (1860–1941) and his American progressive evangelical Protestantism.[22]

Because of his experience within the Disciples of Christ and at Christian University in Missouri, Henry Wise Wood developed a particular social and political theory directly tied to his faith. Wood believed that humans are by nature social beings who are destined to construct a proper social system within which they can flourish. For Wood, history progresses in a linear fashion, characterized by a cosmic struggle between two opposing forces, cooperation and competition. At the end of this evolutionary process would be the creation of the morally perfect individual within a perfectly moral society. The kingdom of heaven on earth, according to Wood, would come about from individual and social regeneration. Individual regeneration involved repentance and, following natural social laws, the moral laws of Christ. Social regeneration would be initiated by those who have accepted the teachings of Christ and desire to build a social system founded upon the call for social cooperation issued by Christ through a gradual, evolutionary process. "Wood adhered to a clear evangelical postmillennial Christian interpretation wherein humanity was to bring about a perfect social system, which he equated to God's kingdom on earth, by way of personal, and eventual social, devotion to the cooperative message of Christ."[23] The agrarians of rural Alberta would handle the practical details of this process.

Wood promoted a rural social gospel movement that would establish the kingdom of God on earth by "large-scale voluntary individual regeneration" and "cooperation of those regenerated individuals within voluntary organizations," but not by government regulation.[24] While emphasizing democratic participation and individual responsibility, Wood rejected increased state ownership and socialism, instead believing that rebirth through Christ would cause the regenerated people to accept the cooperative spirit, issued by Christ, and they would work at the local level to secure policy decisions and economic well-being.[25] After the First World War and the challenges that followed, "southern Alberta farmers hoped that the UFA could organize a wheat pool and force governments to lower producers' costs and assist with irrigation."[26] Farmers were dissatisfied with numerous issues such as the government's handling of prohibition, health policy, debt, the farm mortgage crisis, the lack of credit assistance, and the province's irrigation policies. In 1921, the movement officially politicized and Albertan farmers launched "what would be the most resilient agrarian political crusade in North American history."[27] Although some Latter-day Saints in southern Alberta joined the Canadian Liberal or Conservative parties, the UFA drew many of these Saints into their organization.

Lawrence Peterson (1873–1951) moved from Provo, Utah, to Raymond, Alberta, in 1902 and eventually settled in Barnwell, near Taber. According to the Barnwell Relief Society, the first UFA meeting was held in March 1913 and the twenty-six members selected Peterson as their first president.[28] Other Latter-day Saints who took an active interest in the UFA were William F. LeBaron (1884–1968), A.M. Peterson, N.J. Anderson (1884–1958), and A. Anderson accompanying Peterson to the annual convention in 1915 and 1916. "Latter-day Saint" UFA groups, or locals, were Magrath, Raymond, Leavitt, Stirling, Barnwell, Spring Coulee, Cardston, Taber, and Mountain View.[29] In 1919, UFA members elected Peterson as the director of the entire constituency of Lethbridge.[30]

Another active UFA member and Latter-day Saint was Frank Leavitt (1870–1959) who Peterson acknowledged as offering him great assistance in the year 1919.[31] In his report for that year, Peterson said that the "Cardston Local and those surrounding [ex. Aetna, Leavitt] have carried on a very successful cooperative trading company."[32] And in 1921 he reported on the progress again: "Raymond and Magrath have also obtained a good deal of success along cooperative lines ... Through the elections the farmers have learned the power they have when working together ... I believe that if every U.F.A. member will take his proper place in this great work by helping wherever he finds an opportunity, we shall be able to put Democracy in actions, in the truest sense of the word."[33] Active Latter-day Saint locals in 1921 were the same as 1918 with the additions of Kimball, Taylorville, Spring Coulee, and Aetna.[34]

In 1921, the UFA won 38 seats out of the 61 ridings in the provincial election, taking a majority government, and pushed the Liberals out of power. Latter-day Saints George L. Stringam (1876–1959) and Lawrence Peterson won two of these seats; Stringam for the Cardston Riding and Lawrence Peterson (1873–1951) for the Taber Riding. Cattle rancher George L. Stringam was born and raised in Utah and moved to Alberta in 1910 after purchasing half a section of land north of Glenwood.[35] He participated in politics at the municipal level until 1921 when he entered the race for MLA as a UFA candidate, earning 1,343 votes while Woolf (Liberal) earned 651. Peterson ran in Taber district of the provincial election as a UFA candidate against the Liberal incumbent Archibald J. McLean and won with 2,309 votes over 1,991 for McLean.[36] He won again in 1926 against the Liberal and Conservative candidates for the Taber electoral district.[37]

Cooperation remained a consistent platform of the United Farmers of Alberta. This aspect might have drawn the attention of Latter-day Saints and been a reason for their participation in the movement and political party. An example of cooperation put into practice was the Alberta Wheat Pool. A year before the UFA won the provincial election, the Canadian Council of Agriculture passed a resolution providing for the appointment of a Wheat Pool Committee to be composed of representatives from the four provincial farmers' organizations and the farmers' companies.[38] Establishing a national pool became too difficult to accomplish, but the UFA continued at the provincial level and passed a resolution asking for direct selling of commodities through a means whereby speculation could be eliminated.[39] In 1923, *The U.F.A.* newspaper reported that, "UFA locals in the Cardston, Claresholm, Granum, and Macleod districts are making efforts to organize a local wheat pool."[40] Henry Wise Wood's presidential address also acknowledged that, "the idea of cooperative selling of wheat has been crystalizing in the minds of the Alberta wheat producers for four years."[41] The wheat pool committee organized under the association called Alberta Co-operative Wheat Producers, Limited, which acted as the agent and attorney for the contracting wheat growers. The main features of the Alberta Wheat Pool were that "The association would be a cooperative, non-profit organization, without capital stock. All surpluses, after defraying operating expenses and providing for adequate reserves, would be returned to the members in proportion to the wheat shipped."[42] "It is now up to the individual members of the U.F.A. to put into practice those principles of cooperation which have been so long preached."[43] Grain growers signed a contract that stated

> the undersigned Grower desires to cooperate with others concerned in the production of wheat in the province of Alberta and in the marketing of same, hereinafter referred to as Growers for the purpose of promoting, fostering, and encouraging the business of growing and marketing wheat cooperatively and for eliminating speculation in wheat and for stabilizing the wheat market, for cooperatively and collectively handling the problems of Growers for improving in every legitimate way.[44]

Christian Jensen (1868–1958), another Latter-day Saint, worked both in his Church and Local UFA, acting as the director for the Lethbridge Constituency in the 1920s.[45] He was a main player in the birth of the Alberta Wheat Pool. Jensen sat as a trustee on the board of the Alberta Co-operative Wheat Producers, Ltd., the central selling agency located in Calgary, from its inception in 1923 and as a director for the Lethbridge district of the pool until 1945.[46] In addition to these roles, Jensen served as president of the Canadian Co-operative Wool Growers association from 1937 to 1949 and first president of the Alberta Federation of Agriculture.[47] The cooperative movement in Alberta stemmed from the tradition in England called the Rochdale Plan when an organization of textile workers united and decided that "Dividends, instead of being paid on the basis of capital invested, were paid on a basis of volume of business done, capital being borrowed at a fixed rate of interest. After provision for reserve and educational funds and necessary overhead, all surplus profit was divided among the purchasers in proportion to the volume of their buying."[48]

Cooperation and economic goals were never far from UFA meetings. At a meeting for Cardston and Magrath Locals in 1925, politician William Irvine (1885–1962) said, "the hope of civilization was to be found in the cooperative idea."[49] In 1926, Henry Wise Wood lectured to an audience in Cardston on the economic and political goals of the UFA. Wood explained, "What the UFA aims at is to have all classes cease exploitation of each other, but rather increase their efficiency for the benefit of all."[50] On the topic of the UFA movement, an article in the Cardston *News* elaborated that "It is a great socializing and educational factor in the lives of thousands ... It enters into their daily activities as no other organization, except the [LDS] Church, has ever done ... It is true that some sections of the country were not so much in need of the UFA as a social factor, as particularly the Cardston District, where the Church supplies this need to a very great extent."[51] Then why would Latter-day Saints join the UFA? They joined because most of the Latter-day Saints in southern Alberta were farmers, ranchers, or otherwise involved in agriculture. Furthermore, they might have believed that "the UFA is the most powerful agency in Canada today for the establishment of the Kingdom of God on earth."[52] This may not have been the same as the Latter-day Saint version of the Kingdom of God, but they at least shared the concept of cooperation. During a successful resolution regarding cooperative marketing at the 1926 UFA convention, the report stated that

> the past few years considerable emphasis has been laid upon cooperative marketing of farm projects ... the fruits of the efforts are not being realized notably in the case of the Wheat Pool, and the Southern Alberta Co-operative ... there are still large numbers of farmers, who because of special circumstances or because of indifference, or because of their inability to see the interests of their class, are still outside of these movements: Be it therefore resolved, that this Convention call upon all farmers in the Province to give their support to these movements and thus assure the ultimate victory of the farming industry.[53]

For success of the farming industry equalled, in the minds of UFA members, success for the entire province, no matter what class you were.

In the 1926 election, Stringam returned to the legislature with over 1,300 votes, defeating Conservative candidate Joseph Y. Card and Liberal candidate Walter H. Caldwell (both men were also Latter-day Saints). However, in the town of Cardston itself, Caldwell received 298 votes, Card 200, and Stringam only 193.[54] The smaller, more rural villages voted overwhelmingly in favour of Stringam. He received approximately 96 per cent of the vote in Glenwood, 94 per cent in Leavitt, 59 per cent in Aetna, 56 per cent in Magrath, and 69 per cent in Hill Spring.[55] That year, the UFA maintained its majority government and earned 43 seats. In his speech at the 1930 UFA Political Nominating Convention, Stringam stated, "My Policy is that whatever is best for the Province as a Whole is best for this constituency."[56] Stringam's concept did not drastically differ from the organization of the Church. Sociologist Thomas O'Dea explains the hierarchical structure in *The Mormons*: "[T]he original relationship between the prophet and his disciples evolved into a relationship between the prophet and an oligarchy of leading elders, which merged into and exercised ascendancy over the rank and file of the membership."[57] Responsibility moved from the bottom up while authority came from the top down as a "Living Prophet" remains the highest role in the Church.[58]

Social Credit Movement

The Great Depression engulfed the 1930s and "opened the way for a change in government and ideological direction, in that Social Credit had no interest in the UFA's notion of cooperative 'group government' and was based on a leader-oriented type of democracy."[59] Social Credit theory "blamed the current economic conditions [the Great Depression] on a lack of purchasing power possessed by regular citizens, who were beholden to large financial institutions that controlled credit ... the economy was slowed to a halt because self-interested bankers refused to lend at reasonable rates."[60] Following this theory, the solution was the "state was to take control of credit away from greedy financiers...and provide its citizens with a share or 'dividend' of this "social credit' to allow them to buy goods."[61] But this is what Charles Ora Card had attempted years ago in Cardston. He issued hundreds of scrips to community members to use at the cooperative businesses, but people were unable to pay him back, which compromised the Cardston Co-operative Company. Social scientist S.D. Clark confirms,

> The close relationship between sectarian techniques of religious control and monetary techniques of economic and political control has been most evident, of course, in the Social Credit experiment in Alberta; here the Mormon members of the government in particular had a perfectly good historic example in the use of scrip and the carrying-on of banking operations by the Mormons in Utah.[62]

William Aberhart, founder of the Alberta Social Credit Party, motivated by a fundamentalist, premillennial, religious-based political thought, rejected the idea of a Kingdom of Heaven on earth, and emphasized individual freedom while vilifying socialism.[63] Social Credit appealed to politicians such as Aberhart because it provided a way to fulfil the general Christian duty toward others by guaranteeing an end to the suffering associated with the economic hardtimes, and it protected individual freedoms vital to personal spiritual growth, which, in their opinion, socialist plans did not.[64] For Aberhart and other premillennialist thinkers, the coming of the kingdom of God existed outside the realm of human agency, so Christians should focus on assisting others in their spiritual rebirth before the Rapture.[65] Although Latter-day Saint millennial expectations were not as pessimistic as Aberhart-type premillennialist theories, they did agree on sharing the Christian message with others and individual liberty, and they could also get on board with placing trust in a leader. Clark observes, "the religious-political experiment in Alberta resembled very closely that tried much earlier in Utah; in both cases, religious separatism sought support in political separatism, and encroachments of the federal authority were viewed as encroachments of the worldly society."[66]

"The UFA pursued giving life and form to direct democracy in government, but Social Credit's democracy was more plebiscitary. In its view, governmental policy making, a matter of technical skill and special qualification, was best left to experts."[67] In his essay for *The New Provinces: Alberta and Saskatchewan, 1905–1980*, professor of religious studies Earle Waugh notes a list of reasons why Latter-day Saints in southern Alberta consistently supported Social Credit. First, Aberhart's eschatological teachings matched their idea of building Zion in the American west and, second, appreciated the labour of the ordinary worker in preparation for the Second Coming.[68] In other words, both Latter-day Saints and Aberhart were preparing for the Rapture or Second Coming while still advocating for individual progress, freedom, and spiritual rebirth on earth. As well, Aberhart's political leadership style would have reminded Latter-day Saints of their religious leaders because Aberhart "ruled Alberta from an authoritarian position, and he dealt directly with citizens through his radio broadcast and his frequent public meetings ... all important decisions were left to his personal discretion."[69] Third, the mix of politics and religion was familiar to Latter-day Saints since most came from the formerly theocratic Utah. Also, the notion of a creative work ethic attracted Latter-day Saints to Social Credit because they believed "that individual initiative and activism had transcendent import [and] underlined the necessity of providing the opportunity for sanctified labour."[70] Lastly, Aberhart and Latter-day Saints shared a unique eschatology where they were ideologically premillennialist, but practised a postmillennial enthusiasm.[71]

They believed Jesus Christ would usher in the Millennium, but they did not adopt a pessimistic view of their current situation, the Depression, and instead saw temporal and spiritual advantages to improving their circumstances.

While some Church members climbed on to the Social Credit wagon, the Church itself shifted its own ideology concerning economic well-being. The United Order became a concept to save for implementation when Jesus redeems Zion during the Millennium. Instead, in the 1930s,

> Stake presidents in urban areas contacted nearby farmers who faced prices so low that it was not profitable to harvest their crops. Arrangements were made so that idle urban members could harvest the crops in return for a share thereof. The produce thus obtained was stored in Church-controlled warehouse facilities and distributed according to need. Drawing upon this experience, Welfare farms were soon established under Church ownership in areas surrounding Mormon-populated cities.[72]

In Cardston, Mark A. Coombs (1868–1944) reported that the Alberta Stake Welfare Committee began "preparing to assist those who may be in needy circumstances this winter. ... preparing to begin work at once on a cellar to store produce expected to be received from the various wards of the stake."[73] Bishops of the surrounding wards reported that "excellent cooperation is being given by all the wards of the stake in welfare work, and that canning of fruits and vegetables, and raising of wheat are being carried out as community projects."[74] That August the Alberta Stake began construction of a large storage cellar near the old Bishop's Storehouse and tithing barn.[75] James Forest Wood (1903–95), son of Edward J. Wood, the Alberta Stake president at the time, remembered gardening and canning as welfare projects instead of accepting government assistance.[76] Similarly, John O. Hicken (1905–87) recalled a welfare centre in the 1930s with a canning factory and storehouse.[77]

At the quarterly conference for the Taylor Stake in July 1938, Elder Stringham A. Stevens (1884–1950) of the Church Welfare Committee educated the audience on the Church's welfare plans: "It was not a dole, but it was a project of collecting from the surplus of those who had and transferring it to the districts of those who had not. Then, by means of a works program to give these needy people a chance to earn what they needed."[78] The Church presidency later advised members to rely on the welfare plan from the Church and not from their government, stating that "Such an approval would run contrary to all that has been said over the years since the Welfare Plan was set up [in 1936] ... these isms [Socialism and Communism] will ... destroy the free agency which God gave to us."[79] Myrtle Passey (1893–1983) was president of the Taylor Stake Relief Society from 1939 to 1947 when the main objective was welfare in every phase, both temporal and spiritual, and the plan was "We will take care of our own" and not accept government aid.[80] Assistant Church historian Andrew Jensen recorded the purchase of six acres of irrigated land in 1940 by the Magrath First Ward for the purpose of ward welfare work.[81] Over in Aetna, the Aetna Welfare Committee entered the cattle business and "Every family in the ward are asked to contribute one calf or its equivalent, to be delivered to the committee on the 6th day of May."[82]

At the forefront of the Church Welfare Plan in Canada was soil chemist and dry land farming specialist Asael E. Palmer (1888–1984). Minutes from a meeting of the Canadian Regional Welfare Committee, which Palmer was regional chairman, reveal similar plans involving canning projects spread through all Latter-day Saint stakes in Alberta. By the summer of 1939, the Alberta Stake had seven small units to process vegetables and meat. The Taylor Stake operated one unit and the Lethbridge Stake had five units with a daily output of 1,000 cans.[83]

Church and Politics

Two Latter-day Saints who held prominent roles in the early years of the Social Credit Party of Canada were John H. Blackmore (1890–1971) and Solon Low (1900–62). Blackmore graduated from Calgary Normal School and the University of Alberta and went on to teach for many years. Eventually he received a promotion to principal and led Raymond High School from 1921 to 1935. Blackmore was a faithful and active Latter-day Saint before and during his time in federal politics, until his excommunication in the 1940s. At a sacrament meeting of the Cardston First Ward in July 1934, Blackmore spoke on the topic of genealogy and narrated stories about tests of faith in scripture.[84] The following month he was the principal speaker at the Alberta Stake priesthood meeting and presented on the theme "The Philosophy of Mormonism."[85] Blackmore's visible role in the Church mirrored his visible role in the community, as school principal and, later, as politician. In 1935, Blackmore represented the Lethbridge riding as a Social Credit member, a position he maintained through the next five federal elections, sitting in Parliament for 22 years. In addition to gaining the majority of votes in the southern Alberta riding, Blackmore gained the confidence

120   Thirsty Land into Springs of Water

Figure 5.1   John H. Blackmore, Social Credit poster.
Source: Author's photograph

of his party, which made him the national party leader from 1935 to 1945 (Figure 5.1).

Blackmore's church-related responsibilities did not cease, but they did change. Church leaders released him from his position as member of the Stake Sunday School Board, which he had sat on since 1928, a year after the 1935 election.[86] This was unsurprising since his job as Member of Parliament required residence in Ottawa, Ontario, and so his responsibilities transferred to this branch of the Church. His active role in the Ottawa branch continued through the years.[87] At sacrament meetings in 1937, he acted as one of the speakers on at least two occasions, one in February and one in March, speaking on Christ's Resurrection at the latter event.[88] In the 1940s, Blackmore's church participation increased from just speaking. On 6 June 1942 at a Fast and Testimony Meeting in Albion Hall, Blackmore, along with his brother Harold, bore his testimony to his fellow Latter-day Saints.[89] In September 1945, Blackmore sealed the anointing after Sacrament Services for the Ottawa branch; in May 1946 he blessed and named John Albert Parkinson and spoke about the necessity of baptism.[90] In 1947, Blackmore's Church activities included speaking in meetings, blessing babies, administering the sacrament, and giving the invocation, until he was excommunicated at the end of the year for promoting plural marriage.

Solon E. Low replaced Blackmore as Social Credit Party leader in the House of Commons when he successfully represented Peace River, Alberta, in the 1945 federal election.[91] Like his fellow Social Credit member Blackmore, Low actively participated in The Church of Jesus Christ of Latter-day Saints. For example, Low spoke to the Cardston First and Second Wards at a joint meeting hosted by the Genealogical Committee.[92] During a visit to the Cardston Alberta Temple in May 1942, the newspaper reported that Low "conversed with several delegations while he was here on government matters."[93] In July 1944, Low spoke at the Cardston First Ward sacrament meeting and again at the tabernacle to all Elders and their wives of that same ward.[94] On a Sunday morning in July of 1945, Low spoke at the Elders quorum, once again in the tabernacle.[95] In addition to Presidents Wood, Smith, and Jensen, Low spoke to the Elders Quorum of the Cardston Second Ward at their annual barbeque in August.[96] Low offered his home to young adults' church groups, such as the Gleaners (girls over sixteen) and Scouts, for "fireside chats" (informal gatherings for prayer, music, and lessons) in 1946.[97]

As the examples of Blackmore and Low demonstrate, there was often overlap between church and state for Latter-day Saints in Canada, and they could end up with an electoral representative that also acted as the bishop of their ward. A significant feature of the Church is their reliance on lay participation and leadership. An implication of this is that Latter-day Saint spiritual leaders also have full-time jobs, occupations, and external commitments that can conflict with each other. Leadership in the Church requires no formal training and, instead, depends on experience they might have learned during their life as a member. Blackmore and Low were active Latter-day Saints, but the case of Nathan Eldon Tanner shows an even more extreme example of this situation.

Social Credit defeated the UFA in the election of 1935. Latter-day Saint Nathan Eldon Tanner (1898–1982) became the Social Credit candidate for Cardston in 1935 and ended up serving 17 years in the legislature.[98] Tanner received his education from the Calgary Normal School and University of Alberta. He went on to work as principal of Hill Spring School (1919–27) and Cardston High School for 11 years. In 1936, the premier named him Speaker of the Legislative Assembly and two years later he was appointed Minister of Lands and Mines, a position he held for 15 years.[99] Also prominent in provincial politics at this time was Latter-day Saint Solon Low (1900–62), who was also a teacher by trade and graduate of the University of Alberta and the University of Southern California.[100] Low won the Warner seat in 1935 and received the appointment to the Cabinet as Provincial Treasurer until 1944, when he left provincial politics for federal politics.

Tanner, like Blackmore and Low, began his career as a school teacher. He became a counsellor (ranking just below the bishop) of the Cardston First Ward in 1918 until he became bishop in 1933 until 1935. That was the year he entered provincial politics as a Social Credit candidate. After successfully winning a seat in the legislature, the new legislative assembly selected him as Speaker of the Alberta Legislative Assembly. Tanner transitioned from moderating the meetinghouse to moderating the legislative assembly until the year 1937. Premier William Aberhart appointed him to the Cabinet of Alberta as Minister of Lands and Mines at the beginning of 1937, a position he held until 1952.

Canadians reacted to a Latter-day Saint political representative very differently than the Americans. In 1903, when Apostle Reed Smoot won a seat on the US Senate, the strong negative reaction initiated an investigation and formal trial into both Smoot and the Church that lasted until 1907. Although the outcome was positive for Smoot, he took his seat on the Senate and served a long career in politics, The Church of Jesus Christ of Latter-day Saints came under severe scrutiny during the years of the trial. Church leaders received subpoenas and had to answer intrusive questions regarding past and present polygamous relationships. The non-Latter-day Saint public feared both plural marriage and the loyalty of a Latter-day Saint, especially a high-ranking one such as Reed Smoot, would always fall to the Church over the laws of the land. In Canada, outsiders remained relatively quiet on their politicians' religious views. When Aberhart made Tanner Minister of Lands and Mines, *The Globe and Mail* reported the bare facts that "[Tanner's] parents were Mormons, and he is a bishop in that Church, a position corresponding roughly to that of a congregational minister in the Presbyterian or United Church."[101] Here we have a neutral comparison to mainstream Protestant churches in Canada. That this placement of a Latter-day Saint in a position of prominence occurred over 30 years after the Reed Smoot hearings was not the only difference between the Canadian and American cases. At the time that the Social Credit Party welcomed several Latter-day Saints to the inner circle, the political party's elected members included 14 different religious traditions, making the Latter-day Saints only one of many diverse religious opinions.[102]

Two years after his move into the Cabinet, Tanner was selected president of the Edmonton Branch of the Church (a position equivalent to a bishop, but a branch is smaller than a ward). And so, a major player in Alberta politics and the Social Credit circle also led an active life in his church. During his time in Edmonton, Tanner witnessed how "many new avenues were opened up for church development, old prejudices were broken down and opportunities increased. Amid [his] responsibilities as public servant [he] found time to serve in the Church."[103]

Co-operative Commonwealth Federation

Not all Albertan Latter-day Saints stayed with the Social Credit Party; some were enticed by the ideology of the Co-operative Commonwealth Federation.

> As Aberhart was introducing Social Credit into his weekly radio sermons, a meeting in Calgary in 1932 began the formation of the Co-operative Commonwealth Federation (CCF). The CCF Manifesto, proclaimed in the following year, called for the nationalization of banks and reform of credit institutions, but it went much further and incorporated the ideas of European socialism and organized labour ... The results in the 1935 election, and in many subsequent elections, would show that some 90 per cent of UFA members would transfer their allegiance not to the CCF but to Social Credit.[104]

However, some Latter-day Saint UFA members did switch to CCF. The CCF emerged during the Great Depression and some members of both labour and farm organizations saw the only solution was drastic economic reform. "The C.C.F.'s ideological background had clear socialist elements; and it sprang from the urban labour movement, from the social gospel of the churches, and from radical intellectuals, as well as from the soil of the wheat belt."[105]

John Albert Johansen (1877–1957) and his wife, Anna, moved to Raymond in 1904 and lived there for two years before moving out near Woolford.[106] As an active member of the Church, Johansen was immediately appointed to the Taylor Stake Sunday School Board and, after his move to Woolford, given charge of the Woolford Sunday School as superintendent until 1913. He became second counsellor to Bishop of the Woolford Ward Leo Harris and first counsellor in 1915 to Bishop W. T. Ainscough Sr. until 1924, when he took over as bishop for five years.[107] Johansen farmed two sections of land near Woolford, served on the Woolford district school board for nine years, and was central to the organization of the Cardston Municipal Hospital.[108] In August of 1935, Johansen received the nomination as UFA-CCF (later just CCF) candidate for the Lethbridge federal constituency. In his acceptance speech, Johansen promised to raise the standard of living by ensuring that "The natural resources ... must belong to the people with every individual getting the benefit of what he produced by the application of real work and human effort."[109] That October community members gathered at a meeting in the Cardston School gymnasium in support of the CCF and Johansen. Among the crowd were prominent Latter-day Saints James Walker (1885–1954) and Melvin King (1891–1974).[110] Speaking to the room of supporters, Johansen lectured, "as for 'Competition being the Life of Trade" he refuted this completely by his arguments that "the cooperative movement is the spearhead of a new day.'"[111] That federal election placed Liberal leader William Lyon McKenzie King (1874–1950) in power in Ottawa, but Alberta, once again, was mostly Social Credit. As reported by the *Cardston News* on 15 October 1935, Johansen earned only 700 votes, the Reconstruction candidate Gladstone Virtue earned 424, Lyn E. Fairbairn (Liberal) earned 2,104, J.S. Stewart (Conservative) earned 2,910, and John H. Blackmore (Social Credit) earned 6,473.[112]

In the 1944 provincial election, the CCF candidate for Cardston was Edward Leavitt (1875–1958) of Glenwood.[113] At a CCF meeting in the Cardston school gym (still in the gym and not the tabernacle or meetinghouse), Leavitt spoke on the "Policy of Nationalizing Banks" and promised that "If C.C.F. went into power they would not have to nationalize banks; they would only have to set up branches instead of using the nine chartered banks throughout Canada now in operation. As the finance is now managed, the profits are only in the hands of a few instead of benefitting the people of Canada."[114] Part of the CCF platform included free health insurance and other social services, as well as people's ownership and control of natural resources.[115]

Conclusion

David Horton Elton

The example of David Horton Elton (1877–1963) offers an interesting case of the overlapping concerns of church and state as well as political participation in a non-Latter-day Saint majority city in southern Alberta. Elton, originally from England, edited the *Alberta Star*, one of Cardston's earliest newspapers, and helped organize the Alberta and Eastern British Columbia Press Association.[116] He studied law under W.C. Ives in Lethbridge and was admitted to the bar in 1913. During his legal studies, the Church called Elton to serve as counsellor to the Lethbridge Branch President Robert J. Gordon; Arthur N. Green, whose family moved to the city in 1911, remembered Elton as a leader in the Lethbridge branch of the Church.[117] Professionally, Elton worked for the city of Lethbridge as police magistrate for six years.[118] The Church of Jesus Christ of Latter-day Saints grew in Lethbridge, the city gained a ward, and Elton served as counsellor for Bishop George W. Green, starting in 1914. At this time of prosperity, they entered a period of building their own meetinghouse in Lethbridge at corner of Seventh Avenue and Twelfth Street South. At the first meeting on 18 October 1914 in the new building's basement, Elton gave the special prayer.[119] Around 1917, Elton delivered a lecture on the sociology of Mormonism in Calgary as remembered by Maydell Palmer.[120] In the 1920s, he graduated from law school at the University of Alberta, spoke at the Mutual Improvement Association (MIA) conjoint meeting in Raymond, won an election to the Lethbridge City Council as alderman, lectured on the subject of the first principles of the Gospel in Magrath, and on the topic of success to the Raymond First Ward one Sunday evening.[121]

In the 1930s, Elton aimed higher than alderman and entered the race for the office of mayor. The city's residents elected him in 1935, and he remained in office until 1943. During his tenure as mayor, Elton remained active in his church, speaking at the Glenwood Ward Sunday School on the existence of the spirit life, giving a lecture on a Sunday evening to the Raymond Second Ward, and addressing the priesthood meeting of the Alberta Stake in the Cardston Tabernacle.[122] Elton worked as leader of his city as well as a leader of his religious community. Elton's story shows us how far Latter-day Saints had come since 1887, integrating enough into Canadian society to become elected mayor of the third largest city in the province while still actively participating in the Church.

Political participation at all levels of government demonstrated that Latter-day Saints' accepted their permanency in Canada and their willingness to contribute to issues outside those concerning their immediate communities. Even as they joined their non-Latter-day Saint neighbours at the polls and in the town halls or legislature, they kept some boundaries to identify themselves as Latter-day Saints. For example, the excessive overlap of religious, political, and economic leaders was a characteristic of Latter-day Saint communities because lay leadership meant that spiritual life occupied only one aspect of their lives. They had to support their families and fill their time in other ways, such as with politics.

Latter-day Saints in southern Alberta also achieved distinction from their American counterparts by involving themselves in three distinctly Canadian and Albertan political parties: the UFA, Social Credit Party, and CCF. Participation in these three parties made room for a greater expression of cooperative economics at a higher level. It was one way Latter-day Saints shared in common something critical to their faith – cooperation and unity – with outsiders who agreed on the importance of such qualities. The Wheat Pool, for example, like a Mormon cooperative company, required the pooling together of resources and finances, along with the trust and cooperation of the parties involved who relied on profit for survival or to support their family.

The theme of politics showed the various layers of integration into Canadian society. The Latter-day Saints kept the traditions and practices of the homeland (farm village and communal economics), causing an initial status as "Other" to non-Latter-day Saints. Business and politics, like the other themes of this book, also demonstrated the challenges of integration with the examples of how the minority group negotiated its identity. In this case, lay leadership, an important characteristic of The Church of Jesus Christ of Latter-day Saints, meant their political leaders were often also their spiritual advisers and Church organizers. The person in charge of the spiritual and financial health of the ward or stake might also oversee the town's budget. Latter-day Saints in southern Alberta also found themselves creating some distance between themselves and their American brethren in terms of political ideology. Integration into Canadian society did not mean sacrificing one's entire identity. It meant managing a balance between fitting in (e.g., through political participation) and maintaining boundaries (e.g., through lay participation) that reminded them of their distinctiveness as Latter-day Saints.

The process also made them different than the American Church because of Canadian culture and context. In the United States, explained Yorgason,

> The major turn-of-the-century change was not that Mormons suddenly became capitalists. Many church members had already successfully embraced such principles. Rather, the key transformation was further acceptance of capitalist cultural logic ... Less discussion remained of people sharing responsibility for one another's welfare on a community scale. Moral strictures by 1920 centered on a person's (a man's) responsibility to provide for his family.[123]

Latter-day Saints in Utah reinterpreted their history, focusing more on socially conservative aspects rather than radical ones, and "by merging its destiny with America's destiny and starting to behave like other churches, insulated itself from critiques of power relations between leaders and members."[124] In Alberta, however, the Latter-day Saints aligned with fellow Albertans rather than with Canadians in the east. "By the 1920s, the [American] Mormon culture region's dominant moral order suggested that to question the nation's power and norms was to unleash the forces of anarchy, religious struggle, and unwelcome authoritarianism."[125] In Alberta, to question the nation's power (Ottawa's power), as done by the UFA and Social Credit members, was the norm.

Chapter Six

Architecture

Introduction

Since the first Latter-day Saint settlement in Alberta, several individuals predicted that a temple, the most holy place for Latter-day Saint worship, would be built in Canada. Jonathan Layne (1835–99), one of Cardston's earliest settlers, prophesied that Canada would provide for the Latter-day Saints, just as Cache County, Utah, had done, and the country would eventually house their temples.[1] On his visit to the new Canadian community in 1888, John W. Taylor (1858–1916) made a similar forecast:

> I now speak by the power of prophecy and say that upon this very spot shall be erected a temple to the name of Israel's God and nations shall come from far and near and praise His high and holy name.[2]

These predictions clashed with the expectation that their stay in the North-West Territories was temporary, that it was only until they could legally practise plural marriage in Utah that the Latter-day Saints would remain in Canada. But a temple symbolized permanence. It would be a significant commitment and undertaking for the Canadian Latter-day Saints communities.

To understand the Canadian Latter-day Saint integration experience, in this chapter I will examine the Canadian religious and geographic landscapes with a particular focus on southern rural Alberta, and sacred spaces, such as the meetinghouse, assembly hall, tabernacle, and temple.[3] The question driving this chapter is: What does architecture reveal about the Church in Canada during the period of negotiation? The examination of Latter-day Saint architecture in southern Alberta reveals ways the Latter-day Saints imagined/remembered their homeland and constructed their new home.

Thomas Tweed shares a theoretical framework for the study of sacred architecture in his book *America's Church: The National Shrine and Catholic Presence in the Nation's Capital*. In this study, Tweed identifies the Basilica of the National Shrine of the Immaculate Conception as a threshold for understanding Catholicism in America.[4] I will model my study of early Canadian Latter-day Saint architecture after Tweed's work because he studies a building that represents both integration and religious distinctiveness. The built environment in Cardston and surrounding communities are thresholds for understanding The Church of Jesus Christ of Latter-day Saints in Canada. Ten factors, including location, appearance, context, and function, guide Tweed's study of the shrine and guide my own investigation. Historian Randall M. Miller observes Tweed's placement of the shrine "at the intersection of identity formation, institution building, and social and political interest among Catholics during the twentieth century."[5] These three points of intersection will also direct my own exploration of Canadian Latter-day Saints and the Church's sacred buildings.

From the late nineteenth century to mid-twentieth century, Latter-day Saints in Canada erected several places of worship that are of interest to this study of integration in Canada. However, I will only discuss five buildings in detail: the Cardston Meetinghouse (1888), Cardston Assembly Hall (1893), Raymond Meetinghouse (1903), Alberta Stake Tabernacle (1904–12), and Cardston Alberta Temple (1913–23). The meetinghouses and assembly hall followed earlier models of the simple New England variety, while the tabernacle fell under a more eclectic style of neo-Gothic.[6] These early Canadian buildings shared similarities with both earlier Latter-day Saint spaces and nearby Christian churches. The Alberta Stake Tabernacle's six tall, gothic-arched windows and decorative circular recess both imitated the Kirtland and Nauvoo temple-designs, and matched architectural features of other Alberta churches

Until the construction of the Cardston Alberta Temple, Latter-day Saint worship spaces in the region blended in with Albertan Christian churches in Fort Macleod and Lethbridge. Not only did the Alberta temple depart from nearby church styles, but it also departed from the assorted Victorian styles of earlier Latter-day Saint temples in the United States. As an example of the Prairie School style, drawing inspiration from Frank Lloyd Wright's Unity Temple, what message did the Cardston Alberta Temple communicate to observers? Architects of the Prairie School sought to distance themselves from European elements and develop a truly North American style. However, at this time of integration, the Latter-day Saints strove for undisputed credibility and legitimacy in the eyes of their fellow North Americans. The choice to build the Cardston Alberta Temple in the Prairie School style revealed the Latter-day Saint integration strategy: a combination of both peculiarity and popularity. The architectural style was popular, but not necessarily among non-Latter-day Saint church builders in the region during this time. The Prairie School only enhanced the mysteries of the sacred function of the temple despite its location in the Canadian prairies.

In this chapter I chronicle the history of The Church of Jesus Christ of Latter-day Saints in Canada by placing their architecture in the context of late nineteenth century and early twentieth century shifts in North American Mormonism. This requires a division into four periods: (1) 1887–1903, the period of white settlement of the North-West Territories and Latter-day Saint immigration; (2) 1904–13, the period of accepting their permanent residence and construction of the tabernacle; (3) 1914–18, the period of temple construction, which was interrupted by the First World War; and (4) 1919–23, the completion of temple construction. Within each of these periods, I will use the architecture as a lens to analyse identity formation, institution building, and the social and political interests among Latter-day Saints in Canada.

The Transition from Temporary Refuge to Permanent Residence

In April 1887, before their families arrived in the new settlement, Card and his companions visited nearby Fort Macleod, an outpost for the North-West Mounted Police where Latter-day Saints could register with Customs and pay duties.[7] By the Latter-day Saints' arrival in 1887, the Anglicans of Fort Macleod were rebuilding their church. The Parish of Christ Church formed in 1885, but the original building burned down the following year. The building, still standing there today, is the same one rebuilt the year the Latter-day Saints arrived. Christ Church combined elements of the Gothic Revival and the wooden New England meetinghouse, which equalled a vernacular style often referred to as "Carpenter's Gothic." Christ Church was a white, one-storey structure with lancet arched windows and a single steeple. The Church of England was not the only denomination to institute a missionary program in the territory. In the 1880s, the Roman Catholic Church also established a parish in Fort Macleod. Construction of a wooden church began in 1898, and a Carpenter's Gothic style church resulted a year later.[8] Holy Cross Roman Catholic Church had a simple wood-frame structure, a rose window above the entrance covered in wood tracery, and a spire with a cross atop a single tower. Art historian Barry Magrill explains that "the Gothicized single-cell church" was typical during the settlement of western Canada from Vancouver Island to Manitoba.[9] As part of their introduction to southern Alberta, Latter-day Saints encountered these buildings during their travels and saw an acceptable style for Christian places of worship.

Latter-day Saints also frequently visited Lethbridge, Alberta.[10] This important town provided another example of church architecture typical of the western Canadian frontier. St. Augustine's Church presented features of both the Romanesque and Gothic revivals. The brick material, low height, and adjoining tower suggested Romanesque influences, but the lancet windows indicated a reference to the Gothic. Visiting Anglican authorities consecrated and dedicated St. Augustine's Church on Sunday, 25 March 1888, the same year the Latter-day Saints completed their own meetinghouse in Cardston.[11] The Cardston meetinghouse was a 20.5 by 20-foot square log structure. The meetinghouse functioned as a chapel, school, and community centre. In his diary, Charles Ora Card wrote that they held their first meeting in the building on 29 January 1888 and dedicated it on 2 February, during the fast meeting.[12]

As Card and his companions organized in southern Alberta, growth and development continued in Utah. Latter-day Saints found architectural inspiration in the Gothic, and they were not immune to the Gothic Revival sweeping nineteenth century North America. The first four temples of Utah demonstrate the Church's early preference for Gothic style eclecticism. Manti, Logan, St. George, and Salt Lake City temples had "strongly fortified buttressed walls" and "impressive towers."[13] Churches in the United States favoured Gothic styles for its symbolism and implications. English architect and Roman Catholic convert Augustus W.N. Pugin (1812–52) argues that "the great test of Architectural beauty is the fitness of the design to the purpose for which it is intended, and that the style of a building should so correspond with its use that the spectator may at once perceive the purpose for which it was erected."[14] According to Pugin, the Gothic style, or "Pointed Architecture," expressed the Christian faith in three ways: the cross, trinity, and resurrection.[15] The plan of a Gothic church was in the shape of a cross and the cross symbolized the sacrifice of Jesus Christ. The cross was also found at the top of some church spires. Pugin relates the triangular shapes of the points and arches to the three persons united in the Godhead, the Trinity. In addition, the vertical lines and substantial heights of Gothic buildings alluded to the resurrection of the dead, which is spatially imagined as taking place in Heaven above the Earth. Pugin reflects on the architects of the past and compares them to his contemporaries that returned to pagan styles. In *The True Principles of Pointed or Christian Architecture,* Pugin explains that Classical architecture was inappropriate for nineteenth century religious buildings because it was meant for "idolatrous worship and rites" and designed for a climate completely different than the British Isles.[16] Churches, in Pugin's opinion, required windows and bells; neither of which were found in the Classical styles Pugin describes.[17] Classical architecture was unsatisfactory because it concealed instead of decorated and included unnecessary ornamentation, such as columns or Pagan emblems.[18]

Mediaeval architects were likely members of the churches that commissioned their services. The mediaeval architect received professional and religious "glory from ... creating a sacred space."[19] Pugin recommends that architects follow several rules to emulate architects of the past: abstain from including unnecessary features and guarantee that all ornamentation enriches the construction.[20] In other words, "the external and internal appearance of an edifice should be illustrative of, and in accordance with, the purpose for which it is destined."[21] Moreover, stone is the ideal material for Gothic designs.[22] Pugin believed that architecture had the ability to influence the most sensitive aspects of society. Victorian art critic John Ruskin (1819–1900) took it one step further and argued that morality existed within the structure.[23] The link connecting architecture and morality reinforced the close connection between Gothic Revival and Christianity.

Art historian Phoebe Stanton identifies the attitudes and lasting convictions from the Gothic Revival. A fear of secularism fuelled critics' support of Gothic styles, and this directly correlated to their disapproval of Classical styles.[24] She acknowledges the lasting opinions of Pugin and Ruskin, stating that these men and their followers truly believed that "architecture of an age illustrates its inner nature, strengths, and weaknesses, and the architect may influence, for good or bad, the lives of those around him."[25] In other words, a Christian structure must influence for the improvement of society, the morality. The style to accomplish this was Gothic Revival.

The "revived Gothic," as put by Victorian culture expert Chris Brooks, was a reconstruction of the past. He writes that "its revival has centred on how individuals and societies understood their own place in their own history."[26] Latter-day Saints saw their church as a restoration of the true, authentic church with direct lineage to the time of Christ. According to Brooks, "in a colonial set up, Gothic's connection with ancient community affirmed the identity, the togetherness, of settler societies, sometimes at the expense of cultures and communities they had displaced."[27] With this under consideration, it is unsurprising that Church architect Truman O. Angell (1810–87) and Brigham Young

(1801–77) selected Gothic elements for the first temples in Utah. Prior to his departure for a mission in Europe, Angell received a blessing from President Young on 13 April 1856:

> You shall have power and means to go from place to place; from country to country; and view various specimens of Architecture that you may desire to see ... and be better qualified to continue your work; and you will increase in knowledge upon the temple and other buildings.[28]

Young's blessing suggested that the Church sent Angell to Europe with the purpose of observing and learning as much as possible about European architecture where there remained many examples of the mediaeval Gothic. The first four Utah temples were a testament to this influence.

While the Church finished the Salt Lake City Temple in 1893, growth in Alberta continued with a second wave of immigration due to an irrigation contract between the Church and the Alberta Railway and Irrigation Company. The growing community in Cardston was too large for the original log meetinghouse, and the Church replaced it with a larger building known as the assembly hall.[29] Summarizing the year 1892, Card wrote that he donated $110 towards a new meetinghouse, which became the Cardston Assembly Hall.[30] He describes building the meetinghouse frame to his mother-in-law Zina D.H. Young in a letter dated 17 January 1893:

> Across the westend ... [we] lengthened out the old one about 5 feet and lowered the stage and gave the new one about 16 inches higher than the old and connecting by folding doors.[31]

The assembly hall resembled buildings from the early Utah period. It was a single-room structure with small-paned rectangular windows and plank floors made from easily accessible materials.[32] The early Cardston building also resembled plain early American meetinghouses found in New England.[33] Furthermore, they looked similar to the Anglican and Catholic Carpenter Gothic churches in Fort Macleod. The hall did not have a steeple, like Christ Church or Holy Cross, but it was one-storey, simple and functional.

The Church organized the Cardston Alberta Stake in 1895, and in 1898 and 1899, Church members formed the villages of Magrath and Stirling. Shortly after, Jesse Knight (1845–1921) established the town of Raymond in between the two villages, and quick growth created the need for another meetinghouse. The two-storey, rectangular meetinghouse in Raymond resembled the New England-Colonial shape of the Kirtland and Nauvoo Temples, borrowing the modesty transplanted by the Puritans in seventeenth century New England. It, like the Puritan meetinghouse, was an "unpretentious, unadorned structure built of wood and quite modest in size."[34] The style and similarity with neighbouring congregations played to the Latter-day Saints' favour by remaining inoffensive to non-members and blending in with their surroundings.

In this first period, Latter-day Saints were strangers to the Canadian western frontier. Their main interest was survival. They saw Alberta as a temporary refuge until polygamy was no longer criminalized in the United States. Even in what the Latter-day Saints perceived as a temporary location, they still remained committed to their faith, established wards and meetinghouses in various communities and, ultimately, formed organizations that kept community members involved in the Church. For example, Latter-day Saint women organized the Relief Society before the end of their first year in Cardston.[35] In addition, the Church's Young Men's and Young Women's Mutual Improvement Associations, and the Primary Associations could all be found in southern Alberta wards. The release of Card as president of Cache County Stake in Utah and his calling to be president of the newly formed Alberta Stake in April 1895 symbolized that the Canadian mission was no longer temporary. By 1903, there were enough Latter-day Saints in Alberta to divide into two stakes.

Permanent Residence

The construction of a tabernacle, another essential Latter-day Saint building, offered evidence of the Saints' prosperity in Canada. Latter-day Saints built these larger meetinghouses to hold all the members drawn from a specific area, which could comprise several towns. When the Latter-day Saints in Alberta outgrew their 26 by 40-foot assembly hall, stonemason and general contractor Samuel Smith Newton (1858–1954) designed a new building in the Gothic style, and construction of the Alberta Stake Tabernacle commenced in 1904. The tabernacle had no towers, but it did have a rose window above the main entrance, gabled dormer windows, and lancet windows.[36]

Architectural historian Richard W. Jackson argues that Latter-day Saints in Canada had local autonomy when it came to building construction before 1900 and, even after the turn-of-the-century, Church authorities still rarely restricted architectural choices.[37] They allowed popular styles to dictate. In regards to Latter-day Saint architecture around 1910, Romanesque style replaced the Gothic in popularity, and nearing the 1920s the Prairie style became most popular.[38] Viewers identified the Prairie School style by the characteristic flat roofs, spacious open interiors, native materials, overhanging eaves, thick masonry piers, grouped (ribbon) windows, and a connection between vertical and horizontal forms.[39] Jackson observes more than 50 Latter-day Saint meetinghouses in North America designed in this style and 43 specifically between 1910 and 1919.[40] Architect Allen Dale Roberts claims that some Latter-day Saint architects and members denied and minimized the influence of Frank Lloyd Wright (1867–1959), leader of the Prairie School movement, on their church architecture.[41] The career of Latter-day Saint architect Taylor Woolley (1884–1965) challenges these denials and shows at least one connection between Utah and Wright. Woolley not only joined Wright's Studio in 1908, but also travelled to Italy in 1909 with the famed architect and his son Lloyd (1890–1978).[42]

The Prairie School was an architectural style that supported Latter-day Saint goals. For members, The Church of Jesus Christ of Latter-day Saints offered the single way to gain salvation but, like any living tradition, Mormonism adapted. Wright argued that "form and function are one," which Robert Twombly explains, meant "that there could be only one form for any given function."[43] Wright searched for a style that would suit homes on the prairies and buildings in the United States. And, as his son John Lloyd (1892–1972) explains, it must be organic. In his father's biography, John Lloyd interprets "form and function are one" to mean that "form and function *should* be one" but it was not immune to creativity.[44] The temple was the form and salvation the function. The style of the Church's temples changed, but not the function.

In *Why Architecture Matters*, Paul Goldberger writes that Frank Lloyd Wright believed "that the best way to keep the American agrarian, family tradition strong was to house it in new architectural form created specifically for the American continent rather than transported from elsewhere."[45] The Prairie School was a reaction to international styles and a rejection of historical styles.[46] The American mid-Western prairies, a symbol of democracy, inspired the architects to imitate nature's horizontal lines.[47] The concept of "pure design" required the architect to analyse the different components as geometric shapes and then design these parts like building blocks.[48] The foundation of the Church is similar to the philosophy of Prairie School style. The Church was created on the American continent with strong ties to the land and commitments to the family unit. It was a reaction to and rejection of the new Christianities of the time because Latter-day Saints believed the Heavenly Father told Joseph Smith Jr. that the existing churches were false – specifically, that the Christian church dating back to the time of Christ had erred, and it was up to Smith to organize the correct path.

The promotion of democracy is another characteristic that ties together Mormonism and the Prairie School. The Prairie School liberated architects "from the autocratic styles of the past and [offered] a new creative freedom for the individual."[49] Similarly, Mormonism, according to Nathan O. Hatch, encouraged members "to work together in order to be free individually ... collective expressions of self-respect, instilling hope, purpose, meaning, and identity in thousands of persons whom the dominant culture had defined as marginal."[50] The populist movement aimed to transform "farmers and artisans into thundering prophets intent on shaping the destiny of a nation."[51]

In addition to the philosophical backbone of the Prairie School, other characteristics of the style assisted with the Church's desired goals through architecture's ability to communicate cultural values to following generations.[52] The exterior of buildings are public, accessible, and visually "loud." They are almost unavoidable, and they are certainly durable due to technological advancements and heritage preservation. Building a temple at a new location, in a new architectural style promoted a message of rebirth, a fresh start for the Church. A new phase of Mormonism began with President Joseph F. Smith's Second Manifesto on 6 April 1904. The Church officially prohibited post-Manifesto plural marriages and excommunicated disobedient members. The Church tried to disassociate from polygamy and re-brand "celestial marriage" in terms of longevity rather than multiplicity.[53] John W. Taylor, a strong supporter of both the Canadian settlement and plural marriage, fell victim to these changes and was eventually excommunicated. In 1888, Taylor accompanied Card to Ottawa with the goal of gaining permission to bring plural wives into Canada. The Canadian government denied this request and the visit alerted them to the Latter-day Saints' intentions, which resulted in an amendment to the Criminal Code, making polygamy an indictable offence in Canada. The Church of the twentieth century did not want the dark cloud of polygamy to follow them any longer. The construction of a temple in Alberta provided an opportunity to represent themselves as a group distinct from their past.

Wright's commission to build for the Unity Temple Unitarian congregation in Oak Park, Illinois, offered a reasonable model of inspiration for the architects of the Cardston Alberta Temple. Brooks describes the Unity Temple as a massive cubic form with a slab-like roof.[54] To Wright, his job was to "build a temple to man, appropriate to his uses as a meeting place, in which to study man himself for his God's sake."[55] Practical considerations included cost, purpose, and surrounding environment. He selected concrete because it was a cheap material; he placed the entrance behind the busy street to keep out noise; and he considered the activities housed there, such as Sunday School and special occasions.[56]

Prairie School style entered the Canadian prairies before the construction of the Cardston Alberta Temple. The Canadian Department of the Interior commissioned Francis C. Sullivan (1882–1929), an architect from Kingston, Ontario, and Frank Lloyd Wright to design a pavilion for Banff National Park.[57] Designed in 1911 and constructed by 1913, Sullivan and Wright produced a 200-foot-long shelter made from horizontal wood siding.[58] The pavilion housed numerous activities before its demolition in the 1930s. The Canadian Department of National Defence used it for storage during the First World War, and weekend visitors from Calgary used it for picnicking in the 1920s.[59] The design emphasized the building's horizontality through "the massing, the rough-sawn wooden exterior walls, the dramatically overhanging eaves, the continuous row of leaded-glass windows above the walls, the uninterrupted low-hipped roof, and the secondary hipped roof over the clerestory."[60] Maybe the Cardston Alberta Temple was less of an architectural anomaly than first perceived. Nevertheless, the pavilion was a public, secular building and the temple was a sacred space.

In 1912, Latter-day Saints in Alberta finished the Alberta Stake Tabernacle thereby solidifying their presence in the region. The tabernacle symbolized the success of The Church of Jesus Christ of Latter-day Saints in southern Alberta, but it was not the only growing denomination in town. St. Thomas' Anglican Church stood on First Street West at 20 by 36 feet before it was destroyed by fire.[61] Diversity indicated further integration because it meant non-members considered the Latter-day Saints to be suitable neighbours. The Church's display of success and expansion did not end with the tabernacle. The year of its completion was the same year of the design competition for the Cardston Alberta Temple.

Over ten years after Jonathan Layne's prediction, in Salt Lake City, Church President Joseph F. Smith shared a prophecy concerning the global Church: "I foresee the necessity arising for other temples or places consecrated to the Lord for the performance of the ordinances of God's house, so that the people may have the benefit of the House of the Lord without having to travel hundreds of miles for that purpose."[62] Smith officially announced the Church's plan to build a temple in Canada at the general conference on 4 October 1912.[63]

For their first temple outside the United States, the Church proceeded with a new approach to temple design. They decided to hold a competition rather than commission the appointed Church architect and invited 14 architects to submit designs for consideration. On 24 December 1912, seven of those invited submitted their work to the presiding bishopric, and thus began a new generation of temples in terms of not only appearance but also purpose; temples became reserved for sacred ordinances only.[64] The presiding bishopric displayed the anonymous competition entries at the bishop's building until they selected the winning design. Church authorities announced that Harold W. Burton and Hyrum Pope's entry had won, and they would be the architects for the Cardston temple. Their design was unlike the Utah temples (Figure 6.1).

Even journalists in Salt Lake City close to Church headquarters were confused by the architectural style of the first Canadian temple, stating, "The architecture of the proposed building cannot be identified exactly with any historically accepted style. The aim of the architects was to conform to the peculiar requirements of such a building rather than to imitate any style."[65] A Raymond resident agreed, writing for *Canadian Magazine* in 1913, "The architecture will not correspond to that of any temple erected by the Church in Utah. The authorities seek utility in the Canadian building rather than adherence to any type or revealed plan."[66] The architects allowed the purpose of the building to drive their design and let typical ecclesiastical styles take a back seat. The modern architects of the time, such as Louis Sullivan (1856–1924) and Frank Lloyd Wright, would have described this as "form follows function." The architects designed the temple according to its function, which all Latter-day Saint temples were made to serve. There was no longer a need for an assembly hall because now the temple was reserved for sacred ordinances only. The exterior of the Cardston Alberta Temple differed from the Gothic Utah temples, but the interior rooms and baptismal fonts remained similar and served the same functions.

However, at this time, the Church began to act the opposite in terms of its relationship with other Christian communities. On the exterior, to the outside, they appeared the same, but inside they remained unique, or peculiar. For example, the Church gave up plural marriage and officially punished defiant members who continued to practise it, but then began to re-emphasize the importance of family by initiating the tradition of Family Home Evenings.

The site of the Cardston Alberta Temple remained to be determined. Raymond and Cardston were the two options but, by February 1913, Alberta Stake President Edward J. Wood (1866–1956) received word from Elder Orson F. Whitney (1855–1931) that the Church had selected

Cardston. "It was certainly good news and quite in harmony with my early impressions. My first impressions were that we would have this great blessing – that of temple of the Lord here in Canada, and when it was first spoken of I thought it would sure by come to Cardston."[67] The building committee included Wood as chairman, Taylor Stake President Heber S. Allen (1864–1944), John F. Parrish (1870–1957), and William Baxter, who supervised construction.[68] In April, Wood travelled to Salt Lake City to review the architectural plans and observed that "the building is a different design than others."[69] In a letter to Randolph W. Lineham, Burton revealed that his fellow competitors produced designs similar to the Salt Lake Temple.[70] The Pope and Burton winning design was an anomaly among the Gothic re-creations. The same year that Pope and Burton travelled to Alberta to begin construction on the temple was the same year Sullivan and Wright completed the Banff Park Shelter.

Loyal Residents

Some might assume that global conflict delayed the Latter-day Saints' progress in Canadian society because it interrupted the construction of the Cardston temple. Nevertheless, the First World War provided the Canadian Latter-day Saints with an opportunity to quash their non-Latter-day Saint neighbours' doubts regarding their loyalty and legitimacy. The revision of the Militia Act in 1903 placed complete control of national defence in Canadian hands.[71] About 40,000 men would train in the active militia, while thousands of others would commit to serve only in the event of war.[72] This plan resulted in a Canadian version of the National Guard with trained marksmen all across the country ready to participate in war if needed. Before the conflict in Europe, the Church called Hugh B. Brown (1883–1975), future member of the Quorum of Twelve, to become an officer in the Canadian Army, he eventually qualified for the rank of major, and trained local Latter-day Saints and non-Mormon recruits in the Third Alberta Rangers.[73] Canada was automatically a participant in the conflict when Great Britain declared war on Germany in the late summer of 1914. While work on the temple slowed down, Latter-day Saint residents in southern Alberta demonstrated their loyalty to Canada and Britain by joining the war effort. Many men from Latter-day Saint communities enlisted by the end of 1915, and others were conscripted a year later. Major Brown led the 13th Overseas Mounted Regiment, part of the Canadian overseas expeditionary force, to join the Canadian Army's cavalry in Europe.[74]

The First Depot Battalion, Alberta Regiment, was another unit that included Latter-day Saint soldiers. These men from southern Alberta were conscripted near the end of the First World War. Marion Stoddard Hanson, John Whitaker Head, Schuyler White Hinman, Jeremiah Leavitt, Joseph Leavitt, William Ervin Low, Lehi Harold Marsden, Hyrum Adamson Maughan, and Lorenzo Snow Nelson are just a sample of the men from Latter-day Saint settlements who served as privates in the First Depot Battalion.[75] Some were born in Alberta, others were born in Utah, or their parents were born in Utah. Some Canadian Latter-day Saints demonstrated their commitment to the nation by sacrificing their lives. Others fought and risked their lives to prove where their loyalty lay. They fought side by side with their non-Latter-day Saint neighbours for the same cause.

Meanwhile, as war progressed in Europe, Church authorities back in Salt Lake City announced a new practice that would help maintain "their heritage as a truly distinctive people with a unique message."[76] On 27 April 1915, the First Presidency addressed a letter to stake presidents, bishops, and parents concerning the family. Editors published this letter in the June issue of *The Improvement Era* for all to read: "We advise and urge the inauguration of a 'Home Evening' throughout the Church, at which time fathers and mothers may gather their boys and girls about them in the home and teach them the word of the Lord."[77] This was the introduction of the Family Home Evening. Later, manuals in the early 1960s presented a resistance to feminism and a re-emphasis on patriarchy.[78] These particular values are often cited as "important distinguishing traits" of Latter-day Saints.[79] Latter-day Saints are similar in one way (emphasis on family) and unique in another (Family Home Evening). The balance between popular and particular continued.

Would this pattern of popularity and integration continue with the completion of the Cardston Alberta Temple? Although the war delayed construction of the Cardston Alberta Temple, in 1915, the Church announced plans to build in Laie, Hawaii. Pope and Burton designed this temple in a similar Prairie School style, making it just over half the size of the Alberta temple and of concrete from crushed lava rock in a cream finish. Heber J. Grant (1856–1945) dedicated the Laie Hawaii Temple in 1919. A month before the dedication, he announced a temple for Mesa, Arizona. Architects Don Carols Young Jr. and Ramm Hansen modelled their plans after the Cardston and Laie temples, which made these three all inspired by the Prairie School with hints of Meso-American motifs.

Modern Canadian Citizens

The First World War ended, and temple building continued in Cardston. Construction concluded in 1923, and President Grant dedicated the new temple on 26 August. Pope and Burton's "great achievement," according to architectural historian Paul Anderson, was their skill to combine what Latter-day Saints needed with the best design ideas.[80] He concludes that the architects adapted the building to their surroundings, which were the plains of Alberta: "The pyramid-shaped silhouette was particularly well suited to the temple's location on a low hill in the midst of a broad prairie, since the temple appeared equally strong, well-proportioned, and handsome from all angles."[81] Features of Prairie School architecture inspired the emphasis on the horizontal. The temple was modern because it was not Gothic or Romanesque but was inspired by the work of Frank Lloyd Wright. Even so, the building was also Mormon. It was designed for its function as a sacred site where members in good standing could perform rituals that helped them progress through the plan of salvation.

Joseph Y. Card (1885–1956) attributed the style to ancient cultures in an article for *The Improvement Era* in 1923. He wrote that the new temple "has the Grecian massiveness, a Peruvian touch, and is similar only to the ancient temples of the Astecs [sic] and other aborigines of Central and South America."[82] Another eyewitness account came from May Booth Talmage (1868–1944) after she trekked to Canada from Utah to view the new structure. In an article for the *Young Woman's Journal*, she contended that the temple appeared to be "chiselled out as is a piece of sculpture, rather than a building constructed of separate stones."[83] Scholar John Widtsoe's summary in an article for *Utah Genealogical and Historical Magazine* was similar to the previous observer's account:

> The architecture is baffling but reminds one of the pre-historic temples unearthed in Central and South America. It is in the form of a Greek cross, or, more accurately, of a Maltese cross, with a blunt tower rising from its center. The walls are massive and the foundations secure. The upper courts are covered with flower beds. At a distance, the temple looks as if it had been carved by some gigantic power from a granite block of tremendous proportions.[84]

Writing just over 50 years later, architect Allen Dale Roberts argues that "The development of Mormon architecture is as much a story of change in church philosophy and expansion of church organization as it is a story of the adoption of technological or stylistic improvements."[85] That being said, there must be an explanation for the departure from Gothic Revival and adoption of the Prairie School style. Numerous factors, such as climate, availability of materials, human resources, and growth patterns, affected the Church's architectural plans.[86] After outlining the different periods of Gothic Revival architecture in the Church's history, Roberts reached the modern, or Wright-influenced, period, which he dates from 1910 to 1921. He observes that some Latter-day Saints and Latter-day Saint architects deny Wright's influence on Mormon architecture.[87] The above sample of literature on the Cardston Alberta Temple demonstrated that absence. In an article for *Ensign*, Anderson admits that the Cardston Alberta Temple shows "some similarities to the work of the great modern American architect Frank Lloyd Wright," but he also, like the above authors, compared the temple to pre-Columbian ruins.[88] The desire to connect the temple to ancient temples found in both Central and South America was unsurprising when considering that many Latter-day Saint historians and archaeologists have searched for evidence linking the Book of Mormon to the pre-Columbian Americas. The visual connection acted as a reminder to observers of the authenticity of their sacred text. However, in this book, I am interested in what the influence of Wrightian designs, not just Central and South American styles, communicated to Latter-day Saints and non-members.

Viewers can observe Wright's presence in more than just temple building, and Roberts offers examples that include the Parowan Third Ward chapel and Ensign Ward chapel in addition to the Cardston Alberta Temple.[89] There is no denying the similarities between these buildings and Wright's Unity Temple in Illinois. However, the modern trend in Mormon architecture did not remain popular for long. The key characteristics of Gothic Revival, such as towers, steeples, and Gothic windows, connote qualities of religion and faith for many Christians. Social constructions equating "Gothic" and "churchlike" visually communicated to outsiders that the purpose of the building was religious. Roberts notes that Church members criticized modern architecture for its "awkward" and "unchurchlike" style.[90] It did not communicate the desired message.

Anderson revisits the Cardston Alberta Temple and early twentieth century Church architecture in articles for *Dialogue* and *Journal of Mormon History* (*JMH*). In *Dialogue*, Anderson once again argues that Pope and Burton's inspirations for the temple were both pre-Columbian pyramids and Frank Lloyd Wright. He compliments their achievement in combining popular architectural trends with the needs of the Church.[91] One of the needs of the Latter-day Saints in Canada at this time was integration. The presence of the new temple communicated that they were here to stay, but the architectural style maintained their distinctiveness. They strove for acceptance of their history, both nineteenth century and ancient. Anderson, writing for *JMH* on the topic of modern architecture, identifies that the first wave of Modernism arrived with Louis Sullivan and Frank Lloyd Wright, but by the 1920s and 1930s, when the Church experimented architecturally, Modernism was a fading trend.[92] The Church wanted recognizable characteristics and designs, but they picked ones that were out of date. Roberts counted at least 50 Latter-day Saint buildings constructed in the Prairie School style, including the ones listed above.[93] No less than five architects moved to Utah from Chicago, home of the movement, around 1900 and employed Prairie School style for homeowners.[94] Pope and Burton's winning design for the Cardston Alberta Temple was an example of the influence of the Prairie School style.

Frank Steele, writing for *Juvenile Instructor*, determined that the Cardston Alberta Temple "convinced Canada that the Latter-day Saints are an intensely earnest people, that they are established permanently, [and] that they are substantial citizens."[95] The temple eliminated one reason for Latter-day Saints to return to the United States. The temple did not visually assimilate into the small, rural town, but it fit into Canadian Latter-day Saints' needs. Now that they had a temple in Canada, new missionaries, young couples, and families did not have to travel south of the border to receive sacred ordinances.

Additionally, V.A. Wood interprets the temple's meanings further:

> For the members of the Mormon church the dedication of the Alberta Temple was a time of great anticipation, celebration, and spiritual renewal. It was also the culmination of the hopes, dreams, and sacrifices made by the Mormon pioneers who came to Alberta prior to 1923. To the Church members in Alberta the temple stood in its place of prominence as a symbol of their sacrifice, of the Lord's acceptance of their labours and of the unity and strength of the members of the area.[96]

The Cardston Alberta Temple symbolized success. The Latter-day Saints had come a long way since setting up camp along Lee's Creek in 1887 (Figure 6.1).

Figure 6.1 The Cardston Alberta Temple, West Gate, ca. 1925.

Source: Peel's Prairie Provinces, (peel.library.ualberta.ca), a digital initiative of the University of Alberta Libraries.

Conclusion

The Cardston Alberta Temple is one of several temples without a statue of the angel Moroni. Five of these (St. George, Manti, Laie, Cardston, and Mesa) were completed between 1877 and 1927. Sociologist Armand Mauss determines that the angel represented the charismatic elements of Mormonism such as prophecy, other-worldliness, and spirituality.[97] He observed the disappearing angel at Temple Square in Salt Lake City at a later time than the focus of this book, but the relevance remains. Were these the elements the Latter-day Saints had to abandon to integrate into Canadian society? What would have been more "peculiar"? The angel Moroni atop a tall spire, or the substantial lines of the Prairie School style? The Cardston Alberta Temple might resemble the horizontality of the prairies, but the bright, white granite and immense size within a rural, farming town of about 4,000 residents made the structure a visual oddity.

In the 1930s, Canadian sociology pioneer Carl A. Dawson wrote *Group Settlement: Ethnic Communities in Western Canada* and concludes that the religious dominance of Utah remained apparent in the Canadian settlement. Latter-day Saint men regularly travelled to Utah to attend general conference or visit friends and family members.[98] Latter-day Saints living outside the United States would always have this connection to Utah. Just like Roman Catholics would always be connected to Rome. By understanding the context of their architectural creations, we understand the significance of the Latter-day Saints in Canadian society. Architecture reminded the observer of its creators and users. The Cardston Alberta Temple symbolized the significant contribution of The Church of Jesus Christ of Latter-day Saints to southern Alberta's development. Maybe the choice of Prairie School style went against their program of integration or, perhaps, the Latter-day Saints had reached such a level of integration and acceptance that they were able to experiment without risking their status. The Cardston Alberta Temple drew attention to southern Alberta. It was the first Latter-day Saint temple in Canada, it stood out against surrounding landscape and non-Latter-day Saint buildings, and it provided another talking point about the Church. The new temple attracted visitors and became a sacred destination for Latter-day Saints in Alberta. This would have happened regardless of architectural style.

Theoretically, the relationship between Modern architecture and historical styles mirrored the relationship of the Church and historical Christianity. Modernist architects followed this ideal:

> the rejection of an academic tradition that had degenerated into eclecticism, imprisoned in a history that had come to an end and whose forms could only be endlessly recycled. It did not imply a rejection of tradition ... The architecture of the future would return to the *true* tradition, in which, it was believed, a harmonious and organic unity had existed between all the cultural phenomena of each age.[99]

The period of religious revival and social reforms during what is now known as the Second Great Awakening (ca. 1790-1840) was the context for the arrival of Mormonism in the "burned-over district" of western and central New York state. Joseph Smith, Jr. found himself surrounded by already established Protestant denominations and newly formed Christian sects, all of which combined and recycled different aspects and beliefs of the Christian tradition. In a sense, the region was a marketplace of Christian eclecticism. Smith rejected these and developed what he believed, like the Modernists, was a restoration, a "return to the *true* tradition." In his speech at the dedicatory service of the Cardston Alberta Temple, architect Hyrum Pope confessed that

> the design of a temple of the Lord should certainly be worthy of and in harmony with the genius of the Gospel which has been restored, that it should not be a Gothic cathedral or a classic temple but one which should have all the boldness and all the truth expressed in it for which the gospel stands, for truly this is not a church that has been established by Joseph Smith. This is not a new thought; but it is the gospel, it is the truth which the Lord revealed even to father Adam.[100]

The Modernist architects and Latter-day Saints thought they were returning to, not creating, "the truth." As an example of the Prairie School, the Cardston Alberta Temple reinforced these ideas.

The story of Latter-day Saint settlement in Canada began with plural marriage, Church members seeking asylum, and families needing economic opportunities. They built the first meetinghouses with easily available materials and in recognizable styles. When residence in Canada changed from temporary to permanent, the Church invested money and energy in the creation of a tabernacle for the Alberta Stake in Cardston. This was a more ornate building than previous ones and designed with the influence of the Gothic style. This architectural venture of the Church symbolized their investment in the Canadian Latter-day Saints. In turn, Canadian Latter-day Saints invested in Canada by participating in many facets of Canadian life, including in the First World War. Despite the interruption of the war, the Church designed and constructed what historian of architecture Trevor Boddy describes as "the first consciously 'Modern' major building in the history of Alberta architecture."[101] From the first meetinghouse in Cardston to the first temple in the country, Latter-day Saints in Canada balanced their strong ties to Utah with their desire to create a permanent, safe home in Alberta. The construction of the Cardston Alberta Temple marked not only the end of a long period of struggle and development, but also the beginning of a Canadian Mormonism.

Chapter Seven

Conclusion

Cemeteries: A Final Site of Negotiation

Cemeteries possess a wealth of information about the deceased. According to folklorists Austin and Alta Fife, while visiting a cemetery observers learn about their loved ones' "civic pride; their family groups or clans and the individual members thereof; their professions, trades, occupations, and affiliations; the ethnic groups to which they belonged; the fraternal orders of which they were members; terms of military service; disasters and tragedies they experienced."[1] Folklorist Carol Edison, studying Utahn graves, agrees, "Gravestones, with their visual symbolism and wealth of cultural information, represent a category of expression offering another way to recognize and understand this unique cultural region."[2] Writing about rural cemeteries in the Great Plains, professors of architecture Steve C. Martens and Nancy Volkman describe the sacred sites as "familiar, ritual landscapes that serve a fundamental human need for remembrance, commemoration, and spiritual healing."[3] Within the cemetery, the grave marker "is an important way for us to tell the next generation who we were and to help preserve our collective cultural identity."[4] Like sacred architecture, the cemetery is "a physical space and a spiritual place," but it is the cemetery, according to Elizabethada Wright, an expert on the rhetoric of memorial place, that "confuses the symbolic and physical to allow memories forgotten in other locations to survive – often silently."[5] The gravestones of deceased Latter-day Saints offer additional evidence for understanding the Latter-day Saint experience in southern Alberta. They also provide a final example of how minority religions in Canada continually cross boundaries between integration and otherness as they search for a home in the new land.

The cemetery memorials for the first Latter-day Saint immigrants in southern Alberta do not present anything unexpected for the Victorian era. For example, the headstones of Hans Peterson (1834–90) and Martha Woodward (1863–94) are stone tablets supported by low platforms. Both depict a hand pointing an index finger towards the sky, which several scholars interpret as indicative of the destination of the deceased: heaven (Figure 7.1).[6] In addition to this common Christian symbol, Peterson's headstone includes the familiar epitaph "No pain, no grief, no anxious fear can reach the peaceful sleeper here."[7]

Peterson was a shoemaker, born in Denmark, but immigrated to Utah in 1870 where he married a plural wife. After serving a prison sentence for polygamy, Peterson and his second wife Jennie moved to Alberta. Woodward was a 31-year-old wife and mother who died of tuberculosis in 1894, soon after arriving in the District of Alberta. Peterson and Woodward shared their Latter-day Saint faith and status as immigrants in Canada, but nothing about their headstones displays anything uniquely Latter-day Saint, such as a beehive or the angel Moroni. In addition, the monument memorializing Thomas R. Leavitt (1834–91) is more elaborate in that it includes several standard Victorian symbols such as vines of ivy (representing immortality) running over two columns and an arch, and underneath a planter filled with calla lilies (symbolizing beauty, purity, and marriage).[8] Leavitt's epitaph reads "A precious one from us has gone, A voice we loved is stilled, A place is vacant in our home, Which never can be filled" (Figure 7.2). But, again, there was nothing specific to the Church.

As well, Noah Shurtleff's (1846–92) simple marker lays flush with the lawn, including his full name, dates and locations of birth and death, and "Utah Pioneer 1851 – Canadian Pioneer 1888" (Figure 7.3). Like many of the early Latter-day Saint settlers in Alberta, Shurtleff, at the age of four, travelled from Iowa to Utah Territory with a Mormon migration company. The mention of Utah on his grave is a hint to his faith that not all observers would understand.

Memorials in Latter-day Saint majority community cemeteries blended in as standard Christian graves. In the Stirling Cemetery, the blunt obelisk monument for Utah-born Austin G. Russell (1881–1900) includes oak leaves, acorns, stars, his vita, an epitaph, and his family name (Figure 7.4). The oak leaves symbolize strength, and the acorns symbolize prosperity and spiritual growth.[9] His epitaph states, "Blessed are the dead which die in the Lord," possibly inspired by Revelation in the Christian Bible. Chapter 14 of Revelation comes after an account of great suffering but, according to this prophecy, with the fall of Babylon comes better times for the faithful: "And I heard a voice from heaven

Conclusion 149

Figure 7.1 Hans Peterson's headstone.
Source: Author's photograph

150 Thirsty Land into Springs of Water

Figure 7.2 Thomas R. Leavitt's headstone.
Source: Author's photograph

Conclusion 151

Figure 7.3 Noah Shurtleff's headstone.
Source: Author's photograph

Figure 7.4 Austin G. Russell's obelisk.
Source: Author's photograph

saying unto me, Write, Blessed are the dead which die in the Lord from henceforth: Yea, saith the Spirit, that they may rest from their labours; and their works do follow them."[10] The blessed are those that "either die in the cause of Christ, or rather die in a state of vital union with Christ."[11] This epitaph appears on seven grave markers in the Cardston, Magrath, Raymond, and Stirling cemeteries.

Another popular epitaph was "Asleep in Jesus." The headstone for Orin Leslie Kimball (1889–1901) expands the quote with, "Asleep in Jesus, blessed sleep, From which none ever wake to weep." Inspiration may have come from the Christian bible verse, "For if we believe that Jesus died and rose again, even so them also which sleep in Jesus will God bring with him."[12] The hymn published in 1832 by Margaret Mackey titled *Asleep in Jesus* could also have been related.[13] In his now famous sermon from 1844, Joseph Smith Jr. said, "We have reason to have the greatest hope and consolation for our dead of any people on the earth; for we have seen them walk worthily in our midst, and seen them sink asleep in the arms of Jesus; and those who have died in the faith are now in the celestial kingdom."[14] Despite Smith's speech, "Asleep in Jesus" was appropriate for most Christian denominations, and non-Latter-day Saints would have been familiar with the epitaph, too.

While eventually distancing themselves from plural marriage, Latter-day Saints did not want to separate themselves from their ancestors, whether or not they were connected by plural marriages because the larger the extended family "the greater its sense of achievement and, in a sense, of salvation."[15] In the early twentieth century, one of the most popular carvings on Latter-day Saint grave markers in southern Alberta was the image of a gate. In her poem "Bury Me Quietly When I Die," famous Mormon poetess Eliza R. Snow wrote, "What is death to the good, but an entrance gate / That is placed on the verge of a rich estate."[16] The image of the gate symbolizes the faithful Latter-day Saint's entrance into the Celestial Kingdom. Mary Ann Meyers explains that, for Latter-day Saints, death was not devastating since "life on earth encompassed neither the beginning nor the end of human existence."[17] At the final judgment, when all have been resurrected, Latter-day Saints believe that each person will be assigned one of the three kingdoms of glory: the celestial, the terrestrial, and the telestial. Even within the Celestial Kingdom there are different degrees of glory, and those members in the highest glory receive exaltation. One requirement of the highest degree is the priesthood who, religious studies scholar Douglas Davies explains, hold the keys that "unlock the gates of death and afford access to the several levels of heaven. Through ordination into this higher priesthood and through the temple rites accessible only to such priests, an identity is achieved that possesses the capacity to lead the believer through various post-mortem circumstances into the state of exaltation."[18] The Church teaches holders of the Melchizedek Priesthood that they have the "power and authority to enter into the eternal worlds through the realm of death and in company with their spouses."[19] On numerous gravestones memorializing deceased Latter-day Saints, one finds the image of an open gate, the "gate of death" opened for the deceased with the keys of the priesthood.

In his chapter on Latter-day Saint cemeteries in the United States, Richard Jackson notes the occasional presence of gates on Latter-day Saint graves until 1870, which he interpreted as representing the entrance into paradise.[20] Photographer and writer Douglas R. Keister agrees that gates symbolize passage from one realm to the next, or the Last Judgment.[21] Similarly, in his analysis of the historic cemeteries of Grand Rapids, Michigan, historian Thomas R. Dilley observes an open gate on the 1901 gravestone of John Lodewyk as "an obvious end-of-life image suggesting departure and passage to another realm."[22] In the Cardston Cemetery, the headstone of Fanny Elizabeth Caldwell (1880–1905) presents a wooden picketed gate swung open over a tiled floor and under a brick arch (Figure 7.5).

Her epitaph "She's gone to dwell with saints above, And rest in God's eternal love" is not exclusive to the Church, but it does present a message many Latter-day Saints would understand. For example, the last verse of Abbie A. Bird's poem "To The Memory of Those Who Are Gone," published in *The Young Woman's Journal*, runs, "That when we leave our earthly home/And in seeking friends above,/All will be ready there to greet,/And welcome us with love."[23]

In the Magrath Cemetery, Helen Shaffer's (1859–1909) monument is an obelisk crowned with a carving of an open book, a common Christian symbol, which rests above an engraving on a wall of the obelisk of an opened gate (Figure 7.6). At the base, the epitaph, "Dear wife and mother we lay thee/In the peaceful grave's embrace./But thy memory will be cherished/Till we see thy heavenly face" encourages Latter-day Saints to remain faithful and active in order to reunite in the Celestial Kingdom. These examples from cemeteries in southern Alberta demonstrate a blend of traditional, familiar Christian imagery with hidden Latter-day Saint meaning. To many outsiders, the grave markers would have looked like any others found in Canadian Christian cemeteries. This practice of integration shows a community not yet ready to challenge mainstream pressures to blend-in. It was not necessarily an

Figure 7.5 Fanny Caldwell's headstone.
Source: Author's photograph

Conclusion 155

Figure 7.6 Helen Shaffer's obelisk.
Source: Author's photograph

Figure 7.7 Olinda Pierson's grave marker.
Source: Author's photograph

adaption to Canadian circumstances, but perhaps a reluctance to cross a boundary marking them as different.

Eventually, Latter-day Saints established communities and made homes in southern Alberta, as this book as shown, and they embedded themselves in the social, economic, and political structures of Canada. At the same time, they drew boundaries around themselves in order to maintain an identity of peculiarity, which kept enough tension to keep Latter-day Saints both distinctive from and harmless to their neighbours. When images of the Cardston Alberta Temple began appearing on grave markers, this communicated a new stage of negotiation as Latter-day Saints proudly displayed their unique and sacred architecture on grave markers, which would communicate to anyone passing by the identity of the deceased. Images of the Cardston Alberta Temple began appearing in cemeteries even before the Church completed construction. In the Stirling Cemetery, lying flat to the ground, the grave markers of daughter Olinda Pierson (1896–1918) and father Ola Pierson (1848–1922) picture maple leaves and the Cardston Alberta Temple cut into bronze plaques (Figure 7.7). Although Ola lived 73 years, the flu epidemic of 1918 ended the life of his daughter Olinda early, after only 22 years. The temple on their grave markers symbolizes "the belief that there is a way to achieve victory over death, not just for the individual, but for the family unit, both nuclear and extended."[24]

In her study of Latter-day Saint graves in Utah, what Carol Edison labels as "temple gravestones" she defines as "a folk expression of organizational affiliation and religious belief. [Temple gravestones] speak not only to outsiders as a statement of Mormon religious identity, but also to insiders as a reminder and visual reinforcement of the essence of Mormon belief."[25] The Latter-day Saint temple in Cardston symbolized the permanence of the Church in Canada, and the presence of the temple on grave markers demonstrated a way the Latter-day Saints announced their religious affiliation, no longer favouring standard Christian icons, but embracing the uniquely Latter-day Saint symbol of the temple. In his guide to cemetery symbolism and iconography, Douglas Keister includes the Latter-day Saint temple in his extensive list of symbols and wrote that it represented one thing: Mormonism.[26]

In addition, the image of a temple, writes Edison, "symbolizes the place and the means through which the goal of eternal marriage and family unity is achieved."[27] The construction of the temple in southern Alberta meant that Latter-day Saints could achieve the principle of eternal marriage without journeying to Utah. They could participate in temple rituals, such as sealing ceremonies, in their current homeland. The marriage ceremony performed in a Latter-day Saint temple is called a sealing, which the Encyclopedia of Mormonism simplifies:

> The bride and groom meet with family and friends in a designated sealing room of the temple. The officiator [endowed with the priesthood authority] ... invites [the couple] to come forward and kneel, facing each other across an altar in the middle of the room. The sealer sometimes directs the attention of all present to the mirrors on opposite walls, reflecting endlessly the images of the couple at the altar, and he may comment on the symbolism. Then the sealer pronounces the simple words of the ceremony, which promise, on condition of obedience, lasting bonds with the potential for eternal joy between these two sealed for eternity.[28]

A significant difference from other Christian marriage ceremonies is the absence of "til death do us part" because, for Latter-day Saints, life as a family continues after death, in the spirit world. "For members of the Church, sealings endow life with greater purpose and give marriage a sense of divine partnership with spiritual safeguards ... Sealings can sustain a family in life and console them in death. They establish continuity in life, here and hereafter."[29]

Figure 7.8 The Christensen family grave marker.
Source: Author's photograph

Grave markers displaying a Latter-day Saint temple communicate "basic Mormon beliefs of eternal progression, marriage for time and eternity, and the sealing together of families."[30] The rectangular slab marker for the Christensen family listed the father Peter F. (1863–1930), the mother Mary S. (1872–1947), daughter Zelma Z. (1898–1917), and son Leroy W. (1913–16). In between the parents and above the children was an etching of the Cardston Alberta Temple and not the Manti Temple, where they were probably married since they wed in Manti in 1891 (Figure 7.8).

Another couple who was not married in the Cardston Alberta Temple was John Redford (1866–1941) and Sarah Redford (1866–1954). Despite marrying in 1886 in Logan, Utah, and probably being sealed in the Logan Temple, the Redfords's gravestone in the Leavitt Cemetery not only depicts the Cardston Alberta Temple, but also displays Chief Mountain, a significant feature of the landscape in their adopted home of southern Alberta (Figure 7.9) – perhaps not surprising when considering that four of their nine children were born in Alberta and they spent the rest of their lives there after immigrating between 1895 and 1899.

In the Cardston Cemetery, the granite marker for F. Earl Hurd (1899–1940) and Winnifred Hurd (1903–35) displays the Cardston Alberta Temple, their marriage date of 1 October 1921, and the epitaph "For time and all eternity" (Figure 7.10). The epitaph, like the temple, was

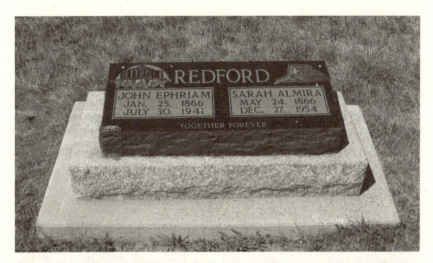

Figure 7.9 The Redfords' gravestone.
Source: Author's photograph

Figure 7.10 The Hurds' gravestone.
Source: Author's photograph

distinctly Latter-day Saint. For Latter-day Saints, marriage in the temple involves the ceremony of sealing, which joined the couple together "for time and all eternity." This was the Latter-day Saint covenant of marriage.[31] As the Church transitioned away from concepts like the plurality of marriage, they began instead emphasizing the eternity of marriage so the use of the epitaph declaring "for time and all eternity" symbolized another negotiation practised by Latter-day Saints. Latter-day Saint cemeteries offer another site of negotiation to study and understand how a minority religion moved between integration, difference, and otherness.

Final Thoughts

Latter-day Saints in southern Alberta crossed boundaries by navigating Canadian society and Canadian expectations, laws, and customs. They also established communities and new homes on Canadian soil. The various examples discussed in this book, including family, gender identity, the built environment, political participation, and business, show how a minority religion plays between otherness, difference, and integration in a constant negotiation of identities as a member of their new community and country, as a member of their religious community, and as a member of their former homeland. In this case, the Latter-day Saint balanced moving aspects of their identity. At times they were othered for their religious beliefs and practices, finding themselves in tension with surrounding communities, making it challenging to integrate or blend in. At other times, they did integrate and adapted some parts of their identity in order to fully or partially participate in Canadian society. The delicate balance demonstrates how adaptation to new circumstances produces new differences – differences from both Canadian society and American Latter-day Saints.

One way in which Latter-day Saints crossed into Canadian society and made a new home for their community was by adapting to Canadian circumstances and embedding themselves in the social, economic, and political structures of Canada. They constructed meetinghouses, an assembly hall, and a tabernacle that looked very similar to other Christian churches in the area, using familiar architectural styles of the time. In addition, Latter-day Saints joined political parties, won elections, and represented their communities at the provincial and federal levels. Latter-day Saint women were also politically and socially active. They joined women's organizations, like Women's Institute and United Farm Women of Alberta, and worked hard to implement social and political change as it impacted their own communities. In both these cases, Latter-day Saints worked together with non-Latter-day Saints to make changes they saw benefiting not only their own community, but society more broadly. In business, Latter-day Saints cooperated with non-Latter-day Saints to plan and complete large-scale irrigation projects that changed agricultural possibilities for all farmers in the area. They also, eventually, abandoned the practice of plural marriage and moved forward embracing monogamy and punishing members that continued the practice.

Acts of integration tell only one part of the story. In fact, Latter-day Saints drew boundaries around themselves in order to maintain an identity of peculiarity. They crossed into Canadian spaces and participated in society, but they also maintained beliefs and practices that provided some tension between their community and outsiders. For example, they constructed the Cardston Alberta Temple in a distinct architectural style that boldly announced their permanence in Canada and separated them from Utah with a different architectural agenda. In addition, they settled towns in the farm village pattern, sometimes using the Plat of Zion, and emphasizing community as well as co-operative interests. The Latter-day Saint commitment to cooperation impacted their early business practices, which did keep them insular for a time. Latter-day Saint women spoke out in support of Church leaders both in terms of their immigration to Canada and practice of plural marriage. They received spiritual gifts, such as speaking in tongues and prophecy, that might have upset neighbouring Christians of different churches and denominations, but they utilized these gifts to support their community, even if it "othered" them from Canadian society. The practice of plural marriage offended Canadians, but the Latter-day Saints came to Alberta with the intention of asking for permission to continue the practice on Canadian soil, which they did not receive. Plural marriage, another belief and practice that othered them from mainstream society, continued, eventually causing internal conflict and disciplinary action after the Church announced the Second Manifesto. A temple, an emphasis on cooperation, the experience of spiritual gifts, and the practice of plural marriage are all examples of how the Latter-day Saints "othered" themselves in their new home of Canada. Some of these beliefs, practices, and activities did change with time, as they decided to participate in Canadian society.

As the Latter-day Saint community in southern Alberta adapted to their new home in Canada, they maintained some differences that separated themselves from both their Canadian neighbours and American brethren. For example, the use of lay leadership in the Church meant that Canadian Latter-day Saints supported politicians who also served as religious leaders in their own communities. It was not uncommon for those elected officials to also be bishops, stake presidents, or leaders of an auxiliary organization. As well, Latter-day Saint women, who eventually joined social and political organizations external to the Church, did maintain a couple of strategies to differentiate themselves from Canadians. Their uses of folk medicines and midwifery in addition to the organization of the Church's Relief Society meant Latter-day Saint women established and maintained specific Latter-day Saint networks around health care, domestic work, and spiritual needs. These specific Latter-day Saints networks were a strategy to build boundaries between themselves and outsiders. Relief Society remains a crucial part of the Church to this day, but folk medicines and midwifery became less common as doctors, nurses, and hospitals reached Latter-day Saint settlements.

Latter-day Saints who immigrated to Canada even found themselves acting differently than their American family members and Church. For example, the architectural style of the Cardston Alberta Temple was the first to break away from the traditional gothic styles of the Utah Temple building strategy. This marked a clear visual distinction between southern Alberta and Utah. As well, the political ideology of Canadian political parties, such as the United Farmers of Alberta, Co-operative Commonwealth Federation, and Social Credit Party, attracted Canadian Latter-day Saints, and they embraced parties fighting for agrarian interests, cooperatives such as a wheat pool, and social services, like health insurance. Latter-day Saints in southern Alberta were constantly negotiating and, therefore, moving between former homelands and new homes. This shows that there is no order to integration, difference, or otherness when a minority religion crosses into new places and establishes new settlements, communities, and homes. We might suspect that otherness comes first, but not always so. As the example of Latter-day Saints demonstrates, sometimes they want to blend in and integrate, gaining social and political power over time as they cross into new social and political spaces beyond the boundaries of their own community, and then differentiate or other themselves from the mainstream. Like the example of Latter-day Saint cemeteries in southern Alberta shows, sometimes they evolved from integrated to distinct. Latter-day Saints in Alberta moved boundaries, created new borders, and eliminated restrictions; they negotiated.

The purpose of this book was to track the process of negotiation, resistance, and integration of Latter-day Saints as they moved into Alberta and encountered a society different from themselves. The example of Latter-day Saints teaches us that minority religions in Canada will search for acceptance, but also resist giving up all the beliefs and practices that make them different from their neighbours or the dominant society. They dwell, they create homes, communities, and connections, and they also cross, back to their homeland and into new environments. Latter-day Saints in southern Alberta integrated into Canadian society and maintained their "peculiar" identity through negotiations evident in their architecture, business practices, political participation, gendered roles, and family structures. Canadian and Albertan societies forced the newcomer to decide what they were willing to give up, maintain, or innovate in their own religion, as well as what they would adopt, reject, or ignore in their adopted society. The Latter-day Saints found success by maintaining some tensions with the dominant society and keeping a distinctive yet acceptable identity through a complicated, multi-dimensional process of negotiation.

Notes

1 Introduction

1 Jane E. Woolf Bates and Zina Woolf Hickman, *Founding of Cardston and Vicinity: Pioneer Problems* (n.p., 1960), 5. Both women died before they could see the published version of their work. Their nephew William L. Woolf made the publication possible in 1960. Historians Charles Ursenbach and Norman Criland printed a second edition in October 1974. Zina and Jane compiled and wrote the history of their community from the years 1887 to 1897, mainly from the memories of Jane who was aged 13 when the family travelled to the North-West Territories as part of the earliest group to arrive at Lee's Creek.
2 Bates and Hickman, *Founding of Cardston and Vicinity*, 61.
3 In 1831, Joseph Smith Jr. asked God about "the gathering" to Zion and received the revelation that "in the barren deserts there shall come forth pools of living water; and the parched ground shall no longer be a thirsty land" (D&C 133: 29).
4 Unless otherwise stated, "the Church" refers to The Church of Jesus Christ of Latter-day Saints.
5 Nathan O. Hatch, *The Democratization of American Christianity* (New Haven: Yale University Press, 1989), 8. For a brief overview of Mormonism, see Richard Lyman Bushman, *Mormonism: A Very Short Introduction* (Oxford: Oxford University Press, 2008). For a more in-depth analysis of Joseph Smith Jr. and the founding of the Church, see Bushman, *Joseph Smith and the Beginnings of Mormonism* (Urbana and Chicago: University of Illinois Press, 1984).
6 Hatch, *The Democratization of American Christianity*, 113.
7 Hatch, *The Democratization of American Christianity*, 120.
8 In August 2018, the Church announced the importance of using the full name of The Church of Jesus Christ of Latter-day Saints and moved away

from terms or nicknames such as "Mormon" and "LDS." This book will try to respect the Church's style guide when referencing Church members and the name of the Church. The author acknowledges that the Church's official opinion is that the term "Mormonism" is inaccurate.

9 Richard E. Bennett, "'Plucking Not Planting': Mormonism in Eastern Canada 1830–1850," in *The Mormon Presence in Canada*, edited by B.Y. Card, Herbert C. Northcott, John E. Foster, Howard Palmer, and George K. Jarvis (Edmonton: University of Alberta Press, 1990), 19; 30.

10 In the Church, the Prophet is a man selected by God, as representative of Jesus Christ, to teach and lead the Church as president and prophet. For a history of the Church in Upper Canada, see Richard E. Bennett, "A Study of the Church of Jesus Christ of Latter-Day Saints in Upper Canada, 1830–1850," (MA thesis, Brigham Young University, 1975). Also see, Richard E. Bennett, ""Plucking Not Planting": Mormonism in Eastern Canada 1830–1850," in *The Mormon Presence in Canada*, edited by B. Y. Card, Herbert C. Northcott, John E. Foster, Howard Palmer, and George K. Jarvis (Edmonton: University of Alberta Press, 1990), 19–34.

11 Jan Shipps, *Mormonism: The Story of a New Religious Tradition* (Urbana and Chicago: University of Illinois Press, 1985), 155–63.

12 Terryl Givens, *The Latter-day Saint Experience in America* (Westport, CT: Greenwood Press, 2004), 43 and 45.

13 Givens, *The Latter-day Saint Experience*, 64.

14 Alvin Finkel, "The Fur Trade and Early European Settlement," in *Working People in Alberta: A History*, ed. Alvin Finkel (Edmonton: Athabasca University Press and Canadian Committee on Labour History, 2012), 33.

15 Census of Canada, 1880–81, Volume 3 (Ottawa: Maclean, Roger & Co., 1883), 114. General Report of the Census of Canada, 1880–81, Volume 4 (Ottawa: Maclean, Roger & Co., 1885), 6–7.

16 Census of the three provisional districts of the North-West Territories, 1884–5: Recensement des trois districts provisoires des Territoires du Nord-Ouest, 1884–5 (Ottawa: MacLean, Roger & Co., 1886), 2; 6–7.

17 Census of Canada, 1890–91, Volume 1 (Ottawa: S.E. Dawson, 1893), 328–9.

18 Gerald Friesen, *The Canadian Prairies: A History* (Toronto: University of Toronto Press, 1987), 245.

19 Gerald Friesen, *The Canadian Prairies: A History* (Toronto: University of Toronto Press, 1987), 464.

20 Census of Canada, 1890–91, Volume 1 (Ottawa: S.E. Dawson, 1893), 181–3.

21 Geo Takach, *Will the Real Alberta Please Stand Up?* (Edmonton: University of Alberta Press, 2010), 64.

22 Takach, *Will the Real Alberta Please Stand Up*, 32.

23 For an understanding of the Americanization thesis in Mormon studies, see Thomas G. Alexander, *Mormonism in Transition: A History of the*

Latter-day Saints, 1890–1930 (Urbana: University of Illinois Press, 1986); Armand L. Mauss, *The Angel and the Beehive: The Mormon Struggle with Assimilation* (Urbana: University of Illinois Press, 1994); Ethan R. Yorgason, *Transformation of the Mormon Culture Region* (Urbana: University of Illinois Press, 2003); Kathleen Flake, *The Politics of American Religious Identity: The Seating of Senator Reed Smoot, Mormon Apostle* (Chapel Hill & London: The University of North Carolina Press, 2004).

24 The term "peculiar" comes from Latter-day Saint sources and is not derogative. In 1892, Church President Wilford Woodruff admitted that "The Latter-day Saints are somewhat peculiar from other religious denominations." See J. Spencer Fluhman, *A Peculiar People: Anti-Mormonism and the Making of Religion in Nineteenth-Century America* (Chapel Hill: University of North Carolina Press, 2012). Throughout this book I will use both "peculiar" and "particular" to describe distinctiveness.

25 The questions come directly from Mark G. McGowan's study of Catholic identity in Toronto from 1887 to 1922. In this book, McGowan traces the development of the English-speaking Catholic community as they embedded themselves in the social, occupational, economic, and political structures of Toronto. In addition, he follows how this community developed and adapted its Catholicism to local circumstances. See McGowan, *The Waning of the Green: Catholics, the Irish, and Identity in Toronto, 1887–1922* (Montreal & Kingston: McGill-Queen's University Press, 1999).

26 Matthew Bowman, *The Mormon People: The Making of an American Faith* (New York: Random House, 2012), ix-x.

27 In addition to Bowman, Mauss, Yorgason, and Flake, for an analysis of rhetoric and the process of assimilation at the institutional level, see Gordon Shepherd and Gary Shepherd, *A Kingdom Transformed: Themes in the Development of Mormonism* (Salt Lake City: University of Utah Press, 1984). Much has been written about the Americanization of the Church. See, for example, Thomas F. O'Dea, *The Mormons* (Chicago: University of Chicago Press, 1963); Clark S. Knowlton, "Social Accommodation in Utah," in *Essays on the American West, 1974–1975*, ed. Thomas G. Alexander (Provo, UT: Brigham Young University Press, 1976); Richard D. Poll, "The Americanism of Utah," *Utah Historical Quarterly* 44, no. 1 (Winter 1976): 76–93.

28 O. Kendall White, Jr., "Mormonism in America and Canada: Accommodation to the Nation-State," *The Canadian Journal of Sociology* 3, no. 2 (1978): 179.

29 Recent publications are evidence of the growing field of Global Mormon Studies. For example, *The Palgrave Handbook of Global Mormonism*, edited by R. Gordon Shepherd, A. Gary Shepherd, and Ryan T. Cragun (Palgrave

Macmillan, 2020). Also see, *Global Mormonism in the 21st Century*, edited by Reid L. Neilson (Brigham Young University Press, 2008).
30 David B. Marshall, "The Latter-day Saints, the Doughnut, and Post-Christian Canada," *Journal of Mormon History* 39, no. 2 (2013): 42.
31 A.A. Den Otter, "A Congenial Environment: Southern Alberta on the Arrival of the Mormons," 53–74; Jessie L. Embry, "Two Legal Wives: Mormon Polygamy in Canada, The United States, and Mexico," 170–85; B. Carmon Hardy, "Mormon Polygamy in Mexico and Canada: A Legal and Historiographical Review," 186–210; Maureen Ursenbach Beecher, "Mormon Women in Southern Alberta: The Pioneer Years," 211–30; Keith Parry, "Mormons as Ethnics: A Canadian Perspective," 353–62. In *The Mormon Presence in Canada*, ed. B.Y. Card et al. (Edmonton: University of Alberta Press, 1990).
32 Andrew H. Hedges, "'I Wondered If I Could Feel at Home': Southern Alberta Through the Eyes of Its Early Saints, 1883–1910," 75–97; Mary Jane Woodger, "Frontier Prophetesses: The Gift of Tongues as Manifested by Latter-day Saint Women in Southern Alberta, 1894–1930," 123–38. In *Regional Studies in Latter-day Saint Church History: Western Canada*, ed. Wright et al. (Provo, UT: Dept. of Church History and Doctrine, Brigham Young University, 2000).
33 *Canadian Mormons: History of the Church of Jesus Christ of Latter-day Saints in Canada*, Prete, Roy A. and Carma T. Prete, eds, (Provo: Religious Studies Center, Brigham Young University, in cooperation with Deseret Book Company, 2017).
34 David B. Marshall, "The Latter-day Saints, the Doughnut, and Post-Christian Canada," *Journal of Mormon History* 39, no. 2 (2013): 37.
35 W.E. Mann, *Sect, Cult, and Church in Alberta* (Toronto: University of Toronto Press, 1955), 8.
36 For further demonstration of the significance of Alberta to Canada's historical narratives, see Clark Banack, *God's Province: Evangelical Christianity, Political Thought, and Conservatism in Alberta* (Montreal: McGill-Queen's University Press, 2016).
37 John Webster Grant, *The Church in the Canadian Era* (Vancouver: Regent College, 1988), 177.
38 Nancy Christie and Michael Gauvreau, *Christian Churches and Their Peoples, 1840–1965: A Social History of Religion in Canada* (Toronto: University of Toronto Press, 2010), 61.
39 Anthony W. Rasporich, "Utopian Ideals and Community Settlements in Western Canada, 1880–1914," in *The Prairie West as Promised Land*, ed. R. Douglas Francis and Chris Kitzan (Calgary: University of Calgary Press, 2007), 146–7. In his chapter for *Prophets, Priests, and Prodigals*, Rasporich, using the diaries of Charles Ora Card, notes that "The fluid boundaries

between eschatology and community-building described for Nauvoo might then be transferred to the Cardston experiment which fused sacred and secular concerns in this enduring new Jerusalem in southern Alberta." Anthony W. Rasporich, "Utopia, Sect and Millennium in Western Canada, 1870–1940," in *Prophets, Priests, and Prodigals: Readings in Canadian Religious History, 1608 to Present*, ed. David B. Marshall and Mark McGowan (Toronto: McGraw-Hill Ryerson, 1992), 223.

40 Mark A. Noll, *A History of Christianity in the United States and Canada* (Grand Rapids: W.B. Eerdmans, 1992), 192–7; 435.
41 Thomas A. Tweed, *Crossing and Dwelling: A Theory of Religion* (Cambridge; London: Harvard University Press, 2008), 54.
42 Tweed, *Crossing and Dwelling*, 82.
43 Tweed, *Crossing and Dwelling*, 62.
44 Tweed, *Crossing and Dwelling*, 123.
45 Robert A. Orsi, "Everyday Miracles: The Study of Lived Religion," in *Lived Religion in America: Toward a History of Practice*, ed. David D. Hall (Princeton, NJ: Princeton University Press, 1997), 7.
46 Robert A. Orsi, "Is the Study of Lived Religion Irrelevant to the World We Live In? Special Presidential Plenary Address, Society for the Scientific Study of Religion, Salt Lake City, November 2, 2002," *Journal for the Scientific Study of Religion* 42, no. 2 (2003): 172.
47 Meredith B. McGuire, *Lived Religion: Faith and Practice in Everyday Life* (Oxford and New York: Oxford University Press, 2008), 4.
48 Jan Shipps, *Mormonism: The Story of a New Religious Tradition* (Urbana and Chicago: University of Illinois Press, 1985), 116.
49 Armand L. Mauss, *The Angel and the Beehive: The Mormon Struggle with Assimilation* (Urbana: University of Illinois Press, 1994), 24–31.
50 Yorgason, *Transformation of the Mormon Culture Region*, 9; 13–14.
51 Peter Beyer, "From Far and Wide: Canadian Religious and Cultural Diversity in Global/Local Context," in *Religion and Diversity in Canada*, ed. Lori G. Beaman and Peter Beyer (Leiden and Boston: Brill, 2008), 13.
52 Peter Beyer, "From Far and Wide: Canadian Religious and Cultural Diversity in Global/Local Context," in *Religion and Diversity in Canada*, ed. Lori G. Beaman and Peter Beyer (Leiden and Boston: Brill, 2008), 14.
53 N.K. Clifford, "His Dominion: A Vision in Crisis," *Studies in Religion* 2, no.4 (1973): 315.
54 N.K. Clifford, "His Dominion: A Vision in Crisis," *Studies in Religion* 2, no.4 (1973): 315.
55 N.K. Clifford, "His Dominion: A Vision in Crisis," *Studies in Religion* 2, no.4 (1973): 318.
56 Gerald Friesen, "The Western Canadian Identity," *Historical Papers / Communications historiques*, 8 no. 1 (1973): 15.

57 R. Douglas Francis, "Changing Imagines of the West," in *The Prairie West: Historical Readings*, edited by R. Douglas Francis and Howard Palmer (Edmonton: Pica Pica Press, 1985), 639.
58 R. Douglas Francis, "In Search of a Prairie Myth: A Survey of the Intellectual and Cultural Historiography of Prairie Canada," *Journal of Canadian Studies* 24 no. 3 (1989): 44–69.
59 R. Douglas Francis and Chris Kitzan, "Introduction," in *The Prairie West as Promised Land*, ed. R. Douglas Francis and Chris Kitzan (Calgary: University of Calgary Press, 2007), x–xi.
60 Francis and Kitzan, "Introduction," xiii–xiv.
61 Francis and Kitzan, "Introduction," xiv.
62 Gerald Friesen, *The Canadian Prairies: A History* (Toronto: University of Toronto Press, 1987), 447.
63 Roger Gibbins, *Prairie Politics and Society: Regionalism in Decline* (Toronto: Butterworths, 1980), 17–35.
64 Howard Palmer, *Patterns of Prejudice: A History of Nativism in Alberta* (Toronto: McClelland and Stewart, 1982), 8–9.
65 Palmer, *Patterns of Prejudice*, 13–14.
66 Palmer, *Patterns of Prejudice*, 40–1.
67 Palmer, *Patterns of Prejudice*, 46.
68 Palmer, *Patterns of Prejudice*, 26.
69 Palmer, *Patterns of Prejudice*, 172–6.
70 Armand L. Mauss, *The Angel and the Beehive: The Mormon Struggle with Assimilation* (Urbana: University of Illinois Press, 1994).
71 "Sealing" is a Latter-day Saint ritual that binds husband, wife, and children as eternal family units.

2 Families

1 North Americans tend to prefer the broad term "polygamy." We will see it used by Latter-day Saints, government officials, politicians, newspaper reporters, and anthropologists. However, the more specific term is "polygyny" because this refers to the marriage of one man to several women. "Polygamy" is defined as marriage between one person and two or more spouses simultaneously. While not incorrect, the term "polygamy" suggests that women could also have more than one spouse, and this was not the case for Latter-day Saints. They only practised polygyny, and it is the more specific term.
2 W. Peter Ward, *Courtship, Love and Marriage in Nineteenth-Century English Canada* (Montreal: McGill-Queen's University Press, 1990), 38.
3 "An Act for Consolidating and Amending the Statutes in This Province Relative to Offences against the Person," 4 & 5 Victoria, ch. 27, sec. 22.

4 W.C. Keele, *The Provincial Justice, or Magistrate's Manual, Being a Complete Digest of the Criminal Law of Canada and a Compendious and General View of the Provincial Law of Upper Canada: With Practical Forms, for the Use of the Magistracy*, 4th ed. (Toronto: Henry Roswell, 1858), 406. The manual stated: "So in an indictment for bigamy, it is necessary to state, with correctness, the time of the second marriage and to aver that the first wife was alive at the time ... the place at which the alleged offence was committed must also be stated." Despite the absence of a "first husband," the section on bigamy stated that the offence was "having two wives or two husbands, at the same time." See Keele, *The Provincial Justice*, 101.
5 "An Act Respecting Offences against the Person," 22 Victoria, ch. 91, sec. 29.
6 "Distribution of Legislative Powers," 30 & 31 Victoria, ch. 3, sec. 91–92. The Statutes of Canada passed in 1869 altered the definition of bigamy to fit the united country of Canada. Under the Act respecting offences against the Person, the Canadian government defined someone guilty of bigamy as follows: "Whosoever, being married, marries any other person during the life of the former husband or wife, whether the second marriage has taken place in Canada, or elsewhere, is guilty of felony, and shall be liable to be imprisoned in the Penitentiary for any term not exceeding seven years and not less than two years, or to be imprisoned in any other gaol or place of confinement for any termless than two years, with or without hard labour." See "An Act Respecting Offences against the Person," 32 & 33 Victoria, ch. 20, sec. 58.
7 Comacchio, *Infinite Bonds*, 3.
8 Comacchio, *Infinite Bonds*, 9.
9 Sarah Carter, "Creating 'Semi-Widows' and 'Supernumerary Wives': Prohibiting Polygamy in Prairie Canada's Aboriginal Communities to 1900," in *Contact Zones: Aboriginal and Settler Women in Canada's Colonial Past*, ed. Katie Pickles and Myra Rutherford (Vancouver: UBC Press, 2005), 131–59.
10 Sarah Carter, "'Complicated and Clouded': The Federal Administration of Marriage and Divorce among the First Nations of Western Canada, 1887–1906," in *Unsettled Pasts: Reconceiving the West through Women's History*, ed. Sarah Carter, Lesley Erickson, Patricia Roome, and Char Smith (Calgary: University of Calgary Press, 2005), 151–78.
11 Sarah Carter, *The Importance of Being Monogamous: Marriage and Nation Building in Western Canada to 1915* (Edmonton: University of Alberta Press, 2008), 5.
12 Carter, *The Importance of Being Monogamous*, 41–50; 83–9. For an account of the continuation of plural marriage in Canada, see Jessie L.

Embry, "Exiles for the Principle: LDS Polygamy in Canada," *Dialogue: A Journal of Mormon Thought* 18, no. 3 (1985): 108–16. Embry reports that even seven years after the First Manifesto, 24 of the 49 members of the high priest quorum in the Alberta Stake had plural marriages and three Latter-day Saint men became polygamists as late as 1903. B. Carmon Hardy calls the early Mormon colonization efforts in Canada a "resistance to national pressures to abandon polygamy," and his work provides a list of post-Manifesto plural marriages performed in Canada, starting in 1892 and ending in 1905. B. Carmon Hardy, *Solemn Covenant: The Mormon Polygamous Passage* (Urbana: University of Illinois Press, 1992).

13 For a closer comparison of Kainai and Latter-day Saint non-monogamous relationships, see my paper titled "On the Border of Monogamy: Understanding Non-Monogamy among the Latter-day Saints and Kainai Nation in Alberta," written for the American Examples Workshop, unpublished.

14 Bradley, *Kidnapped from That Land*, 3–5. Kathryn M. Daynes, "Differing Polygamous Patterns: Nineteenth-Century LDS and Twenty-First Century FLDS Marriage Systems," in *Modern Polygamy in the United States: Historical, Cultural, and Legal Issues*, ed. Cardell K. Jacobson with Lara Burton (New York: Oxford University Press, 2011), 140. For further information on the legislation process, see Ken Driggs, "The Mormon Church-State Confrontation in Nineteenth-Century America," *Journal of Church and State* 30, no. 2 (1988): 273–89; and Richard D. Poll, "The Legislative Antipolygamy Campaign," *BYU Studies* 25, no. 4 (1986): 107–24. Also, see Gordon's *The Mormon Question* for a detailed study of nineteenth-century polygamy and United States law.

15 Brigham Y. Card, "Charles Ora Card and the Founding of the Mormon Settlements in Southwestern Alberta, North-West Territories," in *The Mormon Presence in Canada*, ed. Brigham Y. Card et al. (Edmonton: The University of Alberta Press, 1990), 84. For a biography of Card, see Donald G. Godfrey, *Charles Ora Card: Southern Alberta Pioneer* (Mesa: D.G. Godfrey, Godfrey Family Organization, 1987).

The Revised Statutes of Canada, 1886 came into effect a few months before the Saints arrived in the North-West Territories. Bigamy was still prohibited. See "An Act Respecting Offenses Relating to the Laws of Marriage," 49 Victoria, ch. 161, sec. 4.

16 Card, "Charles Ora Card," 85.
17 Bates and Hickman, *Founding of Cardston*, 5.
18 Bates and Hickman, *Founding of Cardston*, 8.
19 Bates and Hickman, *Founding of Cardston*, 7. One notes the racist implications of the term "Indian infested," as if Indigenous peoples were a

pest that invaded the household rather than the original occupants living their lives in their ancestral lands.
20 Louis Orson Brandley, oral history, interviewed by Charles Ursenbach, Raymond, Alberta, 1976, transcript, Church History Library. Also see Gary L. Boatright, "Strangers in a New and Strange Land: Theodore Brandley and the Settlement of Stirling, Alberta," *Alberta History* 61, no. 2 (2013): 2–10.
21 Jessie L. Embry, "Mormon Polygamy in Canada, the United States and Mexico," 178.
22 Charles Samuel Matkin, Oral history, interviewed by Charles Ursenbach, Magrath, Alberta, 18 July 1975, transcript, Church History Library. Heber James Matkin, Oral history, interviewed by Charles Ursenbach, Lethbridge, Alberta, 1974, transcript, Church History Library.
23 Bennion and Richards, *Joseph Harker Family History*, 265. Harker Family Committee, *Harker Heritage* (Magrath, AB: Verona Harker Merkley, 1993), 27.
24 Leavitt Family Organization, *Thomas Rowell Leavitt*, 35. Josephine Leavitt Allred, oral history, interviewed by Orvilla Allred Steven, Provo, Utah, 1976, transcript, Church History Library.
25 John Maclean, *The Indians, Their Manners and Customs* (Toronto: William Briggs, 1889), 26.
26 John Maclean, *Canadian Savage Folk: The Native Tribes of Canada* (Toronto: William Briggs, 1896), 62.
27 John Maclean, *The Warden of the Plains and Other Stories of Life in the Canadian North-West* (Toronto: William Briggs, 1896), 55.
28 Maclean, *Warden of the Plains*, 56–7.
29 Maclean, *Warden of the Plains*, 58.
30 Maclean, *Warden of the Plains*, 62.
31 George Bird Grinnell, *Blackfoot Lodge Tales: The Story of a Prairie People* (1892; reprint, Lincoln: University of Nebraska Press, 1962), 215–16.
32 Beatrice Blackwood, "Blood Indian Notes," in *Pictures Bring Us Messages/Sinaakssiiksi aohtsimaahpihkookiyaawa: Photographs and Histories from the Kainai Nation*, by Alison K. Brown and Laura Peers, with members of the Kainai Nation (Toronto: University of Toronto Press, 2006), 236.
33 Bruce S. Elliott, *Irish Migrants in the Canadas: A New Approach*, 2nd ed. (Montreal and Kingston: McGill-Queen's University Press, 2004), 208. Another account from nineteenth century Upper Canada: "No dowry and no coming out meant no introductions to eligible young men, and therefore, no likely prospects of suitors, even from the middle class" in Barbara Williams, *A Gentlewoman in Upper Canada: The Journals, Letters, and Art of Anne Langton* (Toronto: University of Toronto Press, 2008), 10.

34 Blackwood, "Blood Indian Notes," 238.
35 Blackwood, "Blood Indian Notes," 238.
36 Esther Schiff Goldfrank, *Changing Configurations in the Social Organization of a Blackfoot Tribe During the Reserve Period* (Seattle: University of Washington Press, 1966), 52–3.
37 Goldfrank, *Changing Configurations in the Social Organization of a Blackfoot Tribe During the Reserve Period*, 53.
38 Official Report of the Debates of the House of Commons of the Dominion of Canada: Fourth Session, Fourth Parliament (Ottawa: Maclean, Roger & Co., 1882), 485.
39 Official Report of the Debates of the House of Commons of the Dominion of Canada: Fourth Session, Fourth Parliament, 486.
40 *The Bystander* (March 1881): 137.
41 "Our Mormon Settlers," *The Macleod Gazette*, 27 September 1887.
42 "Our Mormon Settlers." The statement was incorrect because among the first to settle around Lee's Creek were polygamists. Some of these polygamist early settlers were Charles Ora Card, John A. Woolf, Henry L. Hinman (1837–1921), John W. Taylor (1858–1916), Richard Pilling (1833–1906), Thomas Rowell Leavitt, Josiah Austin Hammer (1855–1922), Thomas Duce (1846–1926), and Ephraim Harker (1854–1932).
43 "Mormons in Canada," *Edmonton Bulletin*, 21 December 1889.
44 "Mormons in Canada."
45 9 November 1888, MSS 1543, Charles Ora Card collection, 19th Century Western & Mormon Manuscripts, L. Tom Perry Special Collections, Harold B. Lee Library, Brigham Young University (hereafter MSS 1543, LTPSC).
46 10 November 1888, MSS 1543, LTPSC.
47 10 November 1888, MSS 1543, LTPSC.
48 10 November 1888, MSS 1543, LTPSC.
49 10 November 1888, MSS 1543, LTPSC.
50 14 November 1888, MSS 1543, LTPSC.
51 16 November 1888, MSS 1543, LTPSC.
52 *The Canada Presbyterian*, 21 November 1888, 760.
53 Official Report of the Debates of the House of Commons of the Dominion of Canada: Third Session-Sixth Parliament (Ottawa: Brown Chamberlin, 1889), 980.
54 Official Report of the Debates of the House of Commons of the Dominion of Canada: Fourth Session-Sixth Parliament (Ottawa: Brown Chamberlin, 1890), 342–3.
55 22 February 1890, MSS 1543, LTPSC.
56 Official Report of the Debates of the House of Commons of the Dominion of Canada: Fourth Session, Sixth Parliament (Ottawa: Brown Chamberlin, 1890), 3173.

Notes to pages 40–5   175

57 Official Report of the Debates of the House of Commons of the Dominion of Canada: Fourth Session, Sixth Parliament (Ottawa: Brown Chamberlin, 1890), 3173. Brigham Young, will, ca. 1887, Church History Library.
58 Official Report of the Debates of the House of Commons of the Dominion of Canada: Fourth Session, Sixth Parliament (Ottawa: Brown Chamberlin, 1890), 3176.
59 Official Report of the Debates of the House of Commons of the Dominion of Canada: Fourth Session, Sixth Parliament (Ottawa: Brown Chamberlin, 1890), 3179.
60 Official Report of the Debates of the House of Commons of the Dominion of Canada: Fourth Session-Sixth Parliament, 3179.
61 Official Report of the Debates of the House of Commons of the Dominion of Canada: Fourth Session, Sixth Parliament, 3179.
62 Debates of the Senate of the Dominion of Canada: Fourth Session, Sixth Parliament (Ottawa: Brown Chamberlin, 1890), 583.
63 Debates of the Senate of the Dominion of Canada: Fourth Session, Sixth Parliament, 584.
64 "An Act further to amend the Criminal Law," 53 Victoria, ch. 37, sec. 10 (Revised Statutes of Canada (R.S.C.), ch. 161, sec. 4).
65 "An Act further to Amend the Criminal Law," 53 Victoria, ch. 37, sec. 11 (R.S.C., ch. 161, sec. 5).
66 "Official Declaration 1," Scriptures, Church of Jesus Christ of Latter-day Saints, https://www.lds.org/scriptures/dc-testament/od/1?lang=eng.
67 26 December 1893, MSS 1543, LTPSC.
68 26 December 1893, MSS 1543, LTPSC.
69 26 December 1893, MSS 1543, LTPSC.
70 Stake conference minutes, 28 November 1897, Cardston Alberta Stake General Minutes, 1894–1974, Church History Library.
71 Relief Society minutes, 2 March 1905, Cardston Ward Relief Society Minutes and Records, 1887–1911, Church History Library.
72 "The Criminal Code, 1892," 55 & 56 Victoria, ch. 29, sec. 275.
73 "The Criminal Code, 1892," 55 & 56 Victoria, ch. 29, sec. 275
74 53 Victoria, ch. 37, sec. 11 (R.S.C., ch. 161, sec. 5).
75 L. W. Herchmer, Commissioner, North-West Mounted Police, Annual Report of Commissioner L. W. Herchmer North-West Mounted Police, 1893, *Sessional Papers of the Dominion of Canada: Volume 11, Fourth Session of the Seventh Parliament, Session 1894* (Ottawa: S.E. Dawson, 1894), 15–10.
76 Herchmer, Annual Report, 1893.
77 Fred W. Wilkins, Report of F. W. Wilkins, D.T.S. Subdivision and Trail Surveys in South-Western Alberta, *Sessional Papers of the Dominion of Canada: Volume 9, Fifth Session of the Seventh Parliament, Session 1895* (Ottawa: S.E. Dawson, 1895), 13–39.

78 Wilkins, Report, 1895.
79 Charles W. Speers, Report of C.W. Speers, General Colonization Agent, *Sessional Papers of the Dominion of Canada: Volume 10, Fifth Session of the Eighth Parliament, Session 1900* (Ottawa: S.E. Dawson, 1900), 13–139–13–140.
80 R. Burton Deane letter to Commissioner Lawrence W. Herchmer, 17 March 1899, microfilm, "Mormons at Cardstone [sic] – Report on polygamous practices amongst," Royal Canadian Mounted Police fonds, Subject files, volume 169, Library and Archives Canada.
81 E.H. Bolderson letter to R. Burton Deane, 10 February 1899, microfilm, "Mormons at Cardstone [sic] – Report on polygamous practices amongst," Royal Canadian Mounted Police fonds, Subject files, volume 169, Library and Archives Canada.
82 "Local and General," *Cardston Record*, 8 February 1899, 4.
83 E.H. Bolderson letter to R. Burton Deane, 10 February 1899, microfilm, "Mormons at Cardstone [sic] – Report on polygamous practices amongst," Royal Canadian Mounted Police fonds, Subject files, volume 169, Library and Archives Canada.
84 "A Big Family," *The Children's Record* 14, no. 8 (August 1899): 123. In the same year Canadian author Lily Dougall (1858–1923) released her book about Joseph Smith, titled *The Mormon Prophet* (Toronto: The W. J. Gage Company, 1899).
85 John H. Blackmore, autobiography, 14 November 1935, "The Story of My Life," John Blackmore fonds, Glenbow Archives, Calgary, Alberta.
86 "Social Credit Group Will Support King if He Implements Promises; Blackmore Sure Dividend Possible," *Lethbridge Daily Herald*, 22 November 1935, 6. Government of Canada, Census of Canada, 1901, Library and Archives Canada, http://data2.collectionscanada.ca/1901/z/z004/jpg/z000178894.jpg. The 1901 Census showed William Blackmore's naturalization date as 1896.
87 Cardston Historical Society, "Biography of John Horn Blackmore." MSS 838, Minutes of Faculty Meetings, 1910–1921, LTPSC. Also see Government of Canada, Census of Manitoba, Saskatchewan, and Alberta, 1916, Library and Archives Canada, http://data2.collectionscanada.ca/006003/t-21951/jpg/31228_4363980-00947.jpg. Blackmore listed as High School teacher. "Old-Timer of Cardston Dead," *Lethbridge Daily Herald*, 12 April 1918, 5. Cardston Historical Society, "Biography of John Horn Blackmore." Also see Ernest G. Mardon, Austin A. Mardon, and Catherine Mardon, *The Mormon Contribution to Alberta Politics*, ed. Talicia Dutchin (Edmonton: Golden Meteorite Press, 2011), 17.
88 "Boy Scouts Lauded by Mormon Apostle at Raymond Meeting," *Lethbridge Daily Herald*, 17 August 1922, 5. "Fathers and Sons of Three Stakes to Stage Outing," *Lethbridge Daily Herald*, 1 May 1924, 5.

89 "Social Credit Group Will Support King," 6.
90 John H. Blackmore, letter to Winston Blackmore, 20 February 1939, John Blackmore fonds, Glenbow Archives, Calgary, Alberta.
91 "Reverence for God," John Blackmore fonds, Glenbow Archives, Calgary, Alberta.
92 Janet Bennion, "History, Culture, and Variability of Mormon Schismatic Groups," in *Modern Polygamy in the United States: Historical, Cultural, and Legal Issues*, ed. Cardell K. Jacobson with Lara Burton (New York: Oxford University Press, 2011), 102–3. Also see Janet Bennion, *Polygamy in Primetime: Media, Gender, and Politics in Mormon Fundamentalism* (Waltham, MA: Brandeis University Press, 2012), 25. Bradley, *Kidnapped from That Land*, 19, 27, 50–2. D. Michael Quinn, "Plural Marriage and Mormon Fundamentalism," in *Fundamentalisms and Society: Reclaiming the Sciences, Education, and the Family*, ed. Martin E. Marty and R. Scott Appleby (Chicago: The University of Chicago Press, 1993), 240–93.
93 Bennion, *Polygamy in Primetime*, 26. Bradley, *Kidnapped from That Land*, 59, 64–85. Ken Driggs, "After the Manifesto: Modern Polygamy and Fundamentalist Mormons," *Journal of Church and State* 32, no. 2 (Spring 1990): 381–2. Ken Driggs, "'This Will Someday Be the Head and Not the Tail of the Church': A History of the Mormon Fundamentalists at Short Creek," *Journal of Church and State* 43, no. 1 (Winter 2001): 65–6. Ken Driggs, "Imprisonment, Defiance, and Division: A History of Mormon Fundamentalism in the 1940s and 1950s," *Dialogue: A Journal of Mormon Thought* 38, no. 1 (2005): 73–80.
94 Doctrine and Covenants 132.
95 Bennion, *Polygamy in Primetime*, 61–5. Bradley, *Kidnapped from That Land*, 1–3. Driggs, "After the Manifesto," 370–1, 375. Gordon, *The Mormon Question*, 22–3. Cardell K. Jacobson and Lara Burton, "Prologue: The Incident at Eldorado, Texas," in *Modern Polygamy in the United States: Historical, Cultural, and Legal Issues*, ed. Cardell K. Jacobson and Lara Burton (New York: Oxford University Press, 2011), xx. Quinn, "Plural Marriage and Mormon Fundamentalism," 243.
96 Lorna Blackmore, Affidavit #1, Sworn 25 June 2010, No. S-097767, Vancouver Registry, in the Supreme Court of British Columbia, in the Matter of: The Constitutional Question Act, R.S.B.C. 1996, C.68, etc. Owen LeBaron (1918–75) was related to the murderer and leader of the Church of the First Born of the Lamb of God Ervil LeBaron (1925–81). Owen and Ervil shared a great-grandfather David LeBaron (1822–1905).
97 Orpha Vance Blackmore, ed., "Life of Harold Horn (Pete) Blackmore" (unpublished manuscript, May 1997), Microsoft Word file.
98 *Lethbridge Herald*, 23 August 1947.

178   Notes to pages 49–52

99   Frank A. Cook letter to Easter Wood, 23 September 1947, Letter to Easter Wood, Ottawa 1st Ward General Minutes, 1926–1973, Church History Library.
100   Hilda Crawshaw, witness Statement, Ottawa 1st Ward General Minutes, 1926–1973, Church History Library.
101   Hilda Crawshaw, witness Statement, Ottawa 1st Ward General Minutes, 1926–1973, Church History Library.
102   Disfellowshipment is a temporary suspension of membership privileges. A disfellowshipped person remains a member but cannot enter temples, hold Church callings, exercise the priesthood, partake in the Sacrament, or participate openly in meetings. See Hafen, "Disciplinary Procedures," 385–7.
103   MSS 3116, Octave W. Ursenbach, Report of a meeting held at Cardston, Alberta, Tuesday, 14 October 1947 with Elder John H. Blackmore of Cardston Alberta, Octave W. Ursenbach papers, LTPSC (hereafter MSS 3116, LTPSC). Also see Willard Smith letter to Octave W. Ursenbach, 17 October 1947, MSS 3116, LTPSC. "I appreciate receiving the very fine report which you prepared of our meeting held last Tuesday evening with Brother Blackmore. I think you covered the facts well without prejudice."
104   Ursenbach, Report of a meeting held at Cardston, Alberta, Tuesday, 14 October 1947 with Elder John H. Blackmore of Cardston Alberta, MSS 3116, LTPSC.
105   Ezra Taft Benson letter to Willard L. Smith, 10 November 1947, MSS 3116, LTPSC. Also see Ward Historical Record Book, 1945–1950, Cardston 1st Ward General Minutes, 1914–1977, Church History Library. "A letter outlining the fundamentalist teachings and activities of JH Blackmoere was read, and Bishop J. Forest Wood told of the meeting of the stake presidency, himself and JH Blackmore and of the instructions he had received from the stake presidency to summon Bro Blackmore to a bishops trial in which he would be tried for his standing in the church" – asked Heber Matkin and A. R. Jensen to serve the summons. Trial set for 26 November at home of David U. Watson.
106   "District News," *Lethbridge Herald*, 3 December 1947, 5.
107   "Excommunication Of Lethbridge M.P. Is Confirmed," *Lethbridge Herald*, 29 December 1947, 6.
108   "I'm One-Wife Man, Also I'm Faithful – Blackmore," *Toronto Daily Star*, 29 December 1947, 4.
109   "Blackmore Won't Go into Details," *Lethbridge Herald*, 30 December 1947, 2.
110   "Says Creston Valley Cases Are Set for Trial," *Lethbridge Herald*, 1 August 1953, 13.

111 "LDS Officials Hold Church Trial in B.C.," *Lethbridge Herald*, 5 August 1953, 11.
112 "10 Ousted From Mormon Faith In B.C. Colony," *Lethbridge Herald*, 21 August 1953, 1.
113 P.D. Clarke, Attorney for Zola B. Jeffs (Plaintiff), Complaint No. 65430, Filed 22 October 1940, District Court of the Third Judicial District in and for Salt Lake County, State of Utah. Utah State Archives, Salt Lake City, Utah.
114 J.W. McKnight, Attorney for Rulon Jeffs (Defendant), Rulon Jeffs' Answer to Complaint No. 65430, Filed 14 December 1940, District Court of the Third Judicial District in and for Salt Lake County, State of Utah. Utah State Archives, Salt Lake City, Utah.
115 Zina Brown letter to Mary Firmage, 3 March 1938, Hugh B. Brown Family Papers, 1835–1982, Church History Library.
116 Zina Brown letter to Mary Firmage, 14 April 1938, Hugh B. Brown Family Papers, 1835–1982, Church History Library.
117 Zina Brown letter to her daughters, 28 April 1938, Hugh B. Brown Family Papers, 1835–1982, Church History Library.
118 Hugh B. Brown letter to Zina Brown, 19 December 1939, Hugh B. Brown Family Papers, 1835–1982, Church History Library.
119 Hugh B. Brown letter to Zina Brown, 27 November 1940, Hugh B. Brown Family Papers, 1835–1982, Church History Library.
120 Hugh B. Brown letter to Zina Brown, 29 January 1941, Hugh B. Brown Family Papers, 1835–1982, Church History Library.
121 Zina Brown letter to Mry Firmage, 2 February 1941, Hugh B. Brown Family Papers, 1835–1982, Church History Library.

3 Women

1 Hannah Simmons Gibb, *Poems & Autobiography of Hannah Simmons Gibb 1855–1941* (Ogden, UT: Family Printer Bruce & Clarabelle Gibb, 1982), 54.
2 Estelle Freedman, "Separatism as Strategy: Female Institution Building and American Feminism, 1870–1930," *Feminist Studies* 5, no. 3 (Autumn 1979): 512. Michelle Zimbalist Rosaldo, "Woman, Culture, and Society: Theoretical Overview," in *Woman, Culture and Society*, eds. Michelle Zimbalist Rosaldo and Lousie Lamphere (Stanford: Stanford University Press, 1974), 17–42.
3 "If public and published documents are few and macro studies difficult, then we must investigate personal and private sources with greater seriousness." This is important for this entire book and comes from Margaret Conrad, "'Sundays Always Make Me Think of Home': Time and Place in Canadian Women's History," in *Rethinking Canada: The Promise of Women's History*, ed. Veronica Strong-Boag and Anita Clair Fellman (Toronto: Copp Clark Pitman Ltd., 1986), 69.

4 However, the Edmunds-Tucker Act of 1887 disfranchised all Utah women. Utah suffragists regained the vote in 1896 when Utah became the third state to have equal suffrage. See Carol Cornwall Madsen, "Woman Suffrage," in *Encyclopedia of Mormonism*, ed. David H. Ludlow (New York: Macmillan, 1992), 1572-3.
5 Yorgason, *Mormon Culture Region*, 74.
6 Yorgason, *Mormon Culture Region*, 54.
7 Cynthia R. Comacchio, "Introduction to Part Two," in *Framing Our Past: Constructing Canadian Women's History in the Twentieth Century*, ed. Sharon Anne Cook, Lorna R. McLean, and Kate O'Rourke (Montreal & Kingston: McGill-Queen's University Press, 2001), 75. Also, "Borders appear to have the biggest impact on a woman's experiences when she occupies an additional category (be it racial or ethnic or religious or sexual) that is already marginalized by the nation state in which she resides or to which she is trying to gain entry." Sheila McManus, "Unsettled Pasts, Unsettling Borders: Women, Wests, Nations," in *One Step Over the Line: Toward a History of Women in the North American Wests*, ed. Elizabeth Jameson and Sheila McManus (Edmonton: The University of Alberta Press, 2008), 41.
8 See the chapter on "Gender and Sexual Orientation," in Claudia L. Bushman, *Contemporary Mormonism: Latter-day Saints in Modern America* (Westport, CT: Praeger, 2006).
9 Mary Farrell Bednarowski, "Widening the Banks of the Mainstream: Women Constructing Theologies," in *Women's Leadership in Marginal Religions: Explorations Outside the Mainstream*, ed. Catherine Wessinger (Urbana and Chicago: University of Illinois Press, 1993), 213.
10 Comacchio, "Introduction," 77.
11 Zina Y. Card, "The Sisters in Canada," *The Woman's Exponent* 19, no. 13 (December 1890): 101.
12 Zina Y. Card, "The Sisters in Canada," *The Woman's Exponent* 19, no. 13 (December 1890): 101.
13 Zina Y. Card, "The Sisters in Canada," *The Woman's Exponent* 19, no. 13 (December 1890): 101.
14 Moroni 10: 8.
15 Doctrine and Covenants 46: 11.
16 The Articles of Faith 1: 7. "Through the end of the nineteenth century, when Mormons gathered in priesthood quorums or in Relief Society ... they regularly participated in speaking in tongues, inspired prophecy, weeping, impromptu laying on of hands ... But in the early twentieth century leaders in the church began to discourage such practices through public letters and instructions to local leaders." See Bowman, *The Mormon People*, 173.
17 6 June 1895, MSS 1543, LTPSC. At Neils Hansen's ranch, "Sister Hammer and Sarah Hinman enjoyed the gift of tongues, and my wife Zina and

Nellie Hinman [soon to be Pitcher] had the gift of interpretation of tongues. Many blessings were pronounced upon those present. Sister Nellie Taylor spoke in an inspired way on the gifts and blessings of the Gospel, and we had a very spiritual meeting and a spiritual feast to the satisfaction of the Sts present ... by request I dedicated Bro Neils Hanson's house and land by prayer." See 15 August 1895, MSS 1543, LTPSC.

18 Church members referred to the Alberta settlements as "the Northern Mission" or "the Canadian Mission." Zina Y. Card related a dream from a sister in Salt Lake City who believed the "Northern Mission ... was dictated by the Spirit of the Lord." See Relief Society minutes, 8 December 1887, Cardston Ward Relief Society Minutes, 1887–1911, Church History Library. In 1889, Card called the LDS settlements "the mission in Canada." See 28 October 1889, MSS 1543, LTPSC.

19 Beecher, "Mormon Women in Southern Alberta," 226. Claudia Bushman wrote: "The women of the early Church were as involved in spiritual experiences as men. The spirit did not come through priesthood leaders alone ... women tended to be more receptive to the spirit. They were particularly blessed in the 'woman's sphere': their children were healed, their husbands blessed, their families provided for." See Bushman, "Mystics and Healers," in *Mormon Sisters: Women in Early Utah*, ed. Claudia Lauper Bushman (Cambridge: Emmeline Press, 1976), 2.

20 20 November 1895, MSS 1543, LTPSC.

21 20 November 1895, MSS 1543, LTPSC.

22 6 February 1896, MSS 1543, LTPSC.

23 8 February 1896, MSS 1543, LTPSC. Hammer moved on to Sena Matkin (1860–1914) and blessed her as "one of the choice Handmaidens of the Lord." Card, also a recipient of Hammer's gifts, documented his blessing in his diary: "[She] said to me lift up my heart & rejoice for the Lord had respect unto my works & pronounced many blessings upon me for I should have every righteous desire of my heart." See also 5 November 1896, MSS 1543, LTPSC. In November at a fast meeting, Sarah Hinman (1871–1969) spoke in tongues and approached Card, putting her hands on his head she stated that he "was a servant of God and had his spirit and said even [his] youngest children would rise up and call [him] blessed." Hinman continued to tell Card he "had been a father to the people." Afterwards, she put her hands on Bishop Farrell's head and said, "Many of the people of his ward had been contrary but he should have power over them and that his wayward children should turn to the faith of truth." According to Card, "She also blessed the brethren recently called on missions ... & those that should be gathered here & their children should rise up & bless them. She also sang in tongues & praised the Lord."

Card "felt [he] had received a greater blessing from the Lord through this humble widow."
24 E. B. Wells, "General Conference, Relief Society," *The Woman's Exponent* 25, no. 20 (April 1897): 134.
25 28 May 1897, MSS 1543, LTPSC. Speaking in tongues, Elizabeth Hammer blessed her husband, the bishop of the ward, Josiah Hammer (1855–1922) "that he should recover & not to fret about his [other] wife & infant son God had taken them & they would come up in the morn of the resurrection. 28 May 1897, MSS 1543, LTPSC. One of Josiah's plural wives Emily died earlier that year on 9 January. Their son Frank (born 25 October 1896) died on 21 March 1897.
26 5 June 1898, MSS 1543, LTPSC.
27 7 May 1899, MSS 1543, LTPSC. Also see 31 August 1899, MSS 1543, LTPSC. Visiting the Caldwell Alberta ward in August, Hammer spoke in tongues and blessed Father Caldwell and his family. Next, the visitors attended the meeting in Leavitt where Hammer blessed Apostle John W. Taylor (1858–1916), vowing "he should enjoy greater wisdom than formerly & be known in future as a great prophet."
28 14 September 1898, MSS 1543, LTPSC.
29 "The Recent Triennial in Washington," *The Young Woman's Journal* 10, no. 5 (May 1899): 195.
30 "The Recent Triennial in Washington," 201.
31 "The Recent Triennial in Washington," 206.
32 Joseph F. Smith, speech, 7 April 1900, *Seventieth Annual Conference of the Church of Jesus Christ of Latter-day Saints* (Salt Lake City: The Deseret News, 1900), 41. The same year Smith recommended to Church President Lorenzo Snow to separate the healing liturgy and allow only men to seal anointing. See Jonathan A. Stapley, "'The Last of the Old School': Joseph F. Smith and Latter-day Saint Liturgy," in *Joseph F. Smith: Reflections on the Man and His Times*, ed. Craig K. Manscill, Brian D. Reeves, Guy L. Dorius, and J. B. Haws (Provo, UT: Religious Studies Center; Salt Lake City: Deseret Book, 2013), 233–47.
33 Relief Society minutes, June 1902, Stirling Ward Relief Society Minutes and Records, 1899–1970, Church History Library. Also see 3 June 1902 and 6 June 1902, MSS 1543, LTPSC. Also see Mary Ann Ross Anderson, autobiographical sketch, "The Story of My Life: Mary Ann Ross Anderson," typescript, Low Family Histories, circa 1960, 2006, Church History Library. Alvira D. Bridge, biography, "Julia E. Hawkes Ririe, 1930–1933," photocopy, Taylor Stake Relief Society History, 1962, Church History Library.
34 MSS 1522, Joseph Y. Card diaries, 12 April 1921, 19th Century Western & Mormon Manuscripts, L. Tom Perry Special Collections, Harold B. Lee Library, Brigham Young University (hereafter cited as MSS 1522, LTPSC).

35 12 April 1921, MSS 1522, LTPSC. "As the society in which the Latter-day Saints lived became increasingly pluralistic, if not secular, the Mormon community no longer created its own internal regulatory mechanism ... rational organization and fixed rules replaced a sense of community as the means of establishing norms which the Saints were expected to observe." See Alexander, *Mormonism in Transition*, 94.
36 Heber Carss Jamieson, *Early Medicine in Alberta: The First Seventy-Five Years* (Edmonton: Canadian Medical Association Alberta division, 1947), 44.
37 Jamieson, *Early Medicine in Alberta*, 63.
38 Robert Lampard, "Cardston Medical Contracts and Canadian Medicare," *Alberta History* 54, no. 4 (2006): 6.
39 College of Physicians and Surgeons, *The North-West Territories medical register: Printed and published under the direction of the Council of the College of Physicians and Surgeons, N.W.T., in accordance with chapter 52 of the consolidated ordinances, North-West Territories, 1899, entitled an ordinance respecting the medical profession in force March 15, 1899* (Prince Albert, NWT: College of Physicians and Surgeons, N.W.T, 1899).
40 Lampard, "Cardston Medical Contracts," 6.
41 Edna Kells, "Story of the Cardston Hospital," *Cardston News*, 17 October 1929, 3.
42 Doctrine and Covenants 42:43.
43 Alexander, *Mormonism in Transition*, 195. George W. Cody and Heidi Hascall, "The History of Naturopathic Medicine: The Emergence and Evolution of an American School of Healing," in *Textbook of Natural Medicine*, 4th ed., ed. Joseph E. Pizzorno and Michael T. Murray (St. Louis: Churchill Livingtone, 2013): 36.
44 Joseph Smith, "President Joseph Smith's Journal," 19 April 1843, Joseph Smith Collection, Church History Library. For further information on the relationship between Mormonism and Thomsonian medical ideology, see Thomas Wolfe, "Steaming Saints: Mormons and the Thomsonian Movement in Nineteenth-Century America," in *Disease and Medical Care in the Mountain West: Essays on Region, History, and Practice*, ed. Martha L. Hildreth and Bruce T. Moran (Reno: University of Nevada Press, 1998): 16–28.
45 Norman Lee Smith, "Herbal Remedies: God's Medicine?" *Dialogue: A Journal of Mormon Thought* 12, no. 3 (1979): 47.
46 M.M. Groo, "R.S. Reports," *The Woman's Exponent* 2, no. 4 (1873): 26.
47 Mrs. L. Green Richards, "R.S. Reports," *The Woman's Exponent* 2, no. 4 (1873): 27.
48 "Household Hints," *The Woman's Exponent* 2, no. 20 (1874): 158. In 1882, the publication recommended "In every house there should be a little nook in which a few simple remedies are kept. Among them

should be extract of ginger, Dover's powder, peppermint, chlorate of potash, bicarbonate of soda, sweet oil, paregoric, camphor, arnica, a bottle of pure whisky, cotton, old muslin for bandages, some sticking plaster, a box of ground muster and some ready-made plasters." See "The Family Doctor-Shop," *The Woman's Exponent* 10, no. 21 (1882): 168. See also Marla Rawlings, *Favorite Utah Pioneer Recipes* (Bountiful, UT: Horizon Publishers, 2000), 124. A common home treatment for colds and sore throats was a mustard plaster made from dry mustard mixed with lard and applied to the throat or chest, then covered with a piece of warmed flannel. An Alberta version of the mustard plaster: "Trim the crust from a thin slice of light bread then sprinkle it thickly with ground mustard. Spread a thin cloth over the mustard and dampen with vinegar or water." See "Health Hints," *Raymond Rustler*, 7 January 1910, 2. In addition, Coughs could be treated with a syrup made from onions: "The onions were sliced, places in a pan, and covered with honey. They then were baked in an oven at 200 degrees until very clear. The mixture was then strained, with the onions being pushed against the strainer to remove any leftover juices from the onion. The syrup was then placed in a bottle and taken as needed for coughs." For a near identical recipe, see "Home Cures," *Magrath Pioneer*, 2 June 1908, 7. A different home remedy, without onions, for cough was "One-half ounce of camphor, one-half ounce of lobelia, one ounce of paregoric. Dose. Fifteen drops three or four times a day." See "Home Cures," *Magrath Pioneer*, 15 March 1910, 3. In addition to onions, vinegar was another staple for home remedies. One tablespoon cured stomach ache, diarrhea, food poisoning and heartburn. Rubbed on the skin it soothed sore muscles, sunburns, insect bites, and hives. Rawlings, *Favorite Utah Pioneer Recipes*, 125.

49 Austin Fife, "Pioneer Mormon Remedies," *Western Folklore* 16, no. 3 (1957): 153–61.
50 Anne Woywitka, "Pioneers in Sickness and in Health," *Alberta History* 49, no. 1 (2001): 16.
51 Sandra Rollings-Magnusson, "Flax Seed, Goose Grease, and Gun Power: Medical Practices by Women Homesteaders in Saskatchewan (1882–1914)," *Journal of Family History* 33, no. 4 (2008): 391.
52 "Simple Salve," *Cardston Record*, 17 September 1898, 3.
53 Zina D. Young, diary, November 1880–July 1892, microfilm, Zina Card Brown family collection, 1806–1972, Church History Library.
54 Magrath and District History Association, *Irrigation Builders* (Magrath, AB: Magrath and District History Association, 1974), 365.
55 Rojanea Jacobs Bingham, family history, ca. 1970, photocopy of typescript, Rojanea J. Bingham History of Dora Hinman Jacobs, circa 1970, Church History Library.

56 Christina Nielsen (1868–1965), Mary Woolf (1877–1955), and Mariah Thomas (1839–1907). Relief Society minutes, 20 April 1905, Cardston Ward Relief Society Minutes, 1887–1911, Church History Library. One lesson Nielsen might have taught was the use of celery tops and roots to make tea for the treatment of nervousness, or the use of nutmeg combined with lard and spread over the lungs to treat cold on the lungs. See "The Home Doctor," *Magrath Pioneer*, 29 May 1907, 2; "Home Cures," *Magrath Pioneer*, 26 May 1908, 3. The 1907 article also suggested applying goose oil to loosen stiff joins; rubbing olive oil and quinine on the back and chest to prevent cold settling on lungs; and wetting a cold sore with camphor and covering it with powdered subnitrate of bismuth. An article in September 1908 explained a remedy for burns: "Saturate a wad of cotton with ammonia and pat the burn with it. Keep doing this until the fire is all drawn out, which will be in ten or fifteen minutes." See "The Home Doctor," *Magrath Pioneer*, 15 September 1908, 6. A poultice of witch hazel, which could be used for chilblains, could also have been shared by one of the Relief Society members. They might have instructed "In a small saucepan put a square, folded flannel cloth. Pour over this enough witch hazel to thoroughly moisten it. Heat and place the flannel cloth over the pain. Cover with dry flannel, and pin a towel over it to keep it in place." Also see "The Home Doctor," *Taber Free Press*, 26 March 1908, 2. A cure for detaching fishbones caught in the throat was to swallow a raw egg, see "Health and Beauty Hints," *Taber Free Press*, 23 April 1908, 7. To treat a cavity in a tooth, one must "saturate a small piece of absorbent cotton in oil of cloves, tincture of myrrh or laudanum and place in the cavity." See "Health and Beauty Hints," *Taber Free Press*, 23 April 1908, 7. The herbalists could also have recommended using red pepper to treat neuralgia by applying a wet cloth with red pepper over top to the area of pain. See "Health Hints," *Raymond Rustler*, 19 March 1909, 7. Latter-day Saints used home remedies for more than mild injuries and common colds. During the influenza epidemic of 1918–19, Rachel Forsyth (1890–1986) remembered "Brother Harris" mixing ground onions and salt in a flour paste and wrapping it in gauze against the chest and back of the sufferer. In addition to this poultice, Harris made his patients drink water until they threw up and then repeated the process. Forsyth claimed no one died that followed this treatment. See Rachel Ackroyd Forsyth History, Magrath Museum. The Brother Harris that Forsyth mentioned was probably Thomas William Harris (1868–1941) who moved his family to Raymond in 1904 and moved to Taber between 1916 and 1921. In the history of Barnwell, Harris was remembered for his home remedies and famous onion poultices during the flu epidemic. See Barnwell Relief Society, *Barnwell History* (Ann Arbor: Edwards Bros., 1952), 25.

57 Chris Rigby Arrington, "Pioneer Midwives," in *Mormon Sister: Women in Early Utah*, ed. Claudia Lauper Bushman (Cambridge: Emmeline Press, 1976), 47.
58 Arrington, "Pioneer Midwives," 47.
59 Vernon Shaw, "Our Letter Box," *Cardston News*, 18 May 1937, 4. Hammer arrived in the District of Alberta with some of the earliest Mormon settlers in 1887, but she soon returned to Utah and completed an eight-month course in obstetrics. By the spring of 1888, Hammer was back in Cardston, a trained midwife. See, Beryl Bectell, *Chief Mountain Country: A History of Cardston and District*, vol. 2 (Cardston: Cardston and District Historical Society, 1987), 12.
60 "Ella Elizabeth Nelson Laid to Rest," *Cardston News*, 11 November 1941, 5.
61 Merrill, "A History of Ella Elizabeth Thomas Nelson." She claimed Nelson's only tools were a pair of scissors, a string cord, a bottle of Lysol or iodine, and a small bottle of chloroform.
62 Merrill, "A History of Ella Elizabeth Thomas Nelson."
63 Merrill, "A History of Ella Elizabeth Thomas Nelson." Nearby in areas around Aetna and Kimball, doctors and nurses were even scarcer, and people remembered "that health care consisted of home remedies, folk medicine, faith, prayer, and Priesthood blessings." Observing the need for health care, Bishop Richard Pilling (1833–1906) asked midwife Eva Hansen (1869–1950) to train the Relief Society sisters in midwifery. One of these women was Annie Jensen (1873–1966) of Aetna. In "Health Care and Midwifery," Hicken recorded that Dr. Brant "would ask Annie to travel with him to administer to the sick, as she always brought a suitcase of supplies, such as fresh clean apron, bandages, towels, baby clothes, blankets, a nightgown for the mother, and a kit of medical supplies." Jensen gained even more medical experience by assisting Dr. Mulloy, the doctor of Cardston, during the Influenza epidemic of 1918–19. See Alice Ruth Hicken, "Health Care and Midwifery," in *Range 25 Country Aetna and Kimball Areas*, ed. Kelvin Jensen and Avon Jensen (2005), no page number. Also see Keith Shaw, ed., *Chief Mountain Country: A History of Cardston and District*, vol. 1 (Cardston, AB: Cardston and District Historical Society, 1978), 355. Early midwives of the Magrath region were Mary Edwards, Mrs. Dora Dudley, and Mrs. Eleanor Spencer. See Walter E. Brown, "Magrath Hospitals," in *Irrigation Builders*, 363.
64 "Funeral Services for Mrs. Ella Milner," *Raymond Recorder*, 4 June 1943, 1.
65 Archibald F. Bennett, Ella M. Bennett, and Barbara Bennett Roach, *Valiant in the Faith: Gardner and Sarah Snow and Their Family* (Murray, UT: Roylance Publishing, 1990), 195–6, Raymond Museum and Historical Society, Raymond, Alberta.

66 Nephi K. Kezerian, "Sick, Blessing the," in *Encyclopedia of Mormonism*, ed. Daniel H. Ludlow (New York: Macmillan, 1992), 1308.
67 Hannah Marie Child Russell, letter to granddaughter Beth, 10 February 1934, in *Roots and Wings*, compiled by Luann De Hart Gray (Boise, ID: L.D.H. Gray, 2000), 206–7.
68 Russell, letter to granddaughter, 208.
69 Bushman, "Mystics and Healers," 2.
70 Mary Ellen Kimball, journal, 2 March 1856, Church History Library, as cited in Linda King Newell, "A Gift Given: A Gift Taken: Washing, Anointing, and Blessing the Sick among Mormon Women," *Sunstone* 22, 3–4 (June 1999): 17.
71 Dorothy Jean Merrill, "A History of Ella Elizabeth Thomas Nelson," contributed by Dorothy Jean Merrill on 15 January 2015, https://www.familysearch.org/photos/artifacts/12705480.
72 Bennett, Bennett, and Road, *Valiant in the Faith*, 194. Summarizing her mother Annie Baker's (1858–1933) gifts, Alice Kraft (1897–1990) wrote that Baker's "healing hands were a gift of God and so she regarded them, ever praying for the physical stamina to meet the needs of the people she was called to serve." Like his mother, Thomas Rowell Leavitt II (1862–1939) claimed he was blessed with the gift of healing – neighbours "called at all hours of the day and night to help administer to sick, and sit beside a sick bed where death hovered near ... Through the power of the priesthood, the sick have been healed almost instantly." See Leavitt Family Organization, *The Life of Thomas Rowell Leavitt and His Descendants* (Lethbridge, Alberta: The Herald Printers, 1975), 51 and 142. In addition, Rojanea Bingham (1917–2011) remembered her mother Dora Jacob (1880–1953) "would rub the afflicted part with consecrated oil and pray that we would regain our wanted health and strength." See Rojanea Jacobs Bingham, family history, ca. 1970, photocopy of typescript, Rojanea J. Bingham History of Dora Hinman Jacobs, circa 1970, Church History Library.
73 Cleo Ririe, "My Mother, Allie Jensen – Nurse, Spiritual Advisor & Confident," in *Stories of Allie Zittella Rogers* (Magrath, AB: s.n., 2005). Cleo's father Christian Jensen (1868–1958) was alive and able to administer to her, but she only mentions her mother's healing gift.
74 Cynthia Wight, diary, October 1910, Hans E.N. Wight fonds, Glenbow Archives, Calgary, Alberta.
75 Charles W. Fossey, personal history, 4 May 1955, "Brief History," Magrath Museum.
76 Beth Johnson, reminiscence, 1952, "Reminiscence," Carol and Beth Johnson Fonds, Glenbow Archives, Calgary, Alberta.
77 Cynthia R. Comacchio, *The Infinite Bonds of Family: Domesticity in Canada, 1850–1940* (Toronto: University of Toronto Press, 1999), 91.

78 Comacchio, *Infinite Bonds*, 103–4.
79 Yorgason, *Mormon Culture Region*, 71.
80 "Relief Society," Handbook 2: Administering the Church, Church of Jesus Christ of Latter-day Saints, https://www.lds.org/handbook/handbook-2-administering-the-church/relief-society?lang=eng.
81 "Relief Society," Handbook 2.
82 Relief Society minutes, 2 February 1888, Cardston Ward Relief Society Minutes and Records, 1887–1911, Church History Library.
83 Relief Society minutes, 2 January 1890, Cardston Ward Relief Society Minutes and Records, 1887–1911, Church History Library.
84 Relief Society minutes, 5 October 1895, Cardston Alberta Stake Relief Society Minutes and Records, 1894–1973, Church History Library.
85 Relief Society minutes, 21 March 1896, Cardston Alberta Stake Relief Society Minutes and Records, 1894–1973, Church History Library.
86 Relief Society minutes, 4 August 1899, Cardston Alberta Stake Relief Society Minutes and Records, 1894–1973, Church History Library.
87 "History of Taylor Stake Relief Society 1902–1962," Taylor Stake Relief Society history, 1962, Church History Library. Also see Jane E. Bates, biography, photocopy of typescript, "Biographical Sketch of Mary Lucretia Hyde Woolf," Virginia F. Bates Layton Collection of Family Biographies, Church History Library.
88 Tina Hatch, "'Changing Times Bring Changing Conditions': Relief Society, 1960 to the Present," *Dialogue: A Journal of Mormon Thought* 37, no. 3 (2004): 68.
89 Hatch, "Relief Society, 1960 to the Present," 66.
90 Leonard J. Arrington and Davis Bitton, *The Mormon Experience: A History of the Latter-day Saints* (New York: Knopf, 1979), 235.
91 Comacchio, *Infinite Bonds*, 148.
92 Comacchio, *Infinite Bonds*, 155.
93 Winnifred Newton Thomas, oral history, interviewed by Jessie L. Embry, Cardston, Alberta, 22 and 23 July 1982, transcript, LDS Polygamy Oral History Project, LTPSC.
94 Winnifred Newton Thomas, oral history, interviewed by Jessie L. Embry, Cardston, Alberta, 22 and 23 July 1982, transcript, LDS Polygamy Oral History Project, LTPSC.
95 J. Harris Walker, biography, "Life History of Fannye Harris Walker," contributed by L. Wolsey on April 13, 2017, https://www.familysearch.org/photos/artifacts/35712448.
96 Joseph F. Smith, Discourse delivered at Logan, 6 February 1881, Reported by George F. Gibbs, "The Persecutions of the Ancient Saints – The Organization of the Church in Our Day – Necessity of Obedience to the Laws of the Gospel, Etc.," *Journal of Discourse Volume 22* (Liverpool: Albert Carrington, 1882): 47.

97 Wilford Woodruff, 25 April 1858, *Wilford Woodruff's Journal* (Salt Lake City: Kraut's Pioneer Press, 1982), https://archive.org/details/WoodruffWilfordJournalSelections.
98 Leavitt Family Organization, *Thomas Rowell Leavitt*, 179
99 Frank H. Pitcher, autobiography, ca. 1978, photocopy of manuscript, Frank H. Pitcher autobiography, circa 1978, Church History Library.
100 Ezra Love Paxman, autobiographical account, ca. 1959, "The Life Story of Ezra Paxman," Ezra Love Paxman fonds, Glenbow Archives, Calgary, Alberta.
101 Willard Montgomery Brooks, oral history, interviewed by Charles Ursenbach, Cardston and Calgary, Alberta, 1974–5, transcript, Church History Library.
102 Mauss, *Angel and the Beehive*, x.
103 Joseph F. Smith, Anthon H. Lund, and Charles W. Penrose, "Editor's Table: Home Evening," 27 April 1915, *Improvement Era* 18 no. 8 (June 1915): 733.
104 Xarissa Merkley Clarke, oral history, interviewed by Marsha C. Martin, 4 December 1982, transcript, LDS Family Life Oral History Project, 1959–84, LTPSC.
105 Eva Dahl Salmon, oral history, interviewed by Margaret E. Young, Lethbridge, Alberta, 8 June 1983, Lethbridge Alberta East Stake oral history program, Church History Library.
106 Winnifred Newton Thomas, oral history, interviewed by Jessie L. Embry, Cardston, Alberta, 22 and 23 July 1982, transcript, LDS Polygamy Oral History Project, LTPSC.
107 Armand L. Mauss, "The Mormon Struggle with Assimilation and Identity: Trends and Developments Since Midcentury," *Dialogue: A Journal of Mormon Thought* 27, no. 1 (1994): 132.
108 Armand L. Mauss, "Assimilation and Ambivalence: The Mormon Reaction to Americanization," *Dialogue: A Journal of Mormon Thought* 22, no. 1 (1989): 41.
109 Hyrum Bennion Jr. and Stella Richards, *Joseph Harker Family History Pioneers Utah Canada Idaho*, ed. Jack H. Adamson (Salt Lake City: Acorn Printing Co., 1949), 244.
110 John W. Bennett and Seena B. Kohl, *Settling the Canadian-American West, 1890–1915: Pioneer Adaption and Community Building an Anthropological History* (Lincoln and London: University of Nebraska Press, 1995), 147.
111 Barbara J. Nicholson, "Feminism in the Prairie Provinces to 1916," (MA thesis, University of Calgary, 1974), 89.
112 Catherine C. Cole and Ann Milovic, "Education, Community Service, and Social Life: The Alberta Women's Institutes and Rural Families,

190 Notes to pages 81–3

1909–1945," in *Standing on New Ground: Women in Alberta*, ed. Catherine A. Cavanaugh and Randi R. Warne (Edmonton: The University of Alberta Press, 1993), 20.
113 Bectell, *Chief Mountain Country*, vol. 2, 5.
114 "Brief History of Cardston Women's Institute," *Cardston News*, 23 August 1934, 1.
115 "Mrs. Huyck Points Out Aims of W.I.," *Cardston News*, 18 March 1926, 1.
116 "Baby Clinic Very Successful," *Raymond Recorder*, 5 July 1934, 2.
117 "News Notes," *Raymond Recorder*, 10 June 1927, 8.
118 *Cardston News*, 30 April 1931, 1.
119 "W.I. Studies Child Welfare," *Cardston News*, 9 June 1939, 1.
120 "Red Cross Is Doing Well," *Raymond Leader*, 15 April 1916, 1.
121 "Institute Holds Annual Meeting," *Raymond Leader*, 16 December 1916, 1
122 "W.I. Meeting," *Raymond Recorder*, 20 June 1941, 1.
123 Bradford James Rennie, *The Rise of Agrarian Democracy: The United Farmers and Farm Women of Alberta, 1909–1921* (Toronto: University of Toronto Press, 2000), 101.
124 Rennie, *The Rise of Agrarian Democracy*, 118.
125 United Farm Women of Alberta, *The U.F.W.A.: The Organization for Alberta Farm Women* (Calgary: United Farm Women of Alberta, 1920), 4, http://peel.library.ualberta.ca/bibliography/4648/3.html.
126 United Farm Women of Alberta, *The U.F.W.A.*, 10.
127 "Thumb-Nail Sketch No. 12: Talitha May Carlson," *Cardston News*, 2 February 1937, 4. 61 members. Even before Carlson climbed the ranks of the UFWA, other LDS women participated at the provincial level too. Jehzell Merkley (1874–1955) of Magrath was the director of the Lethbridge District for the year 1923. After Merkley came, Allie Jensen and she held the position of director for 1924 and 1925. At a board meeting in Calgary on 24 January 1925, the executive committee appointed Jensen convenor of social services, the same role they would give to Carlson in 1927. See United Farm Women of Alberta, convention minutes, 18 January 1923, scanned microfilm, United Farmers of Alberta fonds, Glenbow Archives, Calgary, Alberta (hereafter cited as UFA fonds). Also see Miss J.B. Kidd, "The United Farm Women of Alberta in Convention," *The U.F.A.*, 15 February 1923, 6. United Farm Women of Alberta, convention minutes, 17 January 1924, scanned microfilm, UFA fonds. Also see Miss J.B. Kidd, "The Women's Convention in Retrospect," *The U.F.A.*, 1 February 1924, 7. United Farm Women of Alberta, board meeting minutes, 24 January 1925, scanned microfilm, UFA fonds. Raymond also had a UFWA branch and its members also participated and interacted with non-

Latter-day Saints. In February 1926 Oral King (1893–1948) reported on the annual UFWA convention she attended in Calgary to a gathering of UFWA members at Mabel Heninger's (1896–1967) home. See "U.F.W.A. Meeting," *Raymond Recorder*, 12 February 1926, 8.
128 "Grows from Desire for Decent Standard," *The U.F.A.*, 3 June 1926, 28.
129 "Grows from Desire for Decent Standard," 28. Also see "New Local at Cardston," *The U.F.A.*, 17 June 1926, 9. Carlson was director for Lethbridge until 1930.
130 United Farm Women of Alberta, convention minutes, 18 January 1927, scanned microfilm, UFA fonds.
131 "Interesting Series of Program for Women's Local," *The U.F.A.*, 16 April 1927, 25.
132 Inez R. Bennett, "Lethbridge Constituency Holds First U.F.W.A. Conference," *The U.F.A.*, 1 December 1930, 18.
133 Bennett, "Lethbridge Constituency," 19.
134 United Farm Women of Alberta, convention minutes, 22 January 1930, scanned microfilm, UFA fonds.
135 Megan Sanborn Jones, *Performing American Identity in Anti-Mormon Melodrama* (New York: Routledge, 2009), 142. Also see W. Paul Reeve, *Religion of a Different Color: Race and the Mormon Struggle for Whiteness* (New York: Oxford University Press, 2015).
136 "U.F.W.A. Hold Interesting Meeting," *Raymond Recorder*, 24 July 1931, 1.
137 "U.F.W.A.," *Cardston News*, 22 March 1928, 3. Archibald was also president of the Women's Institute in Glenwood for many years. See, Shaw, *Chief Mountain Country*, 236. "Activities of the U.F.W.A.," *The U.F.A.*, 2 January 1931, 14.
138 "Mrs. Ross Again Heads Local U.F.W.A.," *Raymond Recorder*, 27 November 1931, 1. "U.F. and U.F.W.A. Meeting," *Raymond Recorder*, 4 January 1933, 4. "Raymond U.F.W.A. Local Re-Elects President," *Raymond Recorder*, 14 December 1933, 4. "U.F.W.A. Meeting," *Raymond Recorder*, 1 March 1935, 1.
139 "The U.F.W.A. and Junior Branch," *The U.F.A.*, 1 May 1923, 8.
140 "The United Farm Women of Alberta in Annual Convention," *The U.F.A.*, 26 February 1924, 12.
141 "Federal Conventions," *The U.F.A.*, 15 July 1930, 34.
142 "W. I. Convention of Cardston Constituency Held at Spring Coulee," *Cardston News*, 23 September 1925, 1.
143 "W. I. Studies Immigration," *Cardston News*, 14 July 1932, 1.
144 Brian T. Thorn, *From Left to Right: Maternalism and Women's Political Activism in Postwar Canada* (Vancouver and Toronto: UBC Press, 2016), 6.

4 Business

1. L.W. Herchmer, Annual Report of the Commissioner of the North-West Mounted Police, 1888, in *Report of the Commissioner of the North-West Mounted Police, 1888* (Ottawa: Queen's Printer and Controller of Stationery, A. Senecal, 1889), 22.
2. Lowry Nelson, *The Mormon Village: A Pattern and Technique of Land Settlement* (Salt Lake City: University of Utah Press, 1952), 3.
3. Nelson, *The Mormon Village*, 25.
4. John C. Lehr, "The Mormon Cultural Landscape in Alberta," *Malaspina Papers: Studies in Human and Physical Geography* (1973): 29.
5. Nelson, *The Mormon Village*, 38.
6. John C. Lehr, "Mormon Settlements in Southern Alberta," (MA thesis, University of Alberta, 1971), 12.
7. Nelson, *The Mormon Village*, 38.
8. Nelson, *The Mormon Village*, 224.
9. Lynn A. Rosenvall, "The Church of Jesus Christ of Latter-day Saints in Alberta: A Historical and Geographical Perspective," in *Regional Studies in Latter-day Saint Church History: Western Canada*, ed. Wright et al. (Provo, UT: Dept. of Church History and Doctrine, Brigham Young University, 2000), 5.
10. John C. Lehr, "Mormon Settlement Morphology in Southern Alberta." *Albertan Geographer* no. 8 (1972): 10.
11. Helen Greenland, biographical sketch, 1986, "Magrath, Alberta, Canada," photocopy of typescript, Miller, Peterson, Bolander, and Wells Family Biographies, Church History Library.
12. Stirling Sunset Society, *Stirling: Its Story and People, 1899–1980* (Stirling: Stirling Sunset Society, 1981), 6.
13. Richard H. Jackson, "City Planning" in *Encyclopedia of Mormonism*, ed. Daniel H. Ludlow (New York: Macmillan, 1992), 283.
14. Rosenvall, "The Transfer of Mormon Culture to Alberta," *American Review of Canadian Studies* 12, no. 2 (Summer 1982): 58.
15. 31 May 1890; 28 January 1893; 2 February 1895; 2 November 1895; 8 February 1896, MSS 1543, LTPSC. "Sacrament Meeting" is the main worship service held on the Sabbath for the entire ward membership.
16. Arrington, *Great Basin Kingdom: An Economic History of the Latter-Day Saints, 1830–1900* (Cambridge, MA: Harvard University Press, 1958), 293.
17. Arrington, *Great Basin Kingdom*, 354.
18. Arrington, *Great Basin Kingdom*, 383.
19. William L. Woolf, oral history, interviewed by Maureen Ursenbach Beecher, Salt Lake City, Utah, 1972, transcript, Church History Library.
20. Arrington, *Great Basin Kingdom*, 293

21 Arrington, *Great Basin Kingdom*, 315.
22 Arrington, *Great Basin Kingdom*, 324.
23 Arrington, *Great Basin Kingdom*, 328.
24 L. Dwight Israelsen, "United Orders," in *Encyclopedia of Mormonism*, ed. Daniel H. Ludlow (New York: Macmillan, 1992), 1493–95.
25 Arrington, *Great Basin Kingdom*, 341. Israelsen, "United Orders," 1494.
26 Israelsen, "United Orders," 1494.
27 Relief Society minutes, 11 June 1888, Cardston Ward Relief Society Minutes, 1887–1911, Church History Library.
28 Willard and Bernice Brooks, "Cardston – Historic Firsts," in *Chief Mountain Country: A History of Cardston and District*, ed. Beryl Bectell, vol. 2 (Cardston: Cardston and District Historical Society), 2.
29 27 June 1889, MSS 1543, LTPSC. Also see 15 July 1889, MSS 1543, LTPSC. In Calgary, Card "looked about the Business houses for information that would be of benefit to our Co-operative Store at Cardston."
30 31 May 1890, MSS 1543, LTPSC.
31 "The Mormon Question," *Lethbridge News*, 23 July 1890.
32 David T. Smith, *Religious Persecution and Political Order in the United States* (New York: Cambridge University Press, 2015), 62.
33 Sessional Papers, Third Session, First Legislature of the Legislative Assembly of the North-West Territories, Session 1890, *Journals of the First Legislative Assembly of the North-West Territories* (Regina: R. B. Gordon, 1891), 48–9. In June, Card met again with Haultain and "placed the matter of incorporation of 'The Cardston Company Lmtd' in his hand [and] aided him in forming a prospectus." See 19 June 1890, MSS 1543, LTPSC.
34 Session Papers, 49–51. Also mentioned polygamy and problems in United States with Utah.
35 "The Mormon Cardston Company," *Moose Jaw Herald Times*, 7 November 1890, 2. Speaking of the Zion Co-operative Store in Utah: "It has aided Mormonism, as a religious system, and become a strong factor financially and politically. Were it a company organized for the purpose of engaging in a single industry, and no influences of a religious character were brought to bear upon Mormons to join it, there were no cause for grievance, but here is a company composed solely of religious persons, uniting for the purpose of trade, who are bound by oaths and customs alien to the laws of our Dominion."
36 "The Mormon Cardston Company," *Moose Jaw Herald Times*, 7 November 1890, 2.
37 Brooks and Brooks, "Cardston – Historic Firsts," 2–3.
38 Card "attended a meeting of the Board of our Co-operative store." See 26 January 1891, MSS 1543, LTPSC. Also see 29 January 1891. Card met with E.G. Galt (Manager of AB Coal and Ry Co) "who promised to aid

our settlement in getting a charter to Incorporate a Co-operative Co. for Cardston for the purpose of merchandising and manufacturing."
39 Brooks and Brooks, "Cardston – Historic Firsts," 2.
40 J. Royal, Lieutenant Governor, N.W.T., Report Concerning the Administration of the North-West Territories for the Year 1892, *Annual Report of the Department of the Interior for the Year 1892* (Ottawa: S.E. Dawson, 1893).
41 Samuel B. Steele, Superintendent, Commanding Macleod District, Annual Report of Superintendent S. B. Steele, Commanding Macleod District, 1892, *Sessional Papers of the Dominion of Canada: Volume 9, Third Session of the Seventh Parliament, Session 1893* (Ottawa: S.E. Dawson, 1893): 15–40.
42 6 February 1893, MSS 1543, LTPSC.
43 20 February 1893, MSS 1543, LTPSC.
44 30 January 1894, MSS 1543, LTPSC.
45 30 January 1894, MSS 1543, LTPSC. Also see Shaw, *Chief Mountain Country*, 7.
46 "Cullings From Cardston," *Lethbridge News*, 13 July 1893, 2.
47 Henry C. Klassen, *Eye on the Future: Business People in Calgary and the Bow Valley, 1870–1900* (Calgary: University of Calgary Press, 2002), xxxv–xxxvi.
48 Shaw, *Chief Mountain Country*, 226.
49 Shaw, *Chief Mountain Country*, 226.
50 17 November 1890; 14 January 1891; 12 May 1893, MSS 1543, LTPSC.
51 25 February 1891, MSS 1543, LTPSC. In return, the Latter-day Saints gave their political support if Magrath requested. For example, on 28 February 1891 Magrath encouraged Latter-day Saints to vote for Donald W. Davis (1845–1906) as their representative to Ottawa, and in return they would receive support for "rights in other matters." 28 February 1891, MSS 1543, LTPSC.
52 12 January 1895, MSS 1543, LTPSC.
53 17 January 1895, MSS 1543, LTPSC.
54 Samuel. B. Steele, Annual Report of Superintendent S. B. Steele, Commanding Macleod District, 1895, *Sessional Papers of the Dominion of Canada: Volume 11, Sixth Session of the Seventh Parliament, Session 1896* (Ottawa: S.E. Dawson, 1896).
55 14 January 1896, MSS 1543, LTPSC.
56 1 February 1896, 16 March 1896, and 21 March 1896, MSS 1543, LTPSC.
57 31 December 1896, MSS 1543, LTPSC.
58 "Incorporated: The Alberta Land and Stock Company File Articles," *Salt Lake Herald*, 17 June 1896, 6.
59 John Blue, *Alberta Past and Present: Historical and Biographical Volume 3* (Chicago: Pioneer Historical Publishing, 1924), 111–12. In addition to McCarty, other Utahns that supported the company were Homer Manley Brown (1854–1936), Samuel W. Woolley (1840–1908), William J. Robinson

(1860–1941), William Andrew Larsen (1860–1943), M. Peter Madsen (1856–1917), Hans C. Bonneru (1849–1926), and Hugh Russel Sloan (1856–1920).

60 11 March 1897, MSS 1543, LTPSC. Smith and Cannon currently had fives wives and Woodruff had at least three at the time of this meeting. Lisa Olsen Tait, "'A Modern Patriarchal Family': The Wives of Joseph F. Smith, in the *Relief Society Magazine*, 1915–19," in *Joseph F. Smith: Reflections on the Man and His Times*, ed. Craig K. Manscill, Brian D. Reeves, Guy L. Dorius, and J. B. Haws (Provo, UT: Religious Studies Center; Salt Lake City: Deseret Book, 2013), 74–95. For Joseph F. Smith see Christopher C. Jones, "Joseph F. Smith," in *Mormonism: A Historical Encyclopedia*, ed. W. Paul Reeve and Ardis E. Parshall (Santa Barbara: ABC-CLIO, LLC, 2010), 185. For Wilford Woodruff, see Thomas G. Alexander, "Wilford Woodruff," in *Mormonism: A Historical Encyclopedia*, 217–18.

61 Samuel B. Steele, Annual Report of Superintendent S. B. Steele, Commanding D Division, etc., *Sessional Papers of the Dominion of Canada: Volume 11, Second Session of the Eighth Parliament, Session 1897* (Ottawa: S.E. Dawson, 1897). C.H. Mackintosh Lieutenant Governor, N.W.T., Annual Report of the Department of the Interior for the Year 1893, *Sessional Papers of the Dominion of Canada: Volume 10, Fourth Session of the Seventh Parliament, Session 1894* (Ottawa: S.E. Dawson, 1894). Shaw, *Chief Mountain Country*, 7.

62 14 April 1897, MSS 1543, LTPSC.

63 8 March 1898, MSS 1543, LTPSC.

64 8 May 1898, MSS 1543, LTPSC.

65 6 September 1897, MSS 1543, LTPSC.

66 3 November 1897, MSS 1543, LTPSC.

67 An Ordinance to Incorporate the President and High Council of the Alberta Stake of Zion, No. 43 of 1897, *Ordinances of the North-West Territories Passed in the Third Session of the Third Legislative Assembly* (Regina: John Alexander Reid, Queen's Printer for the Territories, 1898), 574–7.

68 17 December 1897, MSS 1543, LTPSC.

69 28 January 1898, MSS 1543, LTPSC.

70 26 April 1898, MSS 1543, LTPSC. Also see Card's diary entries for 5, 6, 7, 9, 13, and 14 April for further negotiations.

71 21 August 1898, MSS 1543, LTPSC.

72 12 February 1899, MSS 1543, LTPSC.

73 12 June 1899, MSS 1543, LTPSC.

74 Anna Brandley Ostlund, "My Father, Theodore Brandley," 1961, photocopy, Church History Library.

75 R. Burton Deane, Annual Report of Superintendent R. B. Deane, Commanding Macleod District, *Sessional Papers of the Dominion of Canada: Volume 12, Fifth Session of the Eighth Parliament, Session 1900* (Ottawa: S.E. Dawson, 1900).

76 John Blue, *Alberta Past and Present: Historical and Biographical Volume 2* (Chicago: Pioneer Historical Publishing, 1924), 160.
77 Blue, *Alberta Past and Present: Historical and Biographical Volume 2*, 161.
78 20 November 1899, MSS 1543, LTPSC.
79 Lawrence B. Lee, "The Canadian-American Irrigation Frontier, 1884–1914," *Agricultural History* 40, no.4 (1966): 280–1.
80 Lawrence B. Lee, "The Canadian-American Irrigation Frontier, 1884–1914," *Agricultural History* 40, no.4 (1966): 281.
81 Lawrence B. Lee, "The Canadian-American Irrigation Frontier, 1884–1914," *Agricultural History* 40, no.4 (1966): 281.
82 Lawrence B. Lee, "The Canadian-American Irrigation Frontier, 1884–1914," *Agricultural History* 40, no.4 (1966): 281.
83 The board elected Card 1st Director and appointed President of the Cardston Company Ltd. on 4 February 1901.
84 21–26 January 1901, MSS 1543, LTPSC.
85 10 October 1901, MSS 1543, LTPSC.
86 24 October 1901, MSS 1543, LTPSC.
87 Brooks and Brooks, "Cardston – Historic Firsts," 4. Also see "Local Topics," *Lethbridge News*, 27 February 1902, 8.
88 4 September 1902, MSS 1543, LTPSC.
89 "Words of Advice by C.O. Card," *Lethbridge News*, 16 December 1903, 5.
90 Young Women's Mutual Improvement Association (hereafter YWMIA) minutes, 1903, Magrath 1st Ward YWMIA Minutes and Records, 1899–1973, Church History Library.
91 Melchizedek Priesthood minutes, 1916, Raymond Alberta Canada Stake Melchizedek Priesthood Minutes and Records, 1900–1973, Church History Library.
92 Sarah Mercer Taylor notebooks, 3 August 1924, Irene M. Anderson Collection, 1884–1978. Church History Library.
93 Relief Society Minutes, 1946, Leavitt Ward Relief Society Minutes and Records, 1910–1973, Church History Library.
94 13 July 1901, MSS 1543, LTPSC.
95 J. Orwin Hicken, Kay B. Redd, and John L. Evans, *Raymond, 1901–1967* (Lethbridge, AB: Lethbridge Herald Co., 1967), 39.
96 *Golden Jubilee of the Town of Raymond, Alberta* (Raymond, AB: Chamber of Commerce, 1951), 43. "Sugar Beets in the South," *Edmonton Bulletin*, 7 October 1901, 5.
97 11 August 1901, MSS 1543, LTPSC.
98 Hicken, Redd, and Evans, *Raymond, 1901–1967*, 40.
99 *Golden Jubilee*, 43.
100 William G. Hartley, "Mormon Sugar in Alberta: E. P. Ellison and the Knight Sugar Factory, 1901–1917," *Journal of Mormon History* 23, no. 2 (1997): 13.

101 William G. Hartley, "Mormon Sugar in Alberta: E. P. Ellison and the Knight Sugar Factory, 1901–1917," *Journal of Mormon History* 23, no. 2 (1997): 29.
102 *Orders in Council: Proclamations and Regulations Having Force of Law in the Dominion of Canada, Issued During the Years 1881 and 1882* (Ottawa: B. Chamberlin, 1882), cxxv. Also see, Warren M. Elofson, *Frontier Cattle Ranching in the Land and Times of Charlie Russell* (Montreal: McGill-Queen's University Press, 2004), 18.
103 May Archibald, ed., *100 Years Between the Rivers A History of Glenwood, Hartley & Standoff,* (Cardston: Golden Press, 1984), 22.
104 Edward Brado, *Cattle Kingdom: Early Ranching in Alberta* (Surrey: Heritage House, 2004), 67.
105 Brado, *Cattle Kingdom*, 68.
106 Brado, *Cattle Kingdom*, 72. Also see Frank Yeigh, "The Greatness of Saskatchewan and Alberta," *Red Deer News*, 3 July 1907. And see "Mercantile Summary," *The Monetary Times: Trade Review and Insurance Chronicle*, 17 March 1905, 1265.
107 Leroy Victor Kelly, *The Story of the Ranchers and Indians of Alberta* (Toronto: William Briggs, 1913), 359.
108 Journal of Events, Cardston Alberta Stake General Minutes, 1894–1974, Church History Library.
109 May Archibald, ed., *100 Years Between the Rivers A History of Glenwood, Hartley & Standoff,* (Cardston: Golden Press, 1984), 289.
110 Journal of Events, 19 September 1906, Cardston Alberta Stake General Minutes, 1894–1974, Church History Library.
111 "Cochrane Ranch Goes to Mormons," *Edmonton Bulletin*, 29 January 1907, 2.
112 "Local and General," *Magrath Pioneer*, 5 June 1907, 5.
113 Aphrodite Karamitsanis, *Place Names of Alberta Volume II* (Calgary: University of Calgary Press, 1992), 51. Archibald, *100 Years Between the Rivers*, 353.
114 Benjamin James Wood, "Benjamin James Wood and Emma Fern Bigelow," contributed by Kathleen Kuuleilani Holyoak on 8 September 2013, https://www.familysearch.org/photos/artifacts/2448377.
115 "In the summer of 1909 President Wood, President Duce, President Williams and members of the High Council met on the Cochrane Ranch, on the hill by the side of the spring, and dedicated the land to become a home for the members of the church and their children. The town site of Hill Spring was being surveyed by Seymour Smith, assisted by Alex Leishman. The land at first, bought by the church, was sold only to church members. In the spring of 1910 on June 12th, the ward was organized. President Wood and his assistants were present. At that time there was only one house on the town site; it was owned by Carl Tanner,

and at that meeting those present found seats on nail kegs and planks." Franklin Pierce Fisher, autobiography, "To My Children," Magrath Museum, Magrath, Alberta. "Newsy Items of Local & General Interest," *Magrath Pioneer*, 21 June 1910, 5.
116 Arrington, *Great Basin Kingdom*, 410.
117 J. Reuben Clark, Jr., "Private Ownership ... under the United Order," *Conference Report* (October 1942): 54–9.

5 Politics

1 Brigham Y. Card, "Introduction," in *The Mormon Contribution to Alberta Politics*, Ernest G. Mardon, Austin A. Mardon, and Catherine Mardon, edited by Talicia Dutchin (Edmonton: Golden Meteorite Press, 2011), x.
2 Mardon, Mardon, and Mardon, *The Mormon Contribution*, 7.
3 Blue, *Volume 3*, 188. Mardon, Mardon, and Mardon, *The Mormon Contribution*, 51.
4 Blue, *Volume 3*, 188–9.
5 Edward Bell, *Social Classes and Social Credit in Alberta* (Montreal & Kingston: McGill-Queen's University Press, 1994), 10.
6 Bell, *Social Classes and Social Credit*, 10.
7 Blue, *Volume 2*, 318
8 Blue, *Volume 2*, 318
9 Blue, *Volume 2*, 319.
10 Blue, *Volume 3*, 90. Other examples from Magrath, see Blue, *Volume 3*, 102 and *Volume 2*, 425. James B. Ririe (1858–1933), who moved to Magrath in 1899, raised sheep, horses, and cattle, and elected mayor of Magrath for several terms. Christian Jensen (1868–1958) came to Magrath in 1903, became a member of the Conservative Party, then UFA member. Mayor of Magrath around 1909 and Bishop of Aetna 1934 to 1946. Examples from Raymond include John W. Evans (1875–1945), who was Mayor of Raymond from 1912 to 1914, Bishop of Raymond 2nd Ward 1912 to 1924, and second counsellor for the Taylor Stake 1924 to 1936. T.J. O'Brien was simultaneously mayor and counsellor for Raymond 1st Ward from 1915 to 1919. Orrin H. Snow (1869–1948) was second counsellor of Taylor Stake from 1911 to 1924, mayor of Raymond 1923 to 1926, and first counsellor of the Taylor Stake 1924 to 1936. William Jensen (1898–1985) was mayor 1945 to 1952 and bishop of the Raymond second Ward 1947 to 1955.
11 "Mormons in the Economy & In Government," in *The Mormon Presence in Canada*, ed. B.Y. Card et al. (Edmonton: The University of Alberta Press, 1990), 232.
12 Banack, *God's Province*, 63. According to Banack, the UFA emerged out of the conflicts surrounding the American liberal and postmillennial

evangelical Protestant tradition, higher criticism, and the adoption of the Darwin-inspired "evolution-friendly conception of social change driven largely by human action in accordance with the moral teachings of Christ."

13 Bradford James Rennie, *The Rise of Agrarian Democracy: The United Farmers and Farm Women of Alberta, 1909–1921* (Toronto: University of Toronto Press, 2000), 35.
14 "The Farmers' Association," *Saturday News*, 30 December 1905, 6.
15 Alberta Farmers' Association minute book, 1906–1907, United Farmers of Alberta fonds, Glenbow Archives, Calgary, Alberta. Secretaries of the branches were as follows: Cardston – Edward Neale Barker; Raymond – James Francis Johnson (1879–1941); Magrath – George A. Hacking (1876–1955); Stirling – Frederick Zaugg (1869–1956). Prominent members of the Raymond branch were Thomas J. O'Brien (1866–1938) and Francis B. Rolfson (1872–1941).
16 "Consider Farmers' Interests," *Edmonton Bulletin*, 1 August 1908, 6.
17 "Local and General," *Alberta Star*, 26 November 1903, 8. In 1906, Woolford reported to the *Cardston Star* that his oats went 115 bushels to the acre without irrigation. "Local Topics," *Lethbridge News*, 30 October 1906, 4.
18 Vilate Bradshaw, "Biography of Richard William Bradshaw," contributed by richardcarlylebradshaw1 on 9 March 2015, https://www.familysearch.org/photos/artifacts/14085384.
19 "Bore for Gas at Lethbridge," *Edmonton Bulletin*, 22 September 1909, 1.
20 The Society of Equity, sharing similar goals of the AFA, tried to obtain profitable prices for all products of the farm garden or orchard, to build and control storage of produce, to secure equitable rates of transportation, to educate, to prevent the adulteration of food and marketing of same, to establish an equitable banking system, and to improve the highways. See Society of Equity constitution and bylaws, ca. 1906–8, United Farmers of Alberta fonds, Glenbow Archives, Calgary, Alberta.
21 Rennie, *Agrarian Democracy*, 7
22 Banack, *God's Province*, 65.
23 Banack, *God's Province*, 78.
24 Banack, *God's Province*, 85.
25 Banack, *God's Province*, 91–5.
26 Rennie, *Agrarian Democracy*, 180.
27 Rennie, *Agrarian Democracy*, 206.
28 Barnwell Relief Society, *Barnwell History* (Ann Arbor: Edwards Bros., 1952), 70. The Church appointed Peterson bishop of the Barnwell Ward in 1915, and he kept that position until 1925. See Barnwell Relief Society, *Barnwell History*, 145.

29 Lethbridge Constituency, *The United Farmers of Alberta (Inc.) Annual Report and Year Book Containing Reports of Officers and Committees for the Year 1918 Together with Official Minutes of the Eleventh Annual Convention*, 41
30 "Directors Are Chosen for the United Farmers," *The Edmonton Bulletin*, 25 January 1919, 1.
31 Lawrence Peterson, "Lethbridge," *The United Farmers of Alberta (Inc.) Annual Report and Year Book Containing Reports of Officers and Committees For the Year 1919 Together with Official Minutes of the Twelfth Annual Convention*, 18.
32 Lawrence Peterson, "Lethbridge," *Year 1919*, 18.
33 Lawrence Peterson, "Lethbridge," 14 December 1921, Barnwell, in *The United Farmers of Alberta (Inc.) Annual Report and Year Book Containing Reports of Officers and Committees For the Year 1921 Together with Official Minutes of the Fourteenth Annual Convention*, 25.
34 Lethbridge Constituency, *The United Farmers of Alberta (Inc.) Annual Report and Year Book Containing Reports of Officers and Committees For the Year 1921 Together with Official Minutes of the Fourteenth Annual Convention*, 66.
35 "George L. Stringam, M.L.A. U.F.A. Candidate for Cardston Riding," *Cardston News*, 12 June 1930, 1. Also see George Owen Stringham, oral history, interviewed by Charles Ursenbach, Cardston, Alberta, 7 March 1974, transcript, Church History Library.
36 Austin A. Mardon and Ernest G. Mardon, *Alberta's Political Pioneers: A Biographical Account of the United Farmers of Alberta 1921–1935*, ed. Justin Selner, Spencer Dunn, and Emerson Csorba (Edmonton: Golden Meteorite Press, 2010), 140.
37 Mardon and Mardon, *Alberta's Political Pioneers*, 140. Peterson: 1,929 votes; J.J. Horrigan: 709; James Harper Prowse: 551.
38 Henry Wise Wood, speech, January 1924, U.F.A. President's Address, Official Reports of the UFA Annual Convention, 1. UFA fonds.
39 Wood, President's Address, 2.
40 "Southern Farmers Forming Local Wheat Pool," *The U.F.A.*, 16 July 1923, 14.
41 Wood, President's Address, 2–3.
42 W. J. Jackman, "A Wheat Pool for Alberta," *The U.F.A.*, 16 July 1923, 1.
43 Jackman, "A Wheat Pool for Alberta," 10.
44 "The Wheat Pool Contract," *Edmonton Bulletin*, 18 August 1923, 14.
45 The United Farmers of Alberta Inc., Directors for 1922, *Annual Report and Year Book Containing Reports of Officers and Committees For the Year 1921 Together with Official Minutes of the Fourteenth Annual Convention*, 87. Also see The United Farmers of Alberta Inc., convention minutes, 1924, scanned microfilm, UFA fonds. The United Farmers of Alberta Inc., convention minutes, 1935, scanned microfilm, UFA fonds.

46 "Elect Trustees for Alberta Wheat Pool," *Redcliff Review*, 23 August 1923, 1. Also see *Raymond Recorder*, 6 December 1945, 1.
47 "Canadian Churchman Dies," *The Church News*, 1 February 1958, 1. "A Valued Citizen," *Lethbridge Herald*, 23 January 1958, 4. Also see Lalovee R. Jensen, "History of Christian Jensen Jr.," contributed by RS Ririe on 27 May 2013, https://www.familysearch.org/photos/artifacts/1156890.
48 "Co-operation in Alberta: Annual Meeting of Alberta Co-operative League," *Red Deer News*, 11 June 1924, 2.
49 "Campaign Launched in Lethbridge Districts in Preparation for the Annual Convention, *The U.F.A.*, 15 December 1925, 18.
50 "H.W. Wood Explains," *Cardston News*, 4 February 1926, 2. "President Wood at Cardston," *The U.F.A.*, 15 February 1926, 15.
51 "The Aims of the U.F.A.," *Cardston News*, 4 February 1926, 2.
52 "U.F.A. Sunday," *Western Independent*, 12 May 1920, 1.
53 The United Farmers of Alberta Inc., convention minutes, 1926, scanned microfilm, UFA fonds.
54 "How Cardston Constituency Voted," *Cardston News*, 1 July 1926, 1. Caldwell's father David Henry Caldwell (1828–1904) was born in Upper Canada, joined the Church in 1843, moved to Nauvoo, Illinois, and completed the trek to Utah in 1853. David, a farmer, moved his family to Cardston in the summer of 1898. Walter Caldwell also farmed, but, by the 1920s, worked as a butcher. He left Alberta some time before 1930 and moved to Utah. In the 1926 election, Liberal candidate Caldwell advocated for a reduction in taxation and the payment of the provincial debt. Conservative candidate Card worked as a real estate and investment broker, and served as president of the Cardston Board of Trade. Joseph was age two when his father Charles Ora Card started the migration to southern Alberta, but he frequently travelled between the US and Canada, and attended Brigham Young College in Logan, Utah. Walter and Joseph descended from important LDS men, and their lives were not restricted to farming, which might explain their attraction to political parties other than the United Farmers. See, "Liberal Rally at Owendale," *Cardston News*, 24 June 1926, 6.
55 "How Cardston Constituency Voted," 1.
56 "George L. Stringam Wins Farmers' Convention Nomination," *Cardston News*, 29 May 1930, 1.
57 O'Dea, *The Mormons*, 160.
58 O'Dea, *The Mormons*, 185.
59 Nelson Wiseman, *In Search of Canadian Political Culture* (Vancouver: UBC Press, 2007), 242.
60 Banack, *God's Province*, 123.
61 Banack, *God's Province*, 124.

62 S.D. Clark, "The Religious Sect in Canadian Politics," *American Journal of Sociology* 51, no. 3 (1945): 210.
63 Banack, *God's Province*, 27.
64 Banack, *God's Province*, 125.
65 Banack, *God's Province*, 214.
66 S.D. Clark, *The Developing Canadian Community*, 2nd ed. (Toronto: University of Toronto Press, 1968), 134–5. As cited in Wiseman, *In Search of Canadian Political Culture*, 246.
67 Wiseman, *In Search of Canadian Political Culture*, 248.
68 Earle Waugh, "The Almighty Has Not Got This Far Yet: Religious Models in Alberta's and Saskatchewan's History," in *The New Provinces: Alberta and Saskatchewan, 1905–1980*, eds. Howard Palmer and Donald Smith (Vancouver: Tantalus Research Limited, 1973), 206.
69 Waugh, "The Almighty Has Not Got This Far Yet," 207.
70 Waugh, "The Almighty Has Not Got This Far Yet," 207.
71 Waugh, "The Almighty Has Not Got This Far Yet," 207.
72 Garth L. Mangum, "Welfare Services," in *Encyclopedia of Mormonism*, ed. Daniel H. Ludlow (New York: Macmillan, 1992), 1555.
73 "1700 Hear Conference Speakers," *Cardston News*, 12 July 1938, 1.
74 "1700 Hear Conference Speakers," *Cardston News*, 12 July 1938, 1.
75 *Raymond Recorder*, 19 August 1938, 4.
76 James Forest Wood, oral history, interviewed by Charles Ursenbach, Cardston, Alberta, 1974, transcript, Church History Library.
77 John O. Hicken, oral history, interviewed by Charles Ursenbach, Raymond, Alberta, 1974, transcript, Church History Library.
78 "Quarterly Conference," *Raymond Recorder*, 15 July 1938, 1.
79 First Presidency letter to Willard L. Smith, 5 February 1947, Raymond Alberta Canada Stake Manuscript History and Historical Reports, 1903–1975, Church History Library. Also in MSS 3116, LTPSC.
80 Myrtle N. Passey, "Myrtle N. Passey, 1939–1947," Taylor Stake Relief Society History, 1962, Church History Library.
81 Magrath 1st Ward Manuscript History and Historical Reports, 1899–1984, Church History Library.
82 "Aetna," *Cardston News*, 21 February 1939, 2.
83 MSS 6084, Asael E. Palmer papers, 20th Century Western and Mormon Manuscripts, L. Tom Perry Special Collections, Harold B. Lee Library, Brigham Young University.
84 Sacrament Meeting minutes, 24 July 1934, Ward Historical Record Book 1931–1937, Cardston 1st Ward General Minutes, 1914–1977, Church History Library.
85 "Here and There," *Cardston News*, 2 August 1934, 3.
86 Raymond Alberta Canada Stake Manuscript History and Historical Reports, 1903–1975, Church History Library.

87 A branch is the smallest type of organized congregation of the LDS Church (smaller than a ward) and lead by a branch president. Richard O. Cowan, "Branch, Branch President," in *Encyclopedia of Mormonism*, ed. Daniel H. Ludlow (New York: Macmillan, 1992): 219.
88 Ottawa Branch minutes, 7 February 1937 and 28 March 1937, Ottawa 1st Ward General Minutes, 1926–1973, Church History Library. For more evidence of Blackmore's activities, see 22 January 1939 and 5 March 1939, Ottawa 1st Ward General Minutes, 1926–1973, Church History Library.
89 Ottawa Branch minutes, 6 June 1942, Ottawa 1st Ward General Minutes, 1926–1973, Church History Library.
90 Ottawa Branch minutes, 9 September 1945; 5 May 1946; 12 May 1946, Ottawa 1st Ward General Minutes, 1926–1973, Church History Library. Also that month, Blackmore gave a talk on "striving and attaining" at the Third Quarterly Conference. See 12 September 1945, Ottawa 1st Ward General Minutes, 1926–1973, Church History Library.
91 Since Low replaced Blackmore as party leader in 1944, three years before Blackmore's excommunication, we can conclude that Blackmore did not lose his political position due to his conflicts with the Church.
92 "News Notes," *Raymond Recorder*, 29 May 1942, 1.
93 "News Notes," *Raymond Recorder*, 29 May 1942, 4.
94 "News Notes," *Raymond Recorder*, 28 July 1944, 4. Also see, *Cardston News*, 5 July 1945, 1.
95 *Cardston News*, 12 July 1945, 6.
96 "Elders Party," *Cardston News*, 16 August 1945, 6.
97 "Fireside Chat," *Cardston News*, 10 January 1946, 1. Also see, "Fireside Chat," *Cardston News*, 28 November 1946, 1.
98 Mardon, Mardon, and Mardon, *The Mormon Contribution*, 46.
99 Mardon, Mardon, and Mardon, *The Mormon Contribution*, 47. For specifics on what Tanner accomplished as a member of the Alberta Legislature see G. Homer Durham, *N. Eldon Tanner: His Life and Service* (Salt Lake City: Deseret Book Company, 1982).
100 Mardon, Mardon, and Mardon, *The Mormon Contribution*, 33.
101 "Alberta Mines Minister is Mormon Bishop," *The Globe and Mail*, 6 January 1937, 1. Another neutral expression of LDS politicians and their faith is in "Mormon Gets Cabinet Post," *The Globe and Mail*, 2 February 1937, 15.
102 C. Syd Matthews, "14 Religious Sects Have Representation in Alberta House," *The Globe and Mail*, 25 February 1937, 7.
103 Melvin S. Tagg, *A History of the Mormon Church in Canada* (Lethbridge, AB: Lethbridge Stake Historical Committee, 1968), 222.
104 Franklin L. Foster, "John E. Brownlee, 1925–1934," in *Alberta Premiers of the Twentieth Century*, ed. Bradford James Rennie (Regina: Canada Plains Research Center, University of Regina, 2004), 97.

105 Kenneth McNaught, *A Prophet in Politics: A Biography of J. S. Woodsworth* (Toronto: University of Toronto Press, 2001), 255.
106 Government of Canada, Census of Manitoba, Saskatchewan, and Alberta, 1916, Library and Archives Canada, http://www.bac-lac.gc.ca/eng/census/1916/Pages/item.aspx?itemid=260384.
107 Mable Johansen Palmer, "History of John Albert Johansen," contributed by bethanykariannteerlink1 on 1 January 2014, https://www.familysearch.org/photos/artifacts/4217035. Johansen was called to the Alberta Stake High Council in 1929 until 1942.
108 "J.A. Johansen Nominated as Federal U.F.A.–C.C.F. Candidate," *Cardston News*, 13 August 1935, 6.
109 "J.A. Johansen Nominated as Federal U.F.A.–C.C.F. Candidate," 1.
110 "C.C.F. Program Explained at Gym Meeting," *Cardston News*, 8 October 1935, 1.
111 "C.C.F. Program Explained at Gym Meeting," 4.
112 "Alberta Remains Social Credit," *Cardston News*, 15 October 1935, 1.
113 "C.C.F. Rally," *Cardston News*, 30 March 1944, 1. Leavitt was patriarch of the Alberta Stake, he served a mission in Manitoba, he was bishop of the Glenwood ward for 14 years, he was trustee and secretary of the first school board in Glenwood for 4 years, councilman on the board of the Municipal District of Cochrane for 18 years, 8 years as Reeve, member of the United Irrigation District for 13 years (chairman for 3), and from 1939 to 1945 he was chairman of the board and manager of the UID cheese factory. See obituary, 1958, contributed by Dave Olsen on 5 August 2014, https://www.familysearch.org/photos/artifacts/9095194.
114 "C.C.F. Rally," *Cardston News*, 30 March 1944, 1.
115 "Take a Step Forward with the C.C.F.," *Cardston News*, 3 August 1944, 1.
116 Blue, *Volume 2*, 120. Mardon, Mardon, and Mardon, *The Mormon Contribution*, 22.
117 Thomas W. Pratt, oral history, interviewed by Charles Ursenbach, Lethbridge, Alberta, 9–10 March 1974, transcript, Church History Library. Tagg, *Mormon Church in Canada*, 129. Arthur N. Green, oral history, interviewed by Charles Ursenbach, Lethbridge, Alberta, 1973, transcript, Church History Library.
118 Blue, *Volume 2*, 123.
119 Tagg, *Mormon Church in Canada*, 131.
120 Maydell Cazier Palmer, autobiography, 1980, Autobiography of Maydell Cazier Palmer, Church History Library.
121 *Raymond Recorder*, 11 June 1926, 1. Ernest Mardon and Austin Mardon, *Lethbridge Politicians: Federal, Provincial & Civic* (Edmonton: Golden Meteorite Press, 2008), 79. "D.H. Elton, K.C. Addresses M.I.A.'s of Both Wards," *Cardston News*, 6 December 1928, 6. "Splendid Program for Sunday at the 1st Ward," *Raymond Recorder*, 1 February 1929, 1.

122 "D.H. Elton "Cheers" Glenwood Audiences," *Cardston News*, 30 October 1930, 5. "Mayor Elton at Second Ward," *Raymond Recorder*, 6 May 1938, 1. "Special Thanksgiving Services," *Cardston News*, 4 October 1938, 1. *Cardston News*, 13 December 1938, 1.
123 Yorgason, *Mormon Culture Region*, 127–8.
124 Yorgason, *Mormon Culture Region*, 170.
125 Yorgason, *Mormon Culture Region*, 170.

6 Architecture

1 Vi Alfred Wood, *The Alberta Temple: Centre and Symbol of Faith* (Calgary: Detselig Enterprises, 1989), 26. Richard O. Cowan, "The Alberta Temple: Seventy-Five Years of Service," in *Regional Studies in Latter-day Saint Church History Western Canada*, ed. Dennis A. Wright et al. (Provo, UT: Department of Church History and Doctrine, Brigham Young University, 2000), 239.
2 Wood, *The Alberta Temple*, 27. Cowan, "The Alberta Temple," 240.
3 For LDS, a meetinghouse is a multipurpose facility to house worship services and spiritual education. See C. Mark Hamilton, "Meetinghouse," in *Encyclopedia of Mormonism*, ed. Daniel H. Ludlow (New York: Macmillan, 1992): 876–8. A tabernacle performs similar functions but accommodates more people.
4 Thomas A. Tweed, *America's Church: The National Shrine and Catholic Presence in the Nation's Capital* (New York: Oxford University Press, 2011), 7.
5 Randall M. Miller, review of *America's Church: The National Shrine and Catholic Presence in the Nation's Capital*, by Thomas A. Tweed, *Church History* 81, no. 3 (2012): 738.
6 Puritan architecture favoured a square, or rectangle, centralized assembly hall. Puritans' wanted their buildings to be an obvious departure from Anglican and Catholic churches. See Anne C. Loveland and Otis B. Wheeler, *From Meetinghouse to Megachurch: A Material and Cultural History* (Columbia: University of Missouri Press, 2003). See Mark Gelernter, *A History of American Architecture: Buildings in Their Cultural and Technological Context* (Manchester: Manchester University Press, 1999), 174. See Thomas Carter and Peter Goss' definition of "Victorian Gothic, 1880–1910," in *Utah's Historic Architecture, 1847–1940* (Salt Lake City: University of Utah Press, 1988), 120.
7 Charles Ora Card, *The Diaries of Charles Ora Card: The Canadian Years, 1886–1903*, ed. Donald G. Godfrey and Brigham Y. Card (Salt Lake City: University of Utah Press, 1993), 50–51.
8 Edmund R. Dorosz and Holy Cross Centennial Committee, *Holy Cross Roman Catholic Church, Fort Macleod, Alberta, 1898–1998* (Fort Macleod, AB: Our Pet's, 1998), 21.

9 Barry Magrill, *A Commerce of Taste: Church Architecture in Canada, 1867–1914* (Montreal: McGill-Queen's University Press, 2012), 116.
10 The Matkins were freighters between Lethbridge and Cardston. Charles S. Matkin, oral history, interviewed by Charles Ursenbach, Magrath, Alberta, 18 July 1975, transcript, Church History Library, The Church of Jesus Christ of Latter-day Saints, Salt Lake City, Utah. Also, travellers caught the train in Lethbridge and Card frequently travelled there. For example, between October 1889 and February 1890, he visited the town about once a month to pick up Church authorities at the depot or manage business errands. Card, *The Diaries*, 103–7.
11 "St. Augustine's Church," *Lethbridge News*, 29 March 1888. Card, *The Diaries*, 71.
12 Card, *The Diaries*, 61. A Fast and Testimony Meeting occurs on the first Sunday of each month; members bear verbal witness of their feelings of the gospel and follow the meeting with a fast from two consecutive meals and liquids. Mary Jolley, "Fast and Testimony Meeting," in *Encyclopedia of Mormonism*, ed. Daniel H. Ludlow (New York: Macmillan, 1992), 502.
13 Paul L. Anderson, "First of the Modern Temples," *Ensign* (July 1977), https://www.lds.org/ensign/1977/07/first-of-the-modern-temples?lang=eng. Allen Dale Roberts, "Religious Architecture of the LDS Church: Influences and Changes since 1847," *Utah Historical Quarterly* 43, no. 2 (1975): 316.
14 A.W.N. Pugin, *Contrasts*, 2nd ed. (1836, reprint, Leicester: Leicester University Press, 1969), 1.
15 Pugin, *Contrasts*, 3.
16 A.W.N. Pugin, *The True Principles of Pointed or Christian Architecture* (1841, reprinted from the 1853 impression, Oxford: St. Barnabas, 1969), 40–1.
17 Pugin, *True Principles*, 41.
18 Pugin, *True Principles*, 3–4.
19 Pugin, *Contrasts*, 5. Also see Phoebe B. Stanton, *The Gothic Revival & American Church Architecture: An Episode in Taste 1840–1856* (Baltimore: John Hopkins Press, 1968), xvii. Stanton defined "revival" as nostalgia for the past.
20 Pugin, *True Principles*, 1.
21 Pugin, *True Principles*, 35–6.
22 Pugin, *True Principles*, 2.
23 Paul Goldberger, *Why Architecture Matters* (New Haven: Yale University Press, 2009), 29.
24 Stanton, *The Gothic Revival*, xviii.
25 Stanton, *The Gothic Revival*, 7.
26 Chris Brooks, *The Gothic Revival* (London: Phaidon Press, 1999), 4.
27 Brooks, *The Gothic Revival*, 288.

28 MSS 937, Truman Osborn Angell, Autobiography, ca. 1884. L. Tom Perry Special Collections, Harold B. Lee Library, Brigham Young University.
29 "A Tabernacle in the Wilderness: A History of the Alberta Stake Tabernacle," https://history.lds.org/article/cardston-tabernacle. Also see Charles S. Matkin's Oral History, 20. He stated that the assembly hall burned down around 1911. Shaw, *Chief Mountain Country*, 179. According to Shaw, fire destroyed the hall in 1916.
30 Card, *The Diaries*, 210. They were still working on completing the meetinghouse in the summer. See Card, *The Diaries*, 226. Card stated in a Priesthood meeting "the propriety of completing the meetinghouse with faint response to the request."
31 Correspondence, MSS 3192. Charles Ora Card, Letter, 1893. Martha Sonntag Bradley research papers, 20th Century Western & Mormon Manuscripts, LTPSC.
32 C. Mark Hamilton, "Meetinghouse," in *Encyclopedia of Mormonism*, ed. Daniel H. Ludlow (New York: Macmillan Publishing Company, 1992), 876.
33 Paul L. Anderson, "First of the Modern Temples."
34 Loveland and Wheeler, *From Meetinghouse to Megachurch*, 7. The Raymond meetinghouse was also the community's first schoolhouse.
35 Maureen Ursenbach Beecher, "Mormon Women in Southern Alberta: The Pioneer Years," in *The Mormon Presence in Canada*, ed. Brigham Y. Card et al. (Edmonton: University of Alberta Press, 1990), 224.
36 MSS SC 2901, Richard W. Jackson, "Mormon Tabernacles: An Historical Exegesis, 1847–1937," 1997, LTPSC.
37 Richard W. Jackson, *Places of Worship: 150 Years of Latter-day Saint Architecture* (Provo, UT: Religious Studies Center, Brigham Young University, 2003), 136.
38 Jackson, *Places of Worship*, 137.
39 Jackson, *Places of Worship*, 148. Robert Twombly, *Frank Lloyd Wright: His Life and His Architecture* (New York: Wiley, 1979), 97.
40 Jackson, *Places of Worship*, 148.
41 Roberts, "Religious Architecture of the LDS Church," 324.
42 H. Allen Brooks, *The Prairie School: Frank Lloyd Wright and His Midwest Contemporaries* (New York W.W. Norton & Company, 1996), 84. See also Thomas Carter and Peter Goss, *Utah's Historic Architecture*, 143. Architects designed homes in the style of the Prairie School and public buildings, such as the Ladies Literary Club building in Salt Lake City (Ware and Treganza, 1912) and the LDS Branch for the Deaf in Ogden (Leslie Hodgson, 1916).
43 Twombly, *Frank Lloyd Wright*, 315.
44 John Lloyd Wright, *My Father, Frank Lloyd Wright* (New York: Dover Publications, 1992), 120.
45 Goldberger, *Why Architecture Matters*, 22.

46 Brooks, *The Prairie School*, 3 and 5.
47 Brooks, *The Prairie School*, 5.
48 Brooks, *The Prairie School*, 39. Also see Frank Lloyd Wright, *Frank Lloyd Wright: An Autobiography* (Petaluma, CA: Pomegranate Communications, 2005. Originally published in 1943), 157: "Design is abstraction of nature elements in purely geometric forms."
49 Jon C. Teaford, *Cities of the Heartland: The Rise and Fall of the Industrial Midwest* (Bloomington: Indiana University Press, 1993), 149.
50 Hatch, *Democratization*, 58.
51 Hatch, *Democratization*, 188.
52 Goldberger, *Why Architecture Matters*, 34.
53 Flake, *American Religious Identity*, 132.
54 Brooks, *The Prairie School*, 87.
55 Wright, *An Autobiography*, 154.
56 Wright, *An Autobiography*, 154–5.
57 Wright, *An Autobiography*, 274. Also see Brian R. Sinclair and Terence J. Walker, "Frank Lloyd Wright's Banff Pavilion: Critical Inquiry and Virtual Reconstruction," *APT Bulletin* 28, no. 2/3 (1997): 13–21. Banff is about 222 miles from Cardston. Also see Trevor Boddy, *Modern Architecture in Alberta* (Edmonton: Alberta Culture and Multiculturalism; Regina: Canadian Plains Research Center, 1987), 36–40.
58 Wright, *An Autobiography*, 274.
59 Sinclair and Walker, "Banff Pavilion," 14.
60 Sinclair and Walker, "Banff Pavilion," 16.
61 Rev. Rodney Andrews, "A History of St. Thomas' Anglican Church, Cardston," in *Chief Mountain Country: A History of Cardston and District*, ed. Keith Shaw, vol. 1 (Cardston: Cardston and District Historical Society, 1978), 188.
62 Wood, *The Alberta Temple*, 27–8. Cowan, "The Alberta Temple," 239.
63 Cowan, "The Alberta Temple," 240. Alberta Stake President Edward J. Wood recorded, "and to the surprise of us all he announced that the Church would build a Temple in Canada." See Melvin S. Tagg, "The Life of Edward James Wood" (MA thesis, Brigham Young University, 1959), 92.
64 Richard O. Cowan, *Temples to Dot the Earth* (Springville: Cedar Fort, 1997), 122. Under the direct supervisor of the First Presidency, the Presiding Bishop and his two counsellors make up the presiding bishopric and oversee tithing, membership records, and the Aaronic Priesthood. William Gibb Dyer Jr. and H. David Burton, "Presiding Bishopric," in *Encyclopedia of Mormonism*, ed. Daniel H. Ludlow (New York: Macmillan, 1992).
65 "Approved Design for Temple in Alberta Province," *Deseret Semi-Weekly News*, 2 January 1913. Cardston Alberta Temple: An Historical Record, University of Lethbridge.

66 W. McD. Tait, "The Mormon Temple in Canada," *The Canadian Magazine of Politics, Science, Art and Literature* 42 (1913): 488.
67 Edward James Wood, diary, 13 February 1913, microfilm of manuscript, Edward J. Wood Collection, 1884–1982, Church History Library. Olive Wood Nielson, *A Treasury of Edward J. Wood* (Salt Lake City: Publishers Press, 1983), 384.
68 Wood, *The Alberta Temple*, 31.
69 Wood, diary, 1 April 1913. Nielson, *Treasury*, 386.
70 Harold W. Burton, letter, 20 May 1969, photocopy of typescript, Harold W. Burton Papers, 1964–1969, Church History Library.
71 Chris Madsen, *Another Kind of Justice: Canadian Military Law from Confederation to Somalia* (Vancouver: UBC Press, 1999), 37.
72 James A. Wood, *Militia Myths: Ideas of the Canadian Citizen Soldier, 1896–1921* (Vancouver: UBC Press, 2010), 111.
73 Martha Sonntag Bradley and Mary Brown Firmage Woodward, *4 Zinas: A Story of Mothers and Daughters on the Mormon Frontier* (Salt Lake City: Signature Books, 2000), 411 and 417. The Quorum of the Twelve Apostles is a group of twelve men ordained to the Melchizedek Priesthood office of apostle who serve under the direction of the First Presidency. The Quorum of the Twelve supervise the Quorum of the Seventy, oversee the stakes and training of leaders. See William O. Nelson, "Quorum of the Twelve Apostles," in *Encyclopedia of Mormonism*, ed. Daniel H. Ludlow (New York: Macmillan, 1992): 1185–9.
74 Bradley and Woodward, *4 Zinas*, 417.
75 "Private Marion Stoddard Hanson," CEF Soldier Detail, *Canadian Great War Project*, http://www.canadiangreatwarproject.com/searches/soldier Detail.asp?ID=123024.
76 Mauss, *Angel and the Beehive*, x.
77 Joseph F. Smith, Anthon H. Lund, and Charles W. Penrose, "Editor's Table: Home Evening," 27 April 1915, *Improvement Era* 18 no. 8 (June 1915): 733.
78 Armand L. Mauss, "The Mormon Struggle with Assimilation and Identity: Trends and Developments Since Midcentury," *Dialogue: A Journal of Mormon Thought* 27, no. 1 (1994): 132.
79 Armand L. Mauss, "Assimilation and Ambivalence: The Mormon Reaction to Americanization," *Dialogue: A Journal of Mormon Thought* 22, no. 1 (1989): 41.
80 Paul L. Anderson, "The Early Twentieth Century Temples," *Dialogue: A Journal of Mormon Thought* 14, no. 1 (1981): 14.
81 Anderson, "The Early Twentieth Century Temples," 14.
82 Joseph Y. Card, "The Cardston Temple," *Improvement Era* 26, no. 11 (1923): 1003.
83 May Booth Talmage, "Our Visit to the Temple in Canada," *Young Woman's Journal* 34, no. 10 (1923): 518.

84 John A. Widtsoe, "Dedication of the Alberta Temple," *The Utah Genealogical and Historical Magazine* 14–15 (October 1923): 154.
85 Roberts, "Religious Architecture of the LDS Church," 307.
86 Roberts, "Religious Architecture of the LDS Church," 307.
87 Roberts, "Religious Architecture of the LDS Church," 324.
88 Anderson, "First of the Modern Temples."
89 Roberts, "Religious Architecture of the LDS Church," 324.
90 Roberts, "Religious Architecture of the LDS Church," 325.
91 Anderson, "Twentieth Century Temples," 14.
92 Paul L. Anderson, "Mormon Moderne: Latter-day Saint Architecture, 1925–1945," *Journal of Mormon History* 9, no. 1 (1982): 72.
93 Allen Dale Roberts, *Salt Lake City's Historic Architecture* (Charleston: Arcadia Publishing, 2012), 24.
94 Roberts, *Salt Lake City's Historic Architecture*, 123.
95 C. Frank Steele, "The Cardston Temple," *Juvenile Instructor* 58 no. 9 (1923): 439.
96 Wood, *The Alberta Temple*, 73.
97 Mauss, *Angel and the Beehive*, 3.
98 Carl A. Dawson, *Group Settlement: Ethnic Communities in Western Canada* (Toronto: Macmillan, 1936. Reprint, Millwood, NY: Kraus, 1974), 223.
99 Alan Colquhoun, *Modern Architecture* (Oxford: Oxford University Press, 2002), 10.
100 Hyrum C. Pope, speech, 29 August 1923, microfilm, Hyrum C. Pope Papers, Church History Library.
101 Boddy, *Modern Architecture in Alberta*, 33.

7 Conclusion

1 Austin Fife and Alta Fife, "Gravestone Imagery," in *Utah Folk Art: A Catalog of Material Culture*, ed. Hal Cannon and Utah Arts Council (Provo, UT: Brigham Young University Press, 1980), 138.
2 Carol Edison, "Mormon Gravestones: A Folk Expression of Identity and Belief," *Dialogue: A Journal of Mormon Thought* 22, no. 4 (1989): 89. Also see Nancy Millar, *Once Upon a Tomb: Stories from Canadian Graveyards* (Calgary: Fifth House, 1997), 2. Millar said that graveyards are "microcosms of our communities." Richard H. Jackson agrees that "each cemetery is an ever changing volume that records the history, values, and dreams of a people and place." See Richard H. Jackson, "Mormon Cemeteries: History in Stone," in *Nearly Everything Imaginable: The Everyday Life of Utah's Mormon Pioneers*, ed. Ronald W. Walker and Doris R. Dant (Provo, UT: Brigham Young University Press, 1999), 405.
3 Steve C. Martens and Nancy Volkman, "Cemeteries," in *The Encyclopedia of the Great Plains*, ed. David J. Wishart (Lincoln & London: University of Nebraska Press, 2004), 70.

4 John Gary Brown, "Grave Markers," *The Encyclopedia of the Great Plains*, ed. David J. Wishart (Lincoln: University of Nebraska Press, 2004), 303.
5 Elizabethada A. Wright, "Rhetorical Spaces in Memorial Places: The Cemetery as a Rhetorical Memory Place/Space," *Rhetoric Society Quarterly* 35, no. 4 (Fall, 2005): 51. Wright continued, "If one sees cemeteries as a rhetorical space, then there are thousands upon thousands of voices clamouring to be heard, a cacophony of remembrances are calling out" (60).
6 Jackson, "Mormon Cemeteries," 408. Douglas Keister, *Stories in Stone: A Field Guide to Cemetery Symbolism and Iconography* (Layton: Gibbs Smith, 2004), 108. Ren Davis and Helen Davis, *Atlanta's Oakland Cemetery: An Illustrated History and Guide* (Athens and London: The Historic Oakland Foundation and the University of Georgia Press, 2012), 189.
7 Comes from the 2nd verse of a hymn written by Isaac Watts (1674–1748) "A Funeral Ode at the Interrment of the Body, Supposed to be Sung by the Mourners" – "No pain, no grief, no anxious fear / Invade thy bounds; no mortal woes / Can reach the lovely sleeper here." Like many Christian denominations of the time, Mormons adopted these lyrics during their time in Nauvoo, Illinois in 1841. Shane J. Chism, ed., *A Selection of Early Mormon Hymnbooks, 1832–72: Hymn books and Broadsides from the First 40 Years of the Church of Jesus Christ of Latter-day Saints* (Tuscon: [publisher not identified], 2011), 336. The hymn appeared as "Hymn 223" in Emma Smith, ed., *A Collection of Sacred Hymns, for the Church of Jesus Christ of Latter-Day Saints* (Nauvoo, IL: E. Robinson, 1841), 241.
8 American Monument Association, *Memorial Symbolism, Epitaphs and Design Types* (Boston: American Monument Association, 1947), 21. Mike Filey, *Mount Pleasant Cemetery: An Illustrated Guide* (Toronto: Dundurn Press, 1999), 19. Douglas Keister, *Stories in Stone*, 57. Davis and Davis, *Atlanta's Oakland Cemetery*, 188–9.
9 American Monument Association, *Memorial Symbolism*, 21. Keister, *Stories in Stone*, 61. Thomas R. Dilley, *The Art of Memory: Historic Cemeteries of Grand Rapids, Michigan* (Detroit: Wayne State University Press, 2014), 160.
10 Revelation 14:13, KJV.
11 Matthew Henry, *A Commentary on the Holy Bible with Practical Remarks and Observations, Volume IX* (New York and London: Funk & Wagnalls Company, 1850), 804.
12 1 Thessalonins 4:14, KJV. Another possible verse: "But now is Christ risen from the dead, and become the first fruits of them that slept" (1 Cor. 15:20).
13 Margaret Mackay, "Asleep in Jesus," in *A Library of Poetry for Sunday Reading*, ed. Philip Schaff and Arthur Gilman (New York: Dodd, Mead and Company, 1880), 683.
14 Joseph Smith, "The King Follett Sermon," in *History of the Church of Jesus Christ of Latter-day Saints*, ed. B.H. Roberts (Salt Lake City: Church of Jesus Christ of Latter-day Saints, 1948): 6: 315.

15 Douglas J. Davies, *Death, Ritual and Belief: The Rhetoric of Funerary Rites* (London: Cassell, 1997), 112. Mauro Properzi, *Mormonism and the Emotions: An Analysis of LDS Scriptural Texts* (Madison: Fairleigh Dickinson University Press, 2015), 97.
16 Eliza R. Snow, "Bury Me Quietly When I Die," *The Woman's Exponent* 10, no. 13 (1881): 97.
17 Mary Ann Meyers, "Gates Ajar: Death in Mormon Thought and Practice," in *Death in America*, ed. David E. Stannard (Philadelphia: University of Pennsylvania Press, 1975), 114.
18 Douglas J. Davies, *The Mormon Culture of Salvation* (Aldershot: Ashgate Publishing, 2000), 85.
19 Davies, *Mormon Culture of Salvation*, 86.
20 Jackson, "Mormon Cemeteries," 408. Also see Matthew 7:13–14: "Enter ye in the strait gate: for wide is the gate, and broad is the way, that leadeth to destruction, and many there be which go in thereat: Because strait is the gate, and narrow is the way, which leadeth unto life, and few there be that find it" (KJV).
21 Keister, *Stories in Stone*, 116. Also, John 10:9–16, KJV.
22 Dilley, *The Art of Memory*, 163.
23 Abbie A. Bird, "To the Memory of Those Who Are Gone," *The Young Woman's Journal* 8, no. 1 (1896): 1.
24 Edison, "Mormon Gravestones," 92.
25 Edison, "Mormon Gravestones," 92.
26 Keister, *Stories in Stone*, 121.
27 Edison, "Mormon Gravestones," 92.
28 James T. Duke, "Marriage: Eternal Marriage," in *Encyclopedia of Mormonism*, ed. Daniel H. Ludlow (New York: Macmillan, 1992), 858–9. Also see http://ldschurchtemples.org/mormon/marriage/.
29 Paul V. Hyer, "Sealing: Temple Sealings," in *Encyclopedia of Mormonism*, ed. Daniel H. Ludlow (New York: Macmillan, 1992), 1289. Also see, "About the Temple Endowment," Temples, The Church of Jesus Christ of Latter-day Saints, https://www.churchofjesuschrist.org/temples/what-is-temple-endowment?lang=eng.
30 Edison, "Mormon Gravestones," 91.
31 Colleen McDannell and Bernhard Lang, "Modern Heave ... and a Theology," in *Mormons and Mormonism: An Introduction to an American World Religion*, ed. Eric A. Eliason (Urbana and Chicago: University of Illinois Press, 2001), 142.

Bibliography

Primary Sources

Alberta Farmers' Association. Alberta Farmers' Association minute book, 1906–1907. United Farmers of Alberta fonds, Glenbow Archives, Calgary, Alberta.

Alberta Star. "Local and General." 26 November 1903.

Allred, Josephine Leavitt. Oral history. Interview by Orvilla Allred Stevens. Provo, Utah. 1976. Transcript. Church History Library, The Church of Jesus Christ of Latter-day Saints, Salt Lake City, Utah.

Anderson, Irene Ruth Mercer. Irene M. Anderson Collection, 1884–1978. Church History Library, The Church of Jesus Christ of Latter-day Saints, Salt Lake City, Utah.

Anderson, Mary Ann Ross. Autobiographical sketch. "The Story of My Life: Mary Ann Ross Anderson." Typescript Low Family Histories, circa 1960, 2006. Church History Library, The Church of Jesus Christ of Latter-day Saints, Salt Lake City, Utah.

Angell, Truman Osborn. MSS 937. Autobiography. Ca. 1884. L. Tom Perry Special Collections, Harold B. Lee Library, Brigham Young University, Provo, Utah.

Bates, Jane E. Biography. Photocopy of typescript. "Biographical Sketch of Mary Lucretia Hyde Woolf." Virginia F. Bates Layton Collection of Family Biographies. Church History Library, The Church of Jesus Christ of Latter-day Saints, Salt Lake City, Utah.

Bennett, Inez R. "Lethbridge Constituency Holds First U.F.W.A. Conference." *The U.F.A.* 1 December 1930.

Bingham, Rojanea Jacobs. Family history. Ca. 1970. Photocopy of typescript. Rojanea J. Binham History of Dora Hinman Jacobs, circa 1970. Church History Library, The Church of Jesus Christ of Latter-day Saints, Salt Lake City, Utah.

Bird, Abbie A. "To the Memory of Those Who Are Gone." *The Young Woman's Journal* 8, no. 1 (1896): 1.

Blackmore, John Horn. John Blackmore fonds. Glenbow Archives, Calgary, Alberta.

Blackmore, Lorna. Affidavit #1. Sworn 25 June 2010. No. S-097767, Vancouver Registry. In the Supreme Court of British Columbia, in the Matter of: The Constitutional Question Act, R.S.B.C. 1996, C.68, and in the Matter of: The *Canadian Charter of Rights and Freedoms*, and in the Matter of: A reference by the Lieutenant Governor in council set out in order in council no. 533 dated October 22, 2009 concerning the constitutionality of S. 293 of the Criminal Code of Canada, R.S.C. 1985, c. C-46.

Blackmore, Orpha Vance, ed. "Life of Harold Horn (Pete) Blackmore." Unpublished manuscript, last modified May 1997. Microsoft Word file.

Bolderson, E.H. Letter to R. Burton Deane. 10 February 1899. Microfilm. "Mormons at Cardstone [sic] – Report on polygamous practices amongst." Royal Canadian Mounted Police fonds. Subject files, volume 169. Library and Archives Canada, Ottawa, Ontario.

Bradley-Evans, Martha. MSS 3192. Martha Sonntag Bradley research papers. 20th Century Western & Mormon Manuscripts. L. Tom Perry Special Collections, Harold B. Lee Library, Brigham Young University, Provo, Utah.

Bradshaw, Vilate. "Biography of Richard William Bradshaw." Contributed by richardcarlylebradshaw1 on 9 March 2015. https://www.familysearch.org/photos/artifacts/14085384.

Brandley, Louis Orson. Oral history. Interviewed by Charles Ursenbach. Raymond, Alberta. 1976. Transcript. Church History Library, The Church of Jesus Christ of Latter-day Saints, Salt Lake City, Utah.

Brooks, Willard Montgomery. Oral history. Interviewed by Charles Ursenbach. Cardston and Calgary, Alberta. 1974–5. Transcript. Church History Library, The Church of Jesus Christ of Latter-day Saints, Salt Lake City, Utah.

Brown, Hugh Brown. *Hugh B. Brown Family Papers, 1835–1982*. Church History Library, The Church of Jesus Christ of Latter-day Saints, Salt Lake City, Utah.

Burton, Harold W. Harold W. Burton Papers, 1964–9. Church History Library, The Church of Jesus Christ of Latter-day Saints, Salt Lake City, Utah.

The Bystander. March 1881.

The Canada Presbyterian. 21 November 1888.

"Canadian Churchman Dies." *The Church News.* 1 February 1958.

Card, Charles Ora. MSS 1543. Charles Ora Card collection. 19th Century Western & Mormon Manuscripts. L. Tom Perry Special Collections, Harold B. Lee Library, Brigham Young University, Provo, Utah.

Card, Joseph Y. MSS 1522. Joseph Y. Card diaries. 19th Century Western & Mormon Manuscripts. L. Tom Perry Special Collections, Harold B. Lee Library, Brigham Young University, Provo, Utah.

Card, Joseph Y. "The Cardston Temple." *Improvement Era* 26, no. 11 (1923): 1001–1009.
Cardston 1st Ward General Minutes, 1914–1977. Church History Library, The Church of Jesus Christ of Latter-day Saints, Salt Lake City, Utah.
Cardston Alberta Stake General Minutes, 1894–1974. Church History Library, The Church of Jesus Christ of Latter-day Saints, Salt Lake City, Utah.
Cardston Alberta Stake Relief Society Minutes and Records, 1894–1973. Church History Library, The Church of Jesus Christ of Latter-day Saints, Salt Lake City, Utah.
Cardston Historical Society. "Biography of John Horn Blackmore." Families. Accessed 19 April 2016. http://www.cardstonhistoricalsociety.org/families_b.htm.
Cardston News. "W.I. Convention of Cardston Constituency Held at Spring Coulee." 23 September 1925.
Cardston News. "H.W. Wood Explains." 4 February 1926.
Cardston News. "The Aims of the U.F.A." 4 February 1926.
Cardston News. "Mrs. Huyck Points Out Aims of W.I." 18 March 1926.
Cardston News. "Liberal Rally at Owendale." 24 June 1926.
Cardston News. "How Cardston Constituency Voted." 1 July 1926.
Cardston News. "U.F.W.A." 22 March 1928.
Cardston News. "D.H. Elton, K.C. Addresses M.I.A.'s of Both Wards." 6 December 1928.
Cardston News. "George L. Stringam Wins Farmers' Convention Nomination." 29 May 1930.
Cardston News. "George L. Stringam, M.L.A. U.F.A. Candidate for Cardston Riding." 12 June 1930.
Cardston News. "D.H. Elton 'Cheers' Glenwood Audiences." 30 October 1930.
Cardston News. 30 April 1931.
Cardston News. "W.I. Studies Immigration." 14 July 1932.
Cardston News. "Here and There." 2 August 1934.
Cardston News. "Brief History of Cardston Women's Institute." 23 August 1934.
Cardston News. "J.A. Johansen Nominated as Federal U.F.A. – C.C.F. Candidate." 13 August 1935.
Cardston News. "C.C.F. Program Explained at Gym Meeting." 8 October 1935.
Cardston News. "Alberta Remains Social Credit." 15 October 1935.
Cardston News. "Thumb-Nail Sketch No. 12: Talitha May Carlson." 2 February 1937.
Cardston News. "1700 Hear Conference Speakers." 12 July 1938.
Cardston News. "Special Thanksgiving Services." 4 October 1938.
Cardston News. 13 December 1938.
Cardston News. "Aetna." 21 February 1939.
Cardston News. "W.I. Studies Child Welfare." 9 June 1939.

Cardston News. "Ella Elizabeth Nelson Laid to Rest." 11 November 1941.
Cardston News. "C.C.F. Rally." 30 March 1944.
Cardston News. "Take a Step Forward with the C.C.F." 3 August 1944.
Cardston News. 5 July 1945.
Cardston News. 12 July 1945.
Cardston News. "Elders Party." 16 August 1945.
Cardston News. "Fireside Chat." 10 January 1946.
Cardston News. "Fireside Chat." 28 November 1946.
Cardston Record. "Simple Salve." 17 September 1898.
Cardston Record. "Local and General." 8 February 1899.
Cardston Ward Relief Society Minutes and Records, 1887–1911. Church History Library, The Church of Jesus Christ of Latter-day Saints, Salt Lake City, Utah.
Card, Zina Y. "The Sisters in Canada." *The Woman's Exponent* 19, no. 13 (December 1890): 101.
Census of Canada, 1880–81, Volume 3. Ottawa: Maclean, Rogers & Co., 1883.
Census of Canada, 1890–91, Volume 1. Ottawa: S.E. Dawson, 1893.
Census of the three provisional districts of the North-West Territories, 1884–5 = Recensement des trois districts provisoires des Territoires du Nord-Ouest, 1884–5. Ottawa: MacLean, Roger & Co., 1886.
The Children's Record. "A Big Family." 14, no. 8 (August 1899): 123–4.
Church of Jesus Christ of Latter-day Saints. *Seventieth Annual Conference of the Church of Jesus Christ of Latter-day Saints.* Salt Lake City: The Deseret News, 1900.
Church of Jesus Christ of Latter-day Saints. "A Tabernacle in the Wilderness: A History of the Alberta Stake Tabernacle." Last updated 7 June 2012. https://history.lds.org/article/cardston-tabernacle.
Church of Jesus Christ of Latter-day Saints. "Official Declaration 1." Scriptures. Accessed 13 January 2015. https://www.lds.org/scriptures/dc-testament/od/1?lang=eng.
Church of Jesus Christ of Latter-day Saints. "Relief Society." Handbook 2: Administering the Church. Accessed 6 April 2016. https://www.lds.org/handbook/handbook-2-administering-the-church/relief-society?lang=eng.
Church of Jesus Christ of Latter-day Saints. "About the Temple Endowment." Temples. Accessed 30 June 2021. https://www.churchofjesuschrist.org/temples/what-is-temple-endowment?lang=eng
Clark, J. Reuben Jr. "Private Ownership ... under the United Order." *Conference Report* (October 1942): 54–9.
Clarke, P. D. Complaint No. 65430. Filed 22 October 1940. District Court of the Third Judicial District in and for Salt Lake County, State of Utah. Utah State Archives, Salt Lake City, Utah.
Clarke, Xarissa Merkley. Oral history. Interviewed by Marsha C. Martin. 4 December 1982. Transcript. LDS Family Life Oral History Project, 1959–

1984. 20th Century Western & Mormon Manuscripts. L. Tom Perry Special Collections, Harold B. Lee Library, Brigham Young University, Provo, Utah.

College of Physicians and Surgeons. The North-West Territories medical register: Printed and published under the direction of the Council of the College of Physicians and Surgeons, N.W.T., in accordance with chapter 52 of the consolidated ordinances, North-West Territories, 1899, entitled an ordinance respecting the medical profession in force March 15, 1899. Prince Albert: College of Physicians and Surgeons, N.W.T, 1899.

Deane, R. Burton. Letter to Commissioner Lawrence W. Herchmer. 17 March 1899. Microfilm. "Mormons at Cardstone [sic] – Report on polygamous practices amongst." Royal Canadian Mounted Police fonds. Subject files, volume 169. Library and Archives Canada, Ottawa, Ontario.

Deane, R. Burton. Annual Report of Superintendent R. B. Deane, Commanding Macleod District. *Sessional Papers of the Dominion of Canada: Volume 12, Fifth Session of the Eighth Parliament, Session 1900*. Ottawa: S.E. Dawson, 1900.

Debates of the Senate of the Dominion of Canada: Fourth Session – Sixth Parliament. Ottawa; Brown Chamberlin, 1890.

Deseret Semi-Weekly News. "Approved Design for Temple in Alberta Province." 2 January 1913. Cardston Alberta Temple: An Historical Record, University of Lethbridge, Lethbridge, Alberta.

Edmonton Bulletin. "Mormons in Canada." 21 December 1889.

Edmonton Bulletin. "Sugar Beets in the South." 7 October 1901.

Edmonton Bulletin. "Cochrane Ranch Goes to Mormons." 29 September 1907.

Edmonton Bulletin. "Consider Farmers' Interests." 1 August 1908.

Edmonton Bulletin. "Bore for Gas at Lethbridge." 22 September 1909.

Edmonton Bulletin. "Directors Are Chosen for the United Farmers." 25 January 1919.

Edmonton Bulletin. "The Wheat Pool Contract." 18 August 1923.

Edward Jenkins Leavitt obituary. 1958. Contributed by Dave Olsen on 5 August 2014. https://www.familysearch.org/photos/artifacts/9095194.

Fisher, Franklin Pierce. Autobiography. "To My Children." Magrath Museum, Magrath, Alberta.

Fossey, Charles W. "Brief History." Magrath Museum, Magrath, Alberta.

General Report of the Census of Canada, 1880–1, Volume 4. Ottawa: Maclean, Roger & Co.: 1885.

The Globe and Mail. "Alberta Mines Minister Is Mormon Bishop." 6 January 1937.

The Globe and Mail. "Mormon Gets Cabinet Post." 2 February 1937.

Golden Jubilee of the Town of Raymond, Alberta. Raymond, AB: Chamber of Commerce, 1951.

Goldfrank, Esther Schiff. *Changing Configurations in the Social Organization of a Blackfoot Tribe During the Reserve Period*. Seattle: University of Washington Press, 1966.

Government of Canada. Census of Canada, 1901. Library and Archives Canada, Ottawa, Ontario. Accessed 19 April 2016. http://data2.collectionscanada.ca/1901/z/z004/jpg/z000178894.jpg.

Government of Canada. Census of Manitoba, Saskatchewan, and Alberta, 1916. Library and Archives Canada, Ottawa, Ontario. Accessed 19 January 2017. http://www.bac-lac.gc.ca/eng/census/1916/Pages/item.aspx?itemid=260384.

Government of Canada. Census of Manitoba, Saskatchewan, and Alberta, 1916. Library and Archives Canada, Ottawa, Ontario. Accessed 19 April 2016. http://data2.collectionscanada.ca/006003/t-21951/jpg/31228_4363980-00947.jpg.

Green, Arthur Nalder. Oral History. Interviewed by Charles Ursenbach. Lethbridge, Alberta. 1973. Transcript. Church History Library, The Church of Jesus Christ of Latter-day Saints, Salt Lake City, Utah.

Greenland, Helen. Biographical sketch. 1986. "Magrath, Alberta, Canada." Photocopy of typescript. Miller, Peterson, Bolander, and Wells Family Biographies. Church History Library, The Church of Jesus Christ of Latter-day Saints, Salt Lake City, Utah.

Grinnell, George Bird. *Blackfoot Lodge Tales: The Story of a Prairie People.* New York: Scribner, 1892. Reprint, Lincoln: University of Nebraska Press, 1962.

Groo, M.M. "R.S. Reports." *The Woman's Exponent* 2, no. 4 (1873): 26.

Hans, E.N. Wight fonds. Glenbow Archives, Calgary, Alberta.

Herchmer, Lawrence William. Annual Report of the Commissioner of the North-West Mounted Police, 1888. In *Report of the Commissioner of the North-West Mounted Police, 1888,* 7–23. Ottawa: Queen's Printer and Controller of Stationery, A. Senecal, 1889.

Herchmer, Lawrence William. Annual Report of Commissioner L. W. Herchmer North-West Mounted Police, 1893. *Sessional Papers of the Dominion of Canada: Volume 11, Fourth Session of the Seventh Parliament, Session 1894.* Ottawa: S.E. Dawson, 1894.

Hicken, John Orwin. Oral history. Interviewed by Charles Ursenbach. Raymond, Alberta. 1974. Transcript. Church History Library, The Church of Jesus Christ of Latter-day Saints, Salt Lake City, Utah.

Hicken, J. Orwin, Kay B. Redd, and John L. Evans. *Raymond, 1901–1967.* Lethbridge, AB: Lethbridge Herald Co., 1967.

Jackman, W. J. "A Wheat Pool for Alberta." *The U.F.A.* 16 July 1923.

Jackson, Richard W. MSS SC 2901. "Mormon Tabernacles: An Historical Exegesis, 1847–1937." 1997. L. Tom Perry Special Collections, Harold B. Lee Library, Brigham Young University, Provo, Utah.

Jamieson, Heber Carss. *Early Medicine in Alberta: The First Seventy-Five Years.* Edmonton: Canadian Medical Association Alberta division, 1947.

Jensen, Lalovee R. "History of Christian Jensen Jr." https://www.familysearch.org/photos/artifacts/1156890.
Johnson, Beth. Carol and Beth Johnson Fonds, Glenbow Archives, Calgary, Alberta.
Journals of the First Legislative Assembly of the North-West Territories. Regina.: R. B. Gordon, 1891.
Keele, W.C. *The Provincial Justice, or Magistrate's Manual, Being a Complete Digest of the Criminal Law of Canada and a Compendious and General View of the Provincial Law of Upper Canada: With Practical Forms, for the Use of the Magistracy.* 4th ed. Toronto: Henry Roswell, 1858.
Kells, Edna. "Story of the Cardston Hospital." *Cardston News.* 17 October 1929.
Kelly, Leroy Victor. *The Story of the Ranchers and Indians of Alberta.* Toronto: William Briggs, 1913.
Kidd, Miss. J.B. "The United Farm Women of Alberta in Convention." *The U.F.A.* 15 February 1923.
Kidd, Miss. J.B. "The Women's Convention in Retrospect." *The U.F.A.* 1 February 1924.
Knight Academy. MSS 838. Minutes of Faculty Meetings, 1910–1921. L. Tom Perry Special Collections, Harold B. Lee Library, Brigham Young University, Provo, Utah.
Larson, Viola Blackmore. Biography. "Life of John H. Blackmore." Archives of the Cardston Historical Society, Courthouse Museum, Cardston, Alberta.
Leavitt Family Organization. *The Life of Thomas Rowell Leavitt and His Descendants.* Lethbridge, AB: The Herald Printers, 1975.
Leavitt Ward Relief Society Minutes and Records, 1910–1973. Church History Library, The Church of Jesus Christ of Latter-day Saints, Salt Lake City, Utah.
Lethbridge Constituency, *The United Farmers of Alberta (Inc.) Annual Report and Year Book Containing Reports of Officers and Committees for the Year 1918 Together with Official Minutes of the Eleventh Annual Convention.*
Lethbridge Constituency. *The United Farmers of Alberta (Inc.) Annual Report and Year Book Containing Reports of Officers and Committees for the Year 1921 Together with Official Minutes of the Fourteenth Annual Convention.*
Lethbridge Daily Herald. "Old-Timer of Cardston Dead." 12 April 1918.
Lethbridge Daily Herald. "Boy Scouts Lauded by Mormon Apostle at Raymond Meeting." 17 August 1922.
Lethbridge Daily Herald. "Fathers and Sons of Three Stakes to Stage Outing." 1 May 1924.
Lethbridge Daily Herald. "Social Credit Group Will Support King If He Implements Promises; Blackmore Sure Dividend Possible." 22 November 1935.
Lethbridge Herald. 23 August 1947.
Lethbridge Herald. "District News." 3 December 1947.
Lethbridge Herald. "Excommunication of Lethbridge M.P. Is Confirmed." 29 December 1947.

Lethbridge Herald. "Blackmore Won't Go into Details." 30 December 1947.
Lethbridge Herald. "Says Creston Valley Cases Are Set for Trial." 1 August 1953.
Lethbridge Herald. "LDS Officials Hold Church Trial in B.C." 5 August 1953.
Lethbridge Herald. "10 Ousted from Mormon Faith in B.C. Colony." 21 August 1953.
Lethbridge Herald. "A Valued Citizen." 23 January 1958.
Lethbridge News. "St. Augustine's Church." 29 March 1888.
Lethbridge News. "The Mormon Question." 23 July 1890.
Lethbridge News. "Cullings From Cardston." 13 July 1893.
Lethbridge News. "Local Topics." 27 February 1902.
Lethbridge News. "Words of Advice by C.O. Card." 16 December 1903.
Lethbridge News. "Local Topics." 30 October 1906.
Mackay, Margaret. "Asleep in Jesus." In *A Library of Poetry for Sunday Reading*, edited by Philip Schaff and Arthur Gilman, 683. New York: Dodd, Mead and Company, 1880.
Mackintosh, Charles Herbert. Annual Report of the Department of the Interior for the Year 1893. *Sessional Papers of the Dominion of Canada: Volume 10, Fourth Session of the Seventh Parliament, Session 1894*. Ottawa: S.E. Dawson, 1894.
Maclean, John. *The Indians, Their Manners and Customs*. Toronto: William Briggs, 1889.
Maclean, John. *Canadian Savage Folk: The Native Tribes of Canada*. Toronto: William Briggs, 1896.
Maclean, John. *The Warden of the Plains and Other Stories of Line in the Canadian North-West*. Toronto: William Briggs, 1896.
The Macleod Gazette. "Our Mormon Settlers." 27 September 1887.
Magrath 1st Ward Manuscript History and Historical Reports, 1899–1984. Church History Library, The Church of Jesus Christ of Latter-day Saints, Salt Lake City, Utah.
Magrath 1st Ward Young Women's Mutual Improvement Association Minutes and Records, 1899–1973. Church History Library, The Church of Jesus Christ of Latter-day Saints, Salt Lake City, Utah.
Magrath and District History Association. *Irrigation Builders*. Magrath, AB: Magrath and District History Association, 1974.
Magrath Pioneer. "The Home Doctor." 29 May 1907.
Magrath Pioneer. "Local and General." 5 June 1907.
Magrath Pioneer. "Home Cures." 26 May 1908.
Magrath Pioneer. "Home Cures." 2 June 1908.
Magrath Pioneer. "The Home Doctor." 15 September 1908.
Magrath Pioneer. "Home Cures." 15 March 1910.
Magrath Pioneer. "Newsy Items of Local & General interest." 21 June 1910.
Matkin, Charles Samuel. Oral History. Interviewed by Charles Ursenbach. Magrath, Alberta. 18 July 1975. Transcript. Church History Library, The Church of Jesus Christ of Latter-day Saints, Salt Lake City, Utah.

Matkin, Heber James. Oral history. Interviewed by Charles Ursenbach. Lethbridge, Alberta. 1974. Transcript. Church History Library, The Church of Jesus Christ of Latter-day Saints, Salt Lake City, Utah.

Matthews, C. Syd. "14 Religious Sects Have Representation in Alberta House." *The Globe and Mail*. 25 February 1937.

McKight, J.W. Rulon Jeffs' Answer to Complaint No. 65430. Filed 14 December 1940. District Court of the Third Judicial District in and for Salt Lake County, State of Utah. Utah State Archives, Salt Lake City, Utah.

Merrill, Dorothy Jean. "A History of Ella Elizabeth Thomas Nelson." https://www.familysearch.org/photos/artifacts/12705480.

The Monetary Times: Trade Review and Insurance Chronicle. "Mercantile Summary." 17 March 1905.

Moose Jaw Herald Times. "The Mormon Cardston Company." 7 November 1890.

Official Report of the Debates of the House of Commons of the Dominion of Canada: Fourth Session-Fourth Parliament. Ottawa: Maclean, Roger & Co., 1882.

Official Report of the Debates of the House of Commons of the Dominion of Canada: Third Session-Sixth Parliament. Ottawa: Brown Chamberlin, 1889.

Official Report of the Debates of the House of Commons of the Dominion of Canada: Fourth Session-Sixth Parliament. Ottawa: Brown Chamberlin, 1890.

Orders in Council: Proclamations and Regulations Having Force of Law in the Dominion of Canada, Issued During the Years 1881 and 1882. Ottawa: B. Chamberlin, 1882.

Ordinances of the North-West Territories Passed in the Third Session of the Third Legislative Assembly. Regina: John Alexander Reid, Queen's Printer for the Territories, 1898.

Ostlund, Anna Brandley. "My Father, Theodore Brandley." 1961. Photocopy. Church History Library, The Church of Jesus Christ of Latter-day Saints, Salt Lake City, Utah.

Ottawa 1st Ward General Minutes, 1926–1973. Church History Library, The Church of Jesus Christ of Latter-day Saints, Salt Lake City, Utah.

Palmer, Asael E. MSS 6084. Asael E. Palmer papers. 20th Century Western and Mormon Manuscripts. L. Tom Perry Special Collections, Harold B. Lee Library, Brigham Young University, Provo, Utah.

Palmer, Mable Johansen. "History of John Albert Johansen." https://www.familysearch.org/photos/artifacts/4217035.

Palmer, Maydell Cazier. Autobiography. 1980. "Autobiography of Maydell Cazier Palmer." Church History Library, The Church of Jesus Christ of Latter-day Saints, Salt Lake City, Utah.

Paxman, Ezra Love. Autobiographical account. Ca. 1959. "The Life Story of Ezra Paxman." Ezra Love Paxman fonds. Glenbow Archives, Calgary, Alberta.

Peterson, Lawrence. "Lethbridge." *The United Farmers of Alberta (Inc.) Annual Report and Year Book Containing Reports of Officers and Committees for the Year 1919 Together with Official Minutes of the Twelfth Annual Convention.*

Peterson, Lawrence. Lethbridge speech on 14 December 1921, Barnwell, Alberta. *The United Farmers of Alberta (Inc.) Annual Report and Year Book Containing Reports of Officers and Committees for the Year 1921 Together with Official Minutes of the Fourteenth Annual Convention.*

Pitcher, Frank H. Frank H. Pitcher Autobiography, Circa 1978. Church History Library, The Church of Jesus Christ of Latter-day Saints, Salt Lake City, Utah.

Pope, Hyrum C. Speech. 29 August 1923. Microfilm. Hyrum C. Pope Papers. Church History Library, The Church of Jesus Christ of Latter-day Saints, Salt Lake City, Utah.

Pratt, Thomas William. Oral History. Interviewed by Charles Ursenbach. Lethbridge, Alberta. 9–10 March 1974. Transcript. Church History Library, The Church of Jesus Christ of Latter-day Saints, Salt Lake City, Utah.

"Private Marion Stoddard Hanson," CEF Soldier Detail, *Canadian Great War Project*. Last updated 11 November 2016. http://www.canadiangreatwarproject.com.

Rachel Ackroyd Forsyth History, Magrath Museum, Magrath, Alberta.

Raymond, Alberta, Canada Stake Manuscript History and Historical Reports, 1903–1975. Church History Library, The Church of Jesus Christ of Latter-day Saints, Salt Lake City, Utah.

Raymond, Alberta, Canada Stake Melchizedek Priesthood Minutes and Records, 1900–1973. Church History Library, The Church of Jesus Christ of Latter-day Saints, Salt Lake City, Utah.

Raymond Leader. "Red Cross Is Doing Well." 15 April 1916.

Raymond Leader. "Institute Holds Annual Meeting." 16 December 1916.

Raymond Recorder. "U.F.W.A. Meeting." 12 February 1926.

Raymond Recorder. 11 June 1926.

Raymond Recorder. "News Notes." 10 June 1927.

Raymond Recorder. "Splendid Program for Sunday at the 1st Ward." 1 February 1929.

Raymond Recorder. "U.F.W.A. Hold Interesting Meeting." 24 July 1931.

Raymond Recorder. "Mrs. Ross Again Heads Local U.F.W.A." 27 November 1931.

Raymond Recorder. "U.F. and U.F.W.A. Meeting." 4 January 1933.

Raymond Recorder. "Raymond U.F.W.A. Local Re-Elects President." 14 December 1933.

Raymond Recorder. "Baby Clinic Very Successful." 5 July 1934.

Raymond Recorder. "U.F.W.A. Meeting." 1 March 1935.

Raymond Recorder. "Mayor Elton At Second Ward." 6 May 1938.

Raymond Recorder. "Quarterly Conference." 15 July 1938.

Raymond Recorder. 19 August 1938.

Raymond Recorder. "W.I. Meeting." 20 June 1941.
Raymond Recorder. "News Notes." 29 May 1942.
Raymond Recorder. "Funeral Services for Mrs. Ella Milner." 4 June 1943.
Raymond Recorder. "News Notes." 28 July 1944.
Raymond Recorder. 6 December 1945.
Raymond Rustler. "Health Hints." 19 March 1909.
Raymond Rustler. "Health Hints." 7 January 1910.
Redcliff Review. "Elect Trustees for Alberta Wheat Pool." 23 August 1923.
Red Deer News. "Co-operation in Alberta: Annual Meeting of Alberta Co-operative League." 11 June 1924.
Richards, Mrs. L. Green. "R.S. Reports." *The Woman's Exponent* 2 no. 4 (1873): 27.
Royal, Joseph. Report Concerning the Administration of the North-West Territories for the Year 1892. *Annual Report of the Department of the Interior for the Year 1892*. Ottawa: S.E. Dawson, 1893.
Russell, Hannah Marie Child. Letter to granddaughter Beth. In *Roots and Wings*, compiled by Luann De Hart Gray, 206–209. Boise, ID: L.D.H. Gray, 2000.
Salmon, Eva Dahl. Oral history. Interviewed by Margaret Erickson Young. Lethbridge, Alberta. 8 June 1983. Transcript. Lethbridge Alberta East Stake oral history program. Church History Library, The Church of Jesus Christ of Latter-day Saints, Salt Lake City, Utah.
Salt Lake Herald. "Incorporated: The Alberta Land and Stock Company File Articles." 17 June 1896.
Saturday News. "The Farmers' Association." 30 December 1905.
Shaw, Vernon. "Our Letter Box." *Cardston News*. 18 May 1937.
Smith, Emma, editor. *A Collection of Sacred Hymns, for the Church of Jesus Christ of Latter-Day Saints*. Nauvoo, IL: E. Robinson, 1841.
Smith, Joseph. Joseph Smith Collection. Church History Library, The Church of Jesus Christ of Latter-day Saints, Salt Lake City, Utah.
Smith, Joseph. "The King Follett Sermon." Volume 6 in *History of the Church of Jesus Christ of Latter-day Saints*, edited by B. H. Roberts, 302–17. Salt Lake City: Church of Jesus Christ of Latter-day Saints, 1948.
Smith, Joseph F. "The Persecutions of the Ancient Saints – The Organization of the Church in Our Day – Necessity of Obedience to the Laws of the Gospel, Etc." *Journal of Discourse*. Volume 22 (Liverpool: Albert Carrington, 1882): 42–50.
Smith, Joseph F., Anthon H. Lund, and Charles W. Penrose. "Editor's Table: Home Evening." *Improvement Era* 18, no. 8 (June 1915): 733–734.
Snow, Eliza R. "Bury Me Quietly When I Die." *The Woman's Exponent* 10, no. 13 (1881): 97.
Society of Equity. Society of Equity Constitution and Bylaws, ca. 1906–1908. United Farmers of Alberta fonds, Glenbow Archives, Calgary, Alberta.

Speers, Charles W. Report of C.W. Speers, General Colonization Agent. *Sessional Papers of the Dominion of Canada: Volume 10, Fifth Session of the Eighth Parliament, Session 1900.* Ottawa: S.E. Dawson, 1900.

Steele, C. Frank, "The Cardston Temple." *Juvenile Instructor* 58, no. 9 (1923): 439–441.

Steele, Samuel B. Annual Report of Superintendent S.B. Steele, Commanding Macleod District, 1892. *Sessional Papers of the Dominion of Canada: Volume 9, Third Session of the Seventh Parliament, Session 1893.* Ottawa: S.E. Dawson, 1893.

Steele, Samuel B. Annual Report of Superintendent S. B. Steele, Commanding Macleod District, 1895, *Sessional Papers of the Dominion of Canada: Volume 11, Sixth Session of the Seventh Parliament, Session 1896.* Ottawa: S.E. Dawson, 1896.

Steele, Samuel B. Annual Report of Superintendent S. B. Steele, Commanding D Division, Together with those of Inspectors G.E. Sanders, P.C.H. Primrose, A.R. Cuthbert, H.J.A. Davidson, and Mr. John Herron. *Sessional Papers of the Dominion of Canada: Volume 11, Sixth Session of the Eighth Parliament, Session 1897.* Ottawa: S.E. Dawson, 1897.

Stirling Ward Relief Society Minutes and Records, 1899–1970. Church History Library, The Church of Jesus Christ of Latter-day Saints, Salt Lake City, Utah.

Stories of Allie Zittella Rogers. Magrath, AB: [No publisher identified], 2005.

Stringham, George Owen. Oral history. Interviewed by Charles Ursenbach. Cardston, Alberta. 7 March 1974. Transcript. Church History Library, The Church of Jesus Christ of Latter-day Saints, Salt Lake City, Utah.

Taber Free Press. "The Home Doctor." 26 March 1908.

Taber Free Press. "Health and Beauty Hints." 23 April 1908.

Tait, W. McD. "The Mormon Temple in Canada." *The Canadian Magazine of Politics, Science, Art and Literature* 42 (1913): 487–92.

Talmage, May Booth. "Our Visit into the Temple in Canada." *The Young Woman's Journal* 34, no. 10 (1923): 517–22.

Taylor Stake Relief Society History, 1962. Church History Library, The Church of Jesus Christ of Latter-day Saints, Salt Lake City, Utah.

Thomas, Winnifred Newton. Oral history. Interviewed by Jessie L. Embry. Cardston, Alberta. 22 and 23 July 1982. Transcript. LDS Polygamy Oral History Project. L. Tom Perry Special Collections, Harold B. Lee Library, Brigham Young University, Provo, Utah.

Toronto Daily Star. "I'm One-Wife Man, Also I'm Faithful – Blackmore." 29 December 1947.

The U.F.A. "The U.F.W.A. and Junior Branch." 1 May 1923.

The U.F.A. "Southern Farmers Forming Local Wheat Pool." 16 July 1923.

The U.F.A. "The United Farm Women of Alberta in Annual Convention." 26 February 1924.

The U.F.A. "Campaign Launched in Lethbridge Districts in Preparation for the Annual Convention." 15 December 1925.
The U.F.A. "President Wood at Cardston." 15 February 1926.
The U.F.A. "Grows from Desire for Decent Standard." 3 June 1926.
The U.F.A. "New Local at Cardston." 17 June 1926.
The U.F.A. "Interesting Series of Program for Women's Local." 16 April 1927.
The U.F.A. "Federal Conventions." 15 July 1930.
The U.F.A. "Activities of the U.F.W.A." 2 January 1931.
The United Farmers of Alberta Inc. Directors for 1922. *Annual Report and Year Book Containing Reports of Officers and Committees for the Year 1921 Together with Official Minutes of the Fourteenth Annual Convention.*
The United Farmers of Alberta Inc. Convention Minutes. 1924. Scanned microfilm. Official Minutes of the UFA Annual Convention. United Farmers of Alberta fonds, Glenbow Archives, Calgary, Alberta.
The United Farmers of Alberta Inc. Convention Minutes. 1926. Scanned microfilm. Official Minutes of the UFA Annual Convention. United Farmers of Alberta fonds, Glenbow Archives, Calgary, Alberta.
The United Farmers of Alberta Inc. Convention Minutes. 1935. Scanned microfilm. Official Minutes of the UFA Annual Convention. United Farmers of Alberta fonds, Glenbow Archives, Calgary, Alberta.
United Farm Women of Alberta. *The U.F.W.A.: The Organization for Alberta Farm Women*. Calgary: United Farm Women of Alberta, 1920. http://peel.library.ualberta.ca/bibliography/4648/3.html.
United Farm Women of Alberta. Convention Minutes. 18 January 1923. Scanned microfilm. United Farmers of Alberta fonds, Glenbow Archives, Calgary, Alberta.
United Farm Women of Alberta. Board Meeting Minutes. 24 January 1925. Scanned microfilm. United Farmers of Alberta fonds, Glenbow Archives, Calgary, Alberta.
United Farm Women of Alberta. Convention Minutes. 18 January 1927. Scanned microfilm. United Farmers of Alberta fonds, Glenbow Archives, Calgary, Alberta.
United Farm Women of Alberta. Convention Minutes. 22 January 1930. Scanned microfilm. United Farmers of Alberta fonds, Glenbow Archives, Calgary, Alberta.
Ursenbach, Octave W. MSS 3116. Octave W. Ursenbach papers. 20th Century Western & Mormon Manuscripts, L. Tom Perry Special Collections, Harold B. Lee Library, Brigham Young University, Provo, Utah.
Walker, J. Harris. "Life History of Fannye Harris Walker." https://www.familysearch.org/photos/artifacts/35712448.
Wells, E.B. "General Conference, Relief Society." *The Woman's Exponent* 25, no. 20 (April 1897): 133–134.

Western Independent. "U.F.A. Sunday." 12 May 1920.

Widtsoe, John A. "Dedication of the Alberta Temple." *The Utah Genealogical and Historical Magazine* 14–15 (October 1923): 153–160.

Wilkins, Fred W. Report of F.W. Wilkins, D.T.S. Subdivision and Trail Surveys in South-Western Alberta. *Sessional Papers of the Dominion of Canada: Volume 9, Fifth Session of the Seventh Parliament, Session 1895.* Ottawa: S.E. Dawson, 1895.

The Woman's Exponent. "Household Hints." 1874.

The Woman's Exponent. "The Family Doctor-Shop." 1882.

Wood, Benjamin James Wood. "Benjamin James Wood and Emma Fern Bigelow." https://www.familysearch.org/photos/artifacts/2448377.

Wood, Edward James. Edward J. Wood Collection, 1884–1982. Church History Library, The Church of Jesus Christ of Latter-day Saints, Salt Lake City, Utah.

Wood, Henry Wise. Speech. January 1924. U.F.A. President's Address. Official Reports of the UFA Annual Convention 1924. United Farmers of Alberta fonds, Glenbow Archives, Calgary, Alberta.

Wood, James Forest. Oral History. Interviewed by Charles Ursenbach. Cardston, Alberta. 1974. Transcript. Church History Library, The Church of Jesus Christ of Latter-day Saints, Salt Lake City, Utah.

Woodruff, Wilford. *Wilford Woodruff's Journal.* Salt Lake City: Kraut's Pioneer Press, 1982. Accessed 16 February 2017. https://archive.org/details/WoodruffWilfordJournalSelections.

Woolf, William Layne. Oral History. Interviewed by Maureen Ursenbach Beecher. Salt Lake City, Utah, 1972. Church History Library, The Church of Jesus Christ of Latter-day Saints, Salt Lake City, Utah.

Yeigh, Frank. "The Greatness of Saskatchewan and Alberta." *Red Deer News.* 3 July 1907.

Young, Brigham. Will. Ca. 1877. Church History Library, The Church of Jesus Christ of Latter-day Saints, Salt Lake City, Utah.

The Young Woman's Journal. "The Recent Triennial in Washington." (May 1899): 195–215.

Zina Card Brown family. Zina Card Brown Family Collection, 1806–1972. Church History Library, The Church of Jesus Christ of Latter-day Saints, Salt Lake City, Utah.

Secondary Sources

Alexander, Thomas G. *Mormonism in Transition: A History of the Latter-day Saints, 1890–1930.* Urbana: University of Illinois Press, 1986.

Alexander, Thomas G. "Wilford Woodruff." In *Mormonism: A Historical Encyclopedia,* edited by W. Paul Reeve and Ardis E. Parshall, 216–19. Santa Barbara: ABC-CLIO, LLC, 2010.

American Monument Association. *Memorial Symbolism, Epitaphs and Design Types*. Boston: American Monument Association, 1947.

Anderson, Paul L. "First of the Modern Temples." *Ensign* (July 1977). https://www.lds.org/ensign/1977/07/first-of-the-modern-temples?lang=eng.

Anderson, Paul L. "The Early Twentieth Century Temples." *Dialogue: A Journal of Mormon Thought* 14, no. 1 (1981): 9–19.

Anderson, Paul L. "Mormon Moderne: Latter-Day Saint Architecture, 1925–1945." *Journal of Mormon History* 9, no. 1 (1982): 71–84.

Andrews, Rodney. "A History of St. Thomas' Anglican Church, Cardston." In *Chief Mountain Country: A History of Cardston and District*, Volume 1, edited by Keith Shaw, 188. Cardston, AB: Cardston and District Historical Society, 1978.

Archibald, May, ed. *100 Years Between the Rivers: A History of Glenwood, Hartley & Standoff*. Cardston, AB: Golden Press, 1984.

Arrington, Chris Rigby. "Pioneer Midwives." In *Mormon Sisters: Women in Early Utah*, edited by Claudia Lauper Bushman, 43–65. Cambridge: Emmeline Press, 1976.

Arrington, Leonard J. *Great Basin Kingdom: An Economic History of the Latter-Day Saints, 1830–1900*. Cambridge, MA: Harvard University Press, 1958.

Arrington, Leonard J., and Davis Bitton. *The Mormon Experience: A History of the Latter-Day Saints*. New York: Knopf, 1979.

Banack, Clark. *God's Province: Evangelical Christianity, Political Thought, and Conservatism in Alberta*. Montreal: McGill-Queen's University Press, 2016.

Barnwell Relief Society. *Barnwell History*. Ann Arbor: Edwards Bros., 1952.

Bates, Jane E. Woolf, and Zina Woolf Hickman. *Founding of Cardston and Vicinity: Pioneer Problems*. N.p.: William L. Woolf, 1960.

Bectell, Beryl, ed. *Chief Mountain Country: A History of Cardston and District*. Volume 2. Cardston: Cardston and District Historical Society, 1987.

Bednarowski, Mary Farrell. "Widening the Banks of the Mainstream: Women Constructing Theologies." In *Women's Leadership in Marginal Religions: Explorations Outside the Mainstream*, edited by Catherine Wessinger, 211–31. Urbana: University of Illinois Press, 1993.

Beecher, Maureen. "Mormon Women in Southern Alberta: The Pioneer Years." In *The Mormon Presence in Canada*, edited by B.Y. Card, Herbert C. Northcott, John E. Foster, Howard Palmer, and George K. Jarvis, 211–30. Edmonton: University of Alberta Press, 1990.

Bell, Edward. *Social Classes and Social Credit in Alberta*. Montreal: McGill-Queen's University Press, 1994.

Bennett, Archibald F., Ella M. Bennett, and Barbara Bennett Roach. *Valiant in the Faith: Gardner and Sarah Snow and Their Family*. Murray, UT: Roylance Publishing, 1990.

Bennett, John W., and Seena B. Kohl. *Settling the Canadian-American West, 1890–1915: Pioneer Adaption and Community Building An Anthropological History.* Lincoln: University of Nebraska Press, 1995.

Bennett, Richard E. "A Study of the Church of Jesus Christ of Latter-Day Saints in Upper Canada, 1830–1850." Master's thesis, Brigham Young University, 1975.

Bennett, Richard E. "'Plucking Not Planting': Mormonism in Eastern Canada 1830–1850." In *The Mormon Presence in Canada*, edited by B.Y. Card, Herbert C. Northcott, John E. Foster, Howard Palmer, and George K. Jarvis, 19–34. Edmonton: University of Alberta Press, 1990.

Bennion, Hyrum Jr., and Stella Richards. *Joseph Harker Family History: Pioneers, Utah, Canada, Idaho*, edited by Jack H. Adamson. Salt Lake City: Acorn Printing, 1949.

Bennion, Janet. "History, Culture, and Variability of Mormon Schismatic Groups." In *Modern Polygamy in the United States: Historical, Cultural, and Legal Issues*, edited by Cardell K. Jacobson and Lara Burton, 101–24. New York: Oxford University Press, 2011.

Bennion, Janet. *Polygamy in Primetime: Media, Gender, and Politics in Mormon Fundamentalism.* Waltham, MA: Brandeis University Press, 2012.

Blackwood, Beatrice. "Blood Indian Notes." In *'Pictures Bring Us Messages'/ Sinaakssiiksi aohtsimaahpihkookiyaawa: Photographs and Histories from the Kainai Nation*, Alison K. Brown, Laura Peers, and members of the Kainai Nation. Toronto: University of Toronto Press, 2006.

Blue, John. *Alberta Past and Present: Historical and Biographical.* Volumes 1–3. Chicago: Pioneer Historical Publishing, 1924.

Boatright, Gary L. "Strangers in a New and Strange Land: Theodore Brandley and the Settlement of Stirling, Alberta." *Alberta History* 61, no. 2 (2013): 2–10.

Boddy, Trevor. *Modern Architecture in Alberta.* Edmonton: Alberta Culture and Multiculturalism; Regina: Canadian Plains Research Center, 1987.

Bowman, Matthew B. *The Mormon People: The Making of an American Faith.* New York: Random House, 2012.

Bradley, Martha Sonntag. *Kidnapped from That Land: The Government Raids on the Short Creek Polygamists.* Salt Lake City: University of Utah Press, 1993.

Bradley, Martha Sonntag, and Mary Brown Firmage Woodward. *4 Zinas: A Story of Mothers and Daughters on the Mormon Frontier.* Salt Lake City: Signature Books, 2000.

Brado, Edward. *Cattle Kingdom: Early Ranching in Alberta.* Surrey, BC: Heritage House, 2004.

Brooks, Chris. *The Gothic Revival.* London: Phaidon Press, 1999.

Brooks, H. Allen. *The Prairie School: Frank Lloyd Wright and His Midwest Contemporaries.* New York: W.W. Norton, 1996.

Brooks, Willard, and Bernice Brooks. "Cardston – Historic Firsts." In *Chief Mountain Country: A History of Cardston and District*, Volume 2, edited by Beryl Bectell, 1–7. Cardston, AB: Cardston and District Historical Society, 1987.

Brown, John Gary. "Grave Markers." In *The Encyclopedia of the Great Plains*, edited by David J. Wishart, 302–3. Lincoln: University of Nebraska Press, 2004.

Bushman, Claudia Lauper. "Mystics and Healers." In *Mormon Sisters: Women in Early Utah*, edited by Claudia Lauper Bushman, 1–23. Cambridge: Emmeline Press, 1976.

Bushman, Claudia Lauper. *Contemporary Mormonism: Latter-day Saints in Modern America*. Westport, CT: Praeger, 2006.

Bushman, Richard Lyman. *Joseph Smith and the Beginnings of Mormonism*. Urbana and Chicago: University of Illinois Press, 1984.

Bushman, Richard Lyman. *Mormonism: A Very Short Introduction*. Oxford: Oxford University Press, 2008.

Beyer, Peter. "From Far and Wide: Canadian Religious and Cultural Diversity in Global/Local Context." In *Religion and Diversity in Canada*, edited by Lori G. Beaman and Peter Beyer, 9–39. Leiden and Boston: Brill, 2008.

Card, Brigham Y. "Charles Ora Card and the Founding of the Mormon Settlements in Southwestern Alberta, North-West Territories." In *The Mormon Presence in Canada*, edited by Brigham Y. Card, Herbert C. Northcott, John E. Foster, Howard Palmer, and George K. Jarvis, 77–107. Edmonton: University of Alberta Press, 1990.

Card, Brigham Y. *The Diaries of Charles Ora Card: The Canadian Years, 1886–1903*. Edited by Donald G. Godfrey and Brigham Y. Card. Salt Lake City: University of Utah Press, 1993.

Card, Brigham Y. "Introduction." In *The Mormon Contribution to Alberta Politics*, Ernest G. Mardon, Austin A. Mardon, and Catherine Mardon, edited by Talicia Dutchin, ix-xii. Edmonton: Golden Meteorite Press, 2011.

Carter, Sarah. "'Complicated and Clouded': The Federal Administration of Marriage and Divorce Among the First Nations of Western Canada, 1887–1906." In *Unsettled Pasts: Reconceiving the West Through Women's History*, edited by Sarah Carter, Lesley Erickson, Patricia Roome and Char Smith, 151–78. Calgary: University of Calgary Press, 2005.

Carter, Sarah. "Creating "Semi-Widows" and "Supernumerary Wives": Prohibiting Polygamy in Prairie Canada's Aboriginal Communities to 1900." In *Contact Zones: Aboriginal and Settler Women in Canada's Colonial Past*, edited by Katie Pickles and Myra Rutherford, 131–59. Vancouver: UBC Press, 2005.

Carter, Sarah. *The Importance of Being Monogamous: Marriage and Nation Building in Western Canada to 1915*. Edmonton: University of Alberta Press, 2008.

Carter, Thomas, and Peter Coss. *Utah's Historic Architecture, 1847–1940*. Salt Lake City: University of Utah Press, 1988.

Chism, Shane J., ed. *A Selection of Early Mormon Hymnbooks, 1832–1872: Hymn books and Broadsides from the First 40 Years of the Church of Jesus Christ of Latter-day Saints.* Tuscon: [publisher not identified], 2011.

Christie, Nancy, and Michael Gauvreau. *Christian Churches and Their Peoples, 1840–1965: A Social History of Religion in Canada.* Toronto: University of Toronto Press, 2010.

Clark, S.D. "The Religious Sect in Canadian Politics." *American Journal of Sociology* 51, no. 3 (1945): 207–16.

Clark, S.D. *The Developing Canadian Community.* 2nd ed. Toronto: University of Toronto Press, 1968.

Clifford, N. K. "His Dominion: A Vision in Crisis." *Studies in Religion* 2, no. 4 (1973): 315–26.

Cody, George W., and Heidi Hascall. "The History of Naturopathic Medicine: The Emergence and Evolution of an American School of Healing." In *Textbook of Natural Medicine,* 4th ed., edited by Joseph E. Pizzorno and Michael T. Murray, 34–60. St. Louis: Churchill Livingtone, 2013.

Cole, Catherine C., and Ann Milovic. "Education, Community Service, and Social Life: The Alberta Women's Institutes and Rural Families, 1909–1945." In *Standing on New Ground: Women in Alberta,* edited by Catherine A. Cavanaugh and Randi R. Warne, 19–31. Edmonton: University of Alberta Press, 1993.

Colquhoun, Alan. *Modern Architecture.* Oxford: Oxford University Press, 2002.

Comacchio, Cynthia R. *The Infinite Bonds of Family: Domesticity in Canada, 1850–1940.* Toronto: University of Toronto Press, 1999.

Comacchio, Cynthia R. "Introduction to Part Two." In *Framing Our Past: Constructing Canadian Women's History in the Twentieth Century,* edited by Sharon Anne Cook, Lorna R. McLean, and Kate O'Rourke, 75–81. Montreal: McGill-Queen's University Press, 2001.

Conrad, Margaret. ""Sundays Always Make Me Think of Home": Time and Place in Canadian Women's History." In *Rethinking Canada: The Promise of Women's History,* edited by Veronica Strong-Boag and Anita Clair Fellman, 67–81. Toronto: Copp Clark Pitman, 1986.

Cowan, Richard O. "Branch, Branch President." In *Encyclopedia of Mormonism,* edited by Daniel H. Ludlow, 219. New York: Macmillan, 1992.

Cowan, Richard O. *Temples to Dot the Earth.* Springville, UT: Cedar Fort, 1997.

Cowan, Richard O. "The Alberta Temple: Seventy-Five Years of Service." In *Regional Studies in Latter-day Saint Church History: Western Canada,* edited by Dennis A. Wright, Robert C. Freeman, Andrew H. Hedges, and Matthew O. Richardson, 239–50. Provo, UT: Department of Church History and Doctrine, Brigham Young University, 2000.

Davies, Douglas J. *Death, Ritual and Belief: The Rhetoric of Funerary Rites.* London: Cassell, 1997.

Davies, Douglas J. *The Mormon Culture of Salvation.* Aldershot: Ashgate Publishing, 2000.

Davis, Ren, and Helen Davis. *Atlanta's Oakland Cemetery: An Illustrated History and Guide.* Athens, GA: University of Georgia Press, 2012.

Dawson, Carl A. *Group Settlement: Ethnic Communities in Western Canada.* Toronto: Macmillan, 1936. Reprint, Millwood, NY: Kraus, 1974. Page references are to the 1974 edition.

Dawson, Carl A. "Differing Polygamous Patterns: Nineteenth Century LDS and Twenty-First Century FLDS Marriage Systems." In *Modern Polygamy in the United States: Historical, Cultural, and Legal Issues,* edited by Cardell K. Jacobson with Lara Burton, 125–48. New York: Oxford University Press, 2011.

Dilley, Thomas R. *The Art of Memory: Historic Cemeteries of Grand Rapids, Michigan.* Detroit: Wayne State University Press, 2014.

Dorosz, Edmund R., and Holy Cross Centennial Committee. *Holy Cross Roman Catholic Church, Fort Macleod, Alberta, 1898–1998.* Fort Macleod, AB: Our Pet's, 1998.

Dougall, Lily. *The Mormon Prophet.* Toronto: The W.J. Gage Company, 1899.

Driggs, Ken. "The Mormon Church-State Confrontation in Nineteenth-Century America." *Journal of Church and State* 30, no. 2 (1988): 273–89.

Driggs, Ken. "After the Manifesto: Modern Polygamy and Fundamentalist Mormons." *Journal of Church and State* 32, no. 2 (Spring 1990): 367–89.

Driggs, Ken. "'This Will Someday Be the Head and Not the Tail of the Church': A History of the Mormon Fundamentalists at Short Creek." *Journal of Church and State* 43, no. 1 (Winter 2001): 49–80.

Driggs, Ken. "Imprisonment, Defiance, and Division: A History of Mormon Fundamentalism in the 1940s and 1950s." *Dialogue: A Journal of Mormon Thought* 38, no. 1 (2005): 65–95.

Duke, James T. "Marriage: Eternal Marriage." In *Encyclopedia of Mormonism,* edited by Daniel H. Ludlow, 857–9. New York: Macmillan, 1992.

Durham, G. Homer. *N. Eldon Tanner: His Life and Service* (Salt Lake City: Deseret Book Company, 1982.

Dyer, William Gibb, Jr., and H. David Burton. "Presiding Bishopric." In *Encyclopedia of Mormonism,* edited by Daniel H. Ludlow, 1128–30. New York: Macmillan, 1992.

Edison, Carol. "Mormon Gravestones: A Folk Expression of Identity and Belief." *Dialogue: A Journal of Mormon Thought* 22, no. 4 (1989): 89–94.

Elliot, Bruce S. *Irish Migrants in the Canadas: A New Approach.* 2nd ed. Montreal: McGill-Queen's University Press, 2004.

Elofson, Warren M. *Frontier Cattle Ranching in the Land and Times of Charlie Russell.* Montreal: McGill-Queen's University Press, 2004.

Embry, Jessie L. "Exiles for the Principle: LDS Polygamy in Canada." *Dialogue: A Journal of Mormon Thought* 18, no. 3 (1985): 108–16.

Embry, Jessie L. "Two Legal Wives: Mormon Polygamy in Canada, The United States, and Mexico." In *The Mormon Presence in Canada*, edited by B. Y. Card, Herbert C. Northcott, John E. Foster, Howard Palmer, and George K. Jarvis, 170–85. Edmonton: University of Alberta Press, 1990.

Fife, Austin. "Pioneer Mormon Remedies." *Western Folklore* 16, no. 3 (1957): 153–162.

Fife, Austin, and Alta Fife. "Gravestone Imagery." In *Utah Folk Art: A Catalog of Material Culture*, edited by Hal Cannon and Utah Arts Council, 136–49. Provo, UT: Brigham Young University Press, 1980.

Filey, Mike. *Mount Pleasant Cemetery: An Illustrated Guide*. Toronto: Dundurn Press, 1999.

Finkel, Alvin. "The Fur Trade and Early European Settlement." In *Working People in Alberta: A History*, edited by Alvin Finkel, 19–38. Edmonton: Athabasca University Press and Canadian Committee on Labour History, 2012.

Flake, Kathleen. *The Politics of American Religious Identity: The Seating of Senator Reed Smoot, Mormon Apostle*. Chapel Hill: University of North Carolina Press, 2004.

Fluhman, Spencer J. *A Peculiar People: Anti-Mormonism and the Making of Religion in Nineteenth-Century America*. Chapel Hill: University of North Carolina Press, 2012.

Foster, Franklin L. "John E. Brownlee, 1925–1934." In *Alberta Premiers of the Twentieth Century*, edited by Bradford James Rennie, 77–106. Regina: Canada Plains Research Center and University of Regina, 2004.

Francis, R. Douglas. "Changing Imagines of the West." In *The Prairie West: Historical Readings*, edited by R. Douglas Francis and Howard Palmer, 629–49. Edmonton: Pica Pica Press, 1985.

Francis, R. Douglas. "In Search of a Prairie Myth: A Survey of the Intellectual and Cultural Historiography of Prairie Canada." *Journal of Canadian Studies* 24 no. 3 (1989): 44–69.

Francis, R. Douglas, and Chris Kitzan. "Introduction." In *The Prairie West as Promised Land*, edited by R. Douglas Francis and Chris Kitzan, x-xi. Calgary: University of Calgary Press, 2007.

Freedman, Estelle. "Separatism as Strategy: Female Institution Building and American Feminism, 1870–1930." *Feminist Studies* 5, no. 3 (1979): 512–529.

Friesen, Gerald. *The Canadian Prairies: A History*. Toronto: University of Toronto Press, 1987.

Friesen, Gerald. "The Western Canadian Identity." *Historical Papers/ Communications historiques* 8, no. 1 (1973): 13–19.

Gelernter, Mark. *A History of American Architecture: Buildings in Their Cultural and Technological Context*. Manchester: Manchester University Press, 1999.

Gibb, Hannah Simmons. *Poems & Autobiography of Hannah Simmons Gibb 1855–1941*. Ogden, UT: Family Printer Bruce & Clarabelle Gibb, 1982.

Gibbins, Roger. *Prairie Politics and Society: Regionalism in Decline*. Toronto: Butterworths, 1980.

Givens, Terryl. *The Latter-Day Saint Experience in America*. Westport, CT: Greenwood Press, 2004.

Godfrey, Donald G. *Charles Ora Card: Southern Alberta Pioneer*. Mesa: D. G. Godfrey, Godfrey Family Organization, 1987.

Goldberger, Paul. *Why Architecture Matters*. New Haven: Yale University Press, 2009.

Gordon, Sarah Barringer. *The Mormon Question: Polygamy and Constitutional Conflict in Nineteenth Century America*. Chapel Hill: The University of North Carolina Press, 2002.

Grant, John Webster. *The Church in the Canadian Era*. Vancouver: Regent College, 1988.

Hafen, Bruce C. "Disciplinary Procedures." In *Encyclopedia of Mormonism*, edited by Daniel H. Ludlow, 385–7. New York: Macmillan, 1992.

Hamilton, C. Mark. "Meetinghouse." In *Encyclopedia of Mormonism*, edited by Daniel H. Ludlow, 876–8. New York: Macmillan, 1992.

Hatch, Nathan O. *The Democratization of American Christianity*. New Haven: Yale University Press, 1989.

Hatch, Tina. "'Changing Times Bring Changing Conditions': Relief Society, 1960 to the Present." *Dialogue: A Journal of Mormon Thought* 37, no. 3 (2004): 65–98.

Hardy, B. Carmon. "Mormon Polygamy in Mexico and Canada: A Legal and Historiographical Review." In *The Mormon Presence in Canada*, edited by B.Y. Card, Herbert C. Northcott, John E. Foster, Howard Palmer, and George K. Jarvis, 186–210. Edmonton: University of Alberta Press, 1990.

Hardy, B. Carmon. *Solemn Covenant: The Mormon Polygamous Passage*. Urbana: University of Illinois Press, 1992.

Harker Family Committee. *Harker Heritage*. Magrath, AB: Verona Harker Merkley, 1993.

Hartley, William G. "Mormon Sugar in Alberta: E.P. Ellison and the Knight Sugar Factory, 1901–1917." *Journal of Mormon History* 23, no. 2 (1997): 1–29.

Hedges, Andrew H. "'I Wondered If I Could Feel at Home': Southern Alberta Through the Eyes of Its Early Saints, 1883–1910." In *Regional Studies in Latter-day Saint Church History: Western Canada*, edited by Dennis A. Wright, Robert C. Freeman, Andrew H. Hedges, and Matthew O. Richardson, 75–97. Provo, UT: Department of Church History and Doctrine, Brigham Young University, 2000.

Henry, Matthew. *A Commentary on the Holy Bible with Practical Remarks and Observations*. Volume 9. New York: Funk & Wagnalls, 1850.

Hicken, Alice Ruth. "Health Care and Midwifery." In *Range 25 Country Aetna and Kimball Areas*, edited by Kelvin Jensen and Avon Jensen. N.p., 2005.

Hyer, Paul V. "Sealing: Temple Sealings." In *Encyclopedia of Mormonism*, edited by Daniel H. Ludlow, 1289–90. New York: Macmillan, 1992.

Israelsen, L. Dwight. "United Orders." In *Encyclopedia of Mormonism*, edited by Daniel H. Ludlow, 1493–5. New York: Macmillan, 1992.

Jackson, Richard H. "City Planning." In *Encyclopedia of Mormonism*, edited by Daniel H. Ludlow, 283–5. New York: Macmillan, 1992.

Jackson, Richard H. "Mormon Cemeteries: History in Stone." In *Nearly Everything Imaginable: The Everyday Life of Utah's Mormon Pioneers*, edited by Ronald W. Walker and Doris R. Dant, 404–28. Provo, UT: Brigham Young University Press, 1999.

Jackson, Richard W. *Places of Worship: 150 Years of Latter-day Saint Architecture*. Provo, UT: Religious Studies Center, Brigham Young University, 2003.

Jacobson, Cardell K., and Lara Burton. "Prologue: The Incident at Eldorado, Texas." In *Modern Polygamy in the United States: Historical, Cultural, and Legal Issues*, edited by Cardell K. Jacobson and Lara Burton, xvii-xxvi. New York: Oxford University Press, 2011.

Jolley, Mary. "Fast and Testimony Meeting." In *Encyclopedia of Mormonism*, edited by Daniel H. Ludlow, 502. New York: Macmillan, 1992.

Jones, Christopher C. "Joseph F. Smith." In *Mormonism: A Historical Encyclopedia*, edited by W. Paul Reeve and Ardis E. Parshall, 184–7. Santa Barbara: ABC-CLIO, LLC, 2010.

Jones, Megan Sanborn. *Performing American Identity in Anti-Mormon Melodrama*. New York: Routledge, 2009.

Karamitsanis, Aphrodite. *Place Names of Alberta*. Volume 2. Calgary: University of Calgary Press, 1992.

Keister, Douglas. *Stories in Stone: A Field Guide to Cemetery Symbolism and Iconography*. Layton: Gibbs Smith, 2004.

Kezerian, Nephi K. "Sick, Blessing the." In *Encyclopedia of Mormonism*, edited by Daniel H. Ludlow, 1308–9. New York: Macmillan, 1992.

Klassen, Henry C. *Eye on the Future: Business People in Calgary and the Bow Valley, 1870–1900*. Calgary: University of Calgary Press, 2002.

Knowlton, Clark S. "Social Accommodation in Utah." In *Essays on the American West, 1974–1975*, edited by Thomas G. Alexander, 79–108. Provo, UT: Brigham Young University Press, 1976.

Lampard, Robert. "Cardston Medical Contracts and Canadian Medicare." *Alberta History* 54, no. 4 (2006): 5–10.

Lee, Lawrence B. "The Canadian-American Irrigation Frontier, 1884–1914." *Agricultural History* 40, no.4 (1966): 271–84.

Lehr, John C. "The Mormon Cultural Landscape in Alberta." *Malaspina Papers: Studies in Human and Physical Geography* (1973): 25–33.

Lehr, John C. "Mormon Settlement Morphology in Southern Alberta." *Albertan Geographer* no. 8 (1972): 6–13.

Lehr, John C. "Mormon Settlements in Southern Alberta." Master's thesis, University of Alberta, 1971.

Loveland, Anne C., and Otis B. Wheeler. "Woman Suffrage." In *Encyclopedia of Mormonism*, edited by Daniel H. Ludlow, 1572–3. New York: Macmillan, 1992.

Loveland, Anne C., and Otis B. Wheeler. *From Meetinghouse to Megachurch: A Material and Cultural History*. Columbia: University of Missouri Press, 2003.

Madsen, Chris. *Another Kind of Justice: Canadian Military Law from Confederation to Somalia*. Vancouver: UBC Press, 1999.

Magrill, Barry. *A Commerce of Taste: Church Architecture in Canada, 1867–1914*. Montreal: McGill-Queen's University Press, 2012.

Mangum, Garth L. "Welfare Services." In *Encyclopedia of Mormonism*, edited by Daniel H. Ludlow, 1554–8. New York: Macmillan, 1992.

Mann, W.E. *Sect, Cult, and Church in Alberta*. Toronto: University of Toronto Press, 1955.

Mardon, Ernest G. and Austin A. Mardon. *Lethbridge Politicians: Federal, Provincial & Civic*. Edmonton: Golden Meteorite Press, 2008.

Mardon, Ernest G., and Austin A. Mardon. *Alberta's Political Pioneers: A Biographical Account of the United Farmers of Alberta 1921–1935*. Edited by Justin Selner, Spencer Dunn, and Emerson Csorba. Edmonton: Golden Meteorite Press, 2010.

Mardon, Ernest G., Austin A. Mardon, and Catherine Mardon. *The Mormon Contribution to Alberta Politics*. Edited by Talicia Dutchin. Edmonton: Golden Meteorite Press, 2011.

Marshall, David B. "The Latter-day Saints, the Doughnut, and Post-Christian Canada," *Journal of Mormon History* 39, no. 2 (2013): 35–77.

Martens, Steve C., and Nancy Volkman. "Cemeteries." In *The Encyclopedia of the Great Plains*, edited by David J. Wishart, 70–1. Lincoln: University of Nebraska Press, 2004.

Mauss, Armand L. "'Assimilation and Ambivalence: The Mormon Reaction to Americanization.'" *Dialogue: A Journal of Mormon Thought* 22, no. 1 (1989): 30–67.

Mauss, Armand L. *The Angel and the Beehive: The Mormon Struggle with Assimilation*. Urbana and Chicago: University of Illinois Press, 1994.

Mauss, Armand L. "'The Mormon Struggle with Assimilation and Identity: Trends and Developments.'" *Dialogue: A Journal of Mormon Thought* 27, no. 1 (1994): 129–49.

McDannell, Colleen and Bernhard Lang. "Modern Heave ... and a Theology." In *Mormons and Mormonism: An Introduction to an American World Religion*, edited by Eric A. Eliason, 137–46. Urbana: University of Illinois Press, 2001.

McGowan, Mark G. *The Waning of the Green: Catholics, the Irish, and Identity in Toronto, 1887–1922*. Montreal: McGill-Queen's University Press, 1999.

McGuire, Meredith B. *Lived Religion: Faith and Practice in Everyday Life*. Oxford and New York: Oxford University Press, 2008.

McManus, Sheila. "Unsettled Pasts, Unsettling Borders: Women, Wests, Nations." In *One Step Over the Line: Toward a History of Women in the North*

American Wests, edited by Elizabeth Jameson and Sheila McManus, 29–47. Edmonton: University of Alberta Press, 2008.

McNaught, Kenneth. *A Prophet in Politics: A Biography of J.S. Woodsworth*. Toronto: University of Toronto Press, 2001.

Meyers, Mary Ann. "Gates Ajar: Death in Mormon Thought and Practice." In *Death in America*, edited by David E. Stannard, 112–33. Philadelphia: University of Pennsylvania Press, 1975.

Millar, Nancy. *Once Upon a Tomb: Stories from Canadian Graveyards*. Calgary: Fifth House, 1997.

Miller, Randall M. Review of *America's Church: The National Shrine and Catholic Presence in the Nation's Capital* by Thomas A. Tweed. *Church History* 81, no. 3 (2012): 738–40.

Neilson, Reid L., ed. *Global Mormonism in the 21st Century*. Provo: Brigham Young University Press, 2008.

Nelson, Lowry. *The Mormon Village: A Pattern and Technique of Land Settlement*. Salt Lake City: University of Utah Press, 1952.

Nelson, William O. "Quorum of the Twelve Apostles." In *Encyclopedia of Mormonism*, edited by Daniel H. Ludlow, 1185–9. New York: Macmillan, 1992.

Newell, Linda King. "A Gift Given: A Gift Taken: Washing, Anointing, and Blessing the Sick Among Mormon Women." *Sunstone* 22, 3–4 (June 1999): 30–43.

Nicholson, Barbara J. "Feminism in the Prairie Provinces to 1916." Master's thesis, University of Calgary, 1974.

Nielson, Olive Wood. *A Treasury of Edward J. Wood*. Salt Lake City: Publishers Press, 1983.

Noll, Mark A. *A History of Christianity in the United States and Canada*. Grand Rapids: W.B. Eerdmans, 1992.

O'Dea, Thomas F. *The Mormons*. Chicago: University of Chicago Press, 1963.

Orsi, Robert A. "Everyday Miracles: The Study of Lived Religion." In *Lived Religion in America: Toward a History of Practice*, edited by David D. Hall, 3–21. Princeton, NJ: Princeton University Press, 1997.

Orsi, Robert A. "Is the Study of Lived Religion Irrelevant to the World We Live In? Special Presidential Plenary Address, Society for the Scientific Study of Religion, Salt Lake City, November 2, 2002," *Journal for the Scientific Study of Religion* 42, no. 2 (2003): 169–174.

Otter, A.A. Den. "A Congenial Environment: Southern Alberta on the Arrival of the Mormons." In *The Mormon Presence in Canada*, edited by B. Y. Card, Herbert C. Northcott, John E. Foster, Howard Palmer, and George K. Jarvis, 53–74. Edmonton: University of Alberta Press, 1990.

Palmer, Howard. *Patterns of Prejudice: A History of Nativism in Alberta*. Toronto: McClelland and Stewart, 1982.

Parry, Keith. "Mormons as Ethnics: A Canadian Perspective." In *The Mormon Presence in Canada*, edited by B.Y. Card, Herbert C. Northcott, John E. Foster,

Howard Palmer, and George K. Jarvis, 353–62. Edmonton: University of Alberta Press, 1990.

Poll, Richard D. "The Americanism of Utah." *Utah Historical Quarterly* 44, no. 1 (1976): 76–93.

Poll, Richard D. "The Legislative Antipolygamy Campaign." *BYU Studies* 25, no. 4 (1986): 107–124.

Prete, Roy A., and Carma T. Prete, eds. *Canadian Mormons: History of the Church of Jesus Christ of Latter-day Saints in Canada*. Provo: Religious Studies Center, Brigham Young University, in cooperation with Deseret Book Company, 2017.

Properzi, Mauro. *Mormonism and the Emotions: An Analysis of LDS Scriptural Texts*. Madison: Fairleigh Dickinson University Press, 2015.

Pugin, A.W.N. *Contrasts*. 2nd ed. 1836. Reprint, Leicester: Leicester University Press, 1969.

Pugin, A.W.N. *The True Principles of Pointed or Christian Architecture*. London: John Weale, 1841. Reprinted from the 1853 impression. Oxford: St. Barnabas, 1969.

Quinn, D. Michael. "Plural Marriage and Mormon Fundamentalism." In *Fundamentalisms and Society: Reclaiming the Sciences, Education, and the Family*, edited by Martin E. Marty and R. Scott Appleby, 240–93. Chicago: University of Chicago Press, 1993.

Rasporich, Anthony W. "Utopia, Sect and Millennium in Western Canada, 1870–1940." In *Prophets, Priests, and Prodigals; Readings in Canadian Religious History, 1608 to Present*, edited by David B. Marshall and Mark McGowan, 213–41. Toronto: McGraw-Hill Ryerson, 1992.

Rasporich, Anthony W. "Utopian Ideals and Community Settlements in Western Canada, 1880–1914." In *The Prairie West as Promised Land*, edited by R. Douglas Francis and Chris Kitzan, 127–54. Calgary: University of Calgary Press, 2007.

Rawlings, Marla. *Favorite Utah Pioneer Recipes*. Bountiful, UT: Horizon Publishers, 2000.

Reeve, W. Paul. *Religion of a Different Color: Race and the Mormon Struggle for Whiteness*. New York: Oxford University Press, 2015.

Rennie, Bradford James. *The Rise of Agrarian Democracy: The United Farmers and Farm Women of Alberta, 1909–1921*. Toronto: University of Toronto Press, 2000.

Roberts, Allen Dale. "Religious Architecture of the LDS Church: Influences and Changes since 1847." *Utah Historical Quarterly* 43, no. 2 (1975): 301–27.

Roberts, Allen Dale. *Salt Lake City's Historic Architecture*. Charleston: Arcadia Publishing, 2012.

Rollings-Magnusson, Sandra. "Flax Seed, Goose Grease, and Gun Power: Medical Practices by Women Homesteaders in Saskatchewan (1882–1914)." *Journal of Family History* 33, no. 4 (2008): 388–410.

Rosaldo, Michelle Zimbalist. "Woman, Culture, and Society: Theoretical Overview." In *Women, Culture and Society*, edited by Michelle Zimbalist Rosaldo and Louise Lamphere, 17–42. Stanford: Stanford University Press, 1974.

Rosenvall, Lynn A. "The Church of Jesus Christ of Latter-day Saints in Alberta: A Historical and Geographical Perspective." In *Regional Studies in Latter-day Saint Church History: Western Canada*, edited by Dennis A. Wright, Robert C. Freeman, Andrew H. Hedges, and Matthew O. Richardson, 1–12. Provo, UT: Dept. of Church History and Doctrine, Brigham Young University, 2000.

Rosenvall, Lynn A. "The Transfer of Mormon Culture to Alberta." *American Review of Canadian Studies* 12, no. 2 (Summer 1982): 51–63.

Shaw, Keith, ed. *Chief Mountain Country: A History of Cardston and District*. Volume 1. Cardston, AB: Cardston and District Historical Society, 1978.

Shepherd, Gordon, and Gary Shepherd. *A Kingdom Transformed: Themes in the Development of Mormonism*. Salt Lake City: University of Utah Press, 1984.

Shepherd, R. Gordon, A. Gary Shepherd, and Ryan T. Cragun, eds. *The Palgrave Handbook of Global Mormonism*. Palgrave Macmillan, 2020.

Shipps, Jan. *Mormonism: The Story of a New Religious Tradition*. Urbana and Chicago: University of Illinois Press, 1985.

Sinclair, Brian R., and Terence J. Walker. "Frank Lloyd Wright's Banff Pavilion: Critical Inquiry and Virtual Reconstruction." *APT Bulletin* 28, no. 2/3 (1997): 13–21.

Smith, David T. *Religious Persecution and Political Order in the United States*. New York: Cambridge University Press, 2015.

Smith, Norma Lee. "Herbal Remedies: God's Medicine?" *Dialogue: A Journal of Mormon Thought* 12, no. 3 (1979): 37–60.

Stanton, Phoebe B. *The Gothic Revival & American Church Architecture: An Episode in Taste 1840–1856*. Baltimore: John Hopkins Press, 1968.

Stapley, Jonathan A. "'The Last of the Old School': Joseph F. Smith and Latter-day Saint Liturgy." In *Joseph F. Smith: Reflections on the Man and His Times*, edited by Craig K. Manscill, Brian D. Reeves, Guy L. Dorius, and J. B. Haws, 233–47. Provo, UT: Religious Studies Center, 2013.

Stirling Sunset Society. *Stirling: Its Story and People, 1899–1980*. Stirling: Stirling Sunset Society, 1981.

Tagg, Melvin S. "The Life of Edward James Wood." MA thesis, Brigham Young University, 1959.

Tagg, Melvin S. *A History of the Mormon Church in Canada*. Lethbridge, AB: Lethbridge Stake Historical Committee, 1968.

Tait, Lisa Olsen. "'A Modern Patriarchal Family': The Wives of Joseph F. Smith in the *Relief Society Magazine*, 1915–19." In *Joseph F. Smith: Reflections on the Man and His Times*, edited by Craig K. Manscill, Brian D. Reeves, Guy L. Dorius, and J. B. Haws, 74–95. Provo, UT: Religious Studies Center, 2013.

Takach, Geo. *Will the Real Alberta Please Stand Up?* Edmonton: University of Alberta, 2010.

Teaford, Jon C. *Cities of the Heartland: The Rise and Fall of the Industrial Midwest.* Bloomington: Indiana University Press, 1993.

Thorn, Brian T. *From Left to Right: Maternalism and Women's Political Activism in Postwar Canada.* Vancouver: UBC Press, 2016.

Tweed, Thomas A.. *Crossing and Dwelling: A Theory of Religion.* Cambridge: Harvard University Press, 2006.

Tweed, Thomas A. *America's Church: The National Shrine and Catholic Presence in the Nation's Capital.* New York: Oxford University Press, 2011.

Twombly, Robert. *Frank Lloyd Wright: His Life and His Architecture.* New York: Wiley, 1979.

Ward, W. Peter. *Courtship, Love and Marriage in Nineteenth-Century English Canada.* Montreal: McGill-Queen's University Press, 1990.

Waugh, Earle. "The Almighty Has Not Got This Far Yet: Religious Models in Alberta's and Saskatchewan's History." In *The New Provinces: Alberta and Saskatchewan, 1905–1980,* edited by Howard Palmer and Donald Smith, 199–215. Vancouver: Tantalus Research, 1973.

White, O. Kendall. "Mormonism in America and Canada: Accommodation to the Nation-State." *The Canadian Journal of Sociology* 3, no. 2 (1978): 161–81.

Williams, Barbara. *A Gentlewoman in Upper Canada: The Journals, Letters, and Art of Anne Langton.* Toronto: University of Toronto Press, 2008.

Wiseman, Nelson. *In Search of Canadian Political Culture.* Vancouver: UBC Press, 2007.

Wolfe, Thomas. "Steaming Saints: Mormons and the Thomsonian Movement in Nineteenth-Century America." In *Disease and Medical Care in the Mountain West: Essays on Region, History, and Practice,* edited by Martha L. Hildreth and Bruce T. Moran, 16–28. Reno: University of Nevada Press, 1998.

Wood, James A. *Militia Myths: Ideas of the Canadian Citizen Soldier, 1896–1921.* Vancouver: UBC Press, 2010.

Wood, Vi Alfred. *The Alberta Temple: Centre and Symbol of Faith.* Calgary: Detselig Enterprises, 1989.

Woodger, Mary Jane. "Frontier Prophetesses: The Gift of Tongues as Manifested by Latter-day Saint Women in Southern Alberta, 1894–1930." In *Regional Studies in Latter-day Saint Church History: Western Canada,* edited by Dennis A. Wright, Robert C. Freeman, Andrew H. Hedges, and Matthew O. Richardson, 123–38. Provo, UT: Department of Church History and Doctrine, Brigham Young University, 2000

Woywitka, Anne. "Pioneers in Sickness and in Health." *Alberta History* 49, no. 1 (2001): 16–20.

Wright, Elizabethada A. "Rhetorical Spaces in Memorial Places: The Cemetery as a Rhetorical Memory Place/Space." *Rhetoric Society Quarterly* 35, no. 4 (Fall 2005): 51–81.

Wright, Frank Lloyd. *Frank Lloyd Wright: An Autobiography*. Petaluma, CA: Pomegranate Communications, 2005. First published 1943 by Duell, Sloan and Pearce (New York).

Wright, John Lloyd. *My Father, Frank Lloyd Wright*. New York: Dover, 1992.

Yorgason, Ethan R. *Transformation of the Mormon Culture Region*. Urbana: University of Illinois Press, 2003.

Index

1892 Criminal Code, 28, 44, 46, 136. *See also* polygamy

Aetna Welfare Committee, 119
Ainscough, W.T., Sr., 124
Alberta Co-operative Wheat Producers, Limited, 113
Alberta Farmers Association, 82, 110–11
Alberta Federation of Agriculture, 114
Alberta Irrigation Company, 96
Alberta Land and Colonization Company, 92, 97
Alberta Land and Stock Company, 97
Alberta Legislative Assembly, 122
Alberta Liberal Party, 108
Alberta Railway and Coal Company, 96–7, 103
Alberta Railway and Irrigation Company, 100, 133
Alberta Stake, 50, 97, 100, 101, 104, 108, 119, 125, 138; division of, 102; High Council of, 109; incorporation of, 98–9; organization of, 61, 97, 133–4; Relief Society of, 74–5; Welfare Committee of, 118. *See also* Alberta Stake Tabernacle

Alberta Stake Tabernacle, 125, 129, 134, 137
Alberta Society of Equity, 82. *See also* Canadian Society of Equity
Alberta Wheat Pool, 113–14
Alberta Women's Institute, 58, 64, 81, 87
Allen, Heber S., 61, 96, 102, 109, 139. *See also* Taylor Stake
Allen, Simeon F., 96, 98
Americanization thesis, 10–12, 19. *See also* Canadianization
Andersen, Sena Georgina, 32
Anderson, N.J., 112. *See also* United Farmers of Alberta
Angell, Truman O., 132–3. *See also* Gothic Revival; sacred architecture
Anthony, Susan B., 63–4. *See also* Triennial National Council of Women
apostle, 6, 52, 99, 122. *See also* Brown, Hugh B.; Smoot, Reed; Taylor, John; Taylor, John W.
Archibald, Rachel, 63, 85. *See also* spiritual gifts; tongues, speaking in; United Farm Women of Alberta
Articles of Faith (1842), 60. *See also* spiritual gifts

assimilation, 10–12, 19, 23, 85.
  See also Americanization thesis;
  Canadianization; social gospel;
  United Farmers of Alberta; United
  Farm Women of Alberta

Barlow, John Y., 48. See also
  Fundamentalist Church of Jesus
  Christ of Latter-day Saints
Barnwell Relief Society, 112. See
  also Peterson, Lawrence; United
  Farmers of Alberta
Bates, Jane Woolf, 32
Bennion, Alice Jane, 32
Benson, Ezra Taft, 51
bigamy, 28–9, 31, 33, 38–41, 44. See
  also 1892 Criminal Code; Morrill
  Anti-Bigamy Act
Bigelow, Orson, 85
Bingham, Rojanea, 69
Bishop's Storehouse, 118. See also
  Alberta Stake: Welfare Committee
  of; Church Welfare Committee
Blackmore, Harold "Pete," 49
Blackmore, Harold Woolly, 47
Blackmore, John H., 46–7, 49–51, 54,
  119, 124. See also Social Credit Party
  of Canada; Taylor Stake: Mutual
  Improvement Association of
Blackmore, Joseph "Ray," 49
Blackmore, William, 47
Blackmore, Winston, 47
Boehmer, Nesta Kay, 49
Bohmer, Aloha, 49
Book of Mormon, The, 5, 60, 142
Boy Scouts, 19
Boyson, Matilda, 84
Bradshaw, Richard W., 110
Brandley, John Theodore, 32, 99
British American Ranch Company, 104
British North America, 5–6, 29
Brooks, Hattie, 78

Brooks, Willard M., 78
Brown, Hugh B., 52, 139
Brown, James T., 108
Brown, Lydia, 81
Burt, Charles W., 108–9

Cache County (Utah), 128, 134
Caldwell, Fanny Elizabeth, 153
Canadian Co-operative Wool
  Growers association, 114
Canadianization, 10, 12, 84, 86.
  See also Americanization thesis
Canadian Pacific Railway (CPR),
  9, 110
Canadian Regional Welfare
  Committee, 119
Canadian Society of Equity, 111
Cannon, George Q., 97
Cannon, Leonora, 5–6
Card, Brigham Y., 107
Card, Charles Ora: arrest of by
  U.S. Marshals Service, 31; and
  Latter-day Saint settlement in
  Alberta, 7; and Magrath sugar
  factory, 102; as member of pro-
  polygamy delegation to Canadian
  government, 37; as president
  of Alberta Stake, 61; as stake
  patriarch, 101; owner of general
  store, 94; town planning for
  Cardston, 91. See also Cardston
  Company Limited; Cardston
  Meetinghouse; cooperative
  economic organizations
Card, Joseph Y., 65, 115, 141
Card, Zina Young, 52, 58, 61–4, 68, 94
Cardston Alberta Temple: depiction
  of on grave markers, 156, 158;
  lack of Moroni statue, 144;
  Meso-American motifs of, 140,
  142; overlap of between church
  and state, 121; as symbol of

contribution to Canadian society, 145–6. *See also* Canadianization; integration; Modernist architecture; Prairie School; sacred architecture; Wright, Frank Lloyd
Cardston Assembly Hall, 129, 133
Cardston Cemetery, 153, 158
Cardston Company Limited, 94–6, 98, 101
Cardston Creamery Company, 109
Cardston Farming Company, 109
Cardston First Ward, 108–9, 119, 121–2
Cardston Meetinghouse, 129, 131
Cardston Milling Company, 100
Cardston Municipal Hospital, 124
Cardston Relief Society, 43, 94
Cardston Riding, 109, 113
Cardston Roller Mills, 100
Cardston Second Ward, 65, 109, 121
Cardston Third Ward, 50
Carlson, Eva, 85
Carlson, Talitha, 83–5
Carter, Sarah Elizabeth, 32
Celestial Kingdom, 48, 152–3
Christensen, Leroy W., 158
Christensen, Mary S., 158
Christensen, Peter F., 158
Christensen, Zelma Z., 158
Church Welfare Committee, 118
Church Welfare Plan, 119
Civil War, 6, 31
Clarke, Xarissa Merkley, 79
Cochrane, Matthew, 104
Cochrane Ranch, 102, 104–5
Cochrane Ranch Company, 104
Communism, 90, 105, 119
Cook, Frank A., 49
Coombs, Mark A., 118
Co-operative Commonwealth Federation, 25, 123, 162
cooperative economic organizations, 15

Corporation of the Alberta Stake of Zion, 104
Crawshaw, Hilda, 49–50

Daines, Sarah, 75
Dennis, William Taylor, 84
Doctrine and Covenants, The, 60, 102
domesticity, 57, 76, 80
Dowdle, Harriet Martha, 32
Drury, Permelia Julia, 32
Duce, Thomas, 65

Edmunds Act (1882), 6, 31
Edmunds-Tucker Act (1887), 6, 31
Ellison, E.P., 103
Ellison Milling, 100
Elton, David Horton, 125

faith healing, 55, 67, 70–4, 82, 86. *See also* spiritual gifts
family home evening, 77, 79–80, 88, 140
First Manifesto, 30, 42–4, 50, 52, 58. *See also* Second Manifesto; Woodruff, Wilford W.
First Nations, 30. *See* Indigenous peoples
First Presidency, 51, 97; affirmation of women's right to faith healing, 71; deeding of church-owned lands to Alberta Stake, 100; inauguration of Family Home Evening, 79, 140; and organization of Alberta stake, 61; public suppression of women's spiritual experiences, 65
First World War, 83, 112, 137, 146; and Cardston temple construction, 130, 141; maternalism as key to social renewal after, 57, 73, 76; as occasion for LDS demonstration of national loyalty, 139–40

Fort Macleod, 66, 104, 129–30, 133
Fossey, Ida, 73
Fundamentalist Church of Jesus Christ of Latter-day Saints (FLDS), 47–53

Galt, Elliott T., 96
Galt Hospital (Lethbridge), 73
general conference, 62, 64, 137, 145
Genealogical Committee, 121
Gibb, Hannah Simmons, 55, 84
Gibb, John Lye, 84
Gibb, Sarah, 84
Gleaners, 121
Glenwood Ward, 105, 125
Gospel of Jesus Christ, 50
Gothic Revival, 130–2, 142. *See also* Angell, Truman O.; sacred architecture
Grant, Heber J., 140
Great Depression, 57, 105, 116, 123

Hammer, Elizabeth, 61–2, 70
Hammer, Josiah, 108
Harker, Ephraim, 32
Harker, Levi, 73, 100, 109
Harker-Head Company Store, 100. *See* Magrath Mercantile Store
Harris, Leo, 124
Head, Jasper J., 100
Hendry, Thomas Archibald, 43, 52
herbalism, 66–9, 71, 73, 76
Hicken, John O., 118
Hill, Deloise Bennion, 79
Hinman, Henry L., 43, 98
Hodson, Zola Brown Jeffs, 46, 52–4
Horn, Mary Christina Ada, 47
House of Commons, 36, 41, 47, 107, 121
H.S. Allen & Company, 100
Hurd, F. Earl, 158

Hurd, Winnifred, 158
Hyde, Sarah, 61

Ibey, Robert, 95, 100–1
immigration: and the Alberta Liberal Party, 108; assistance for from Canadian government, 30; Charles Ora Card appointed as sub agent for Dominion lands, 99; and identity formation, 13, 20–1; and irrigation projects, 100; of non-Latter-day Saints from Ontario, 9, 23; and plural marriage, 29, 35, 37, 41; second wave of into Alberta, 133; women's involvement in discourse about, 80, 84–7, 161. *See also* Alberta Women's Institute; United Farm Women of Alberta
Improvement Era, The, 79, 140–1
Indigenous peoples, 27, 29–30, 33–6, 45, 67–8. *See also* First Nations; Kainai, Niitsitapi
industrialization, 29, 77
integration: and architecture, 129–30, 143, 145; and cemeteries, 147, 153, 160; and cooperation with non-Latter-day Saints, 106–7; and Latter-day Saint women's roles in, 55, 64, 69, 72, 76–7, 87; and political participation, 107, 126; and religious diversity, 137. *See also* Americanization thesis; Canadianization; immigration; monogamy; sacred architecture; spiritual gifts
irrigation, 3, 90, 95–6, 98–102, 104, 133. *See also* Mormon Farm Village
Irvine, William, 114

Jacobs, Dora, 69
Jeffs, David, 53
Jeffs, Rulon, 52–3

Jeffs, Warren, 53
Jensen, Allie, 72, 84
Jensen, Andrew, 119
Jensen, Christian, 84, 114
Jensen, Cleo, 72
Jesus Christ, 90, 118, 131
Johansen, John Albert, 124
Johnson, Anna Mae, 49
Johnson, Beth, 73
Juvenile Instructor, 143

Kainai Nation, 13, 15, 30, 33, 35, 45.
    See also First Nations; Indigenous peoples
Keeler, Margaret, 32, 99
Kimball, Heber C., 71
Kimball, Orin Leslie, 152
King, Melvin, 124
King, William Lyon McKenzie, 124
Kingdom of God, 21, 112, 115, 117
Kinsman, Sarah, 72
Kirtland (Ohio), 5–6, 60, 91
Kirtland Temple (Ohio), 129, 134
Knight, Jesse, 102–3, 133
Knight, Oscar Raymond, 103
Knight Sugar Company Limited, 103

Laie Hawaii Temple, 140, 144
Layne, Jonathan, 128, 137
Leavitt Cemetery, 158
Leavitt, Edward, 124
Leavitt, Frank, 112
Leavitt, Mary Alice, 78
Leavitt, Ralph, 78
Leavitt, Thomas Rowell, 32, 148
LeBaron, William F., 112
Lee's Creek Relief Society, 74
Legislative Assembly of the North-West Territories, 101
Lloyd, John, 135
Logan Utah Temple, 131, 158
Low, James P., 100

Low, Solon, 119, 122
Lyman, Francis M., 37

Macleod District, 97, 113
Magrath, Charles Alexander, 96
Magrath Cemetery, 153
Magrath First Ward, 119
Magrath Mercantile Company, 100
Magrath Ward, 102, 109
Magrath Ward Young Women's Mutual Improvement Association, 102
Manti Utah Temple, 131, 144, 158
Matkin, Samuel, 32, 62
McCarty, Charles, 45–6, 97, 102
McKay, David O., 51
Melchizedek Priesthood, 71, 153
Mercer, Margery, 46
Mercer, Mary, 45
Merkley, Alva, 79
Merkley, Jehzell, 79, 84
Mesa Arizona Temple, 140, 144
Mexico, 31, 33, 40, 64, 92
midwifery, 55, 66–74, 82, 162
Millennium, 118
Milner, Sarah Ella, 70
Modernist architecture, 143, 145–6
monogamy: "de facto," 32;
    and Indigenous peoples, 30;
    replacement of plural marriage with, 27, 46, 49, 54, 57, 64, 161.
    See also non-monogamy; plural marriage; polygamy
"Mormon culture region," 20, 24
Mormon Farm Village, 90
Morrill Anti-Bigamy Act (1862), 6, 31

Nauvoo Illinois Temple, 129, 134
Nelson, Ella, 70, 72
Newton, Amy, 77
Newton, Samuel Smith, 77, 134
Nielson, Bertha, 53

Niitsitapi, 30, 33–4. *See also* First Nations; Indigenous peoples
non-monogamy, 29–30, 33–5, 37–8, 41, 45, 52. *See also* monogamy; plural marriage; polygamy
North-West Irrigation Company, 103
North-West Mounted Police (NWMP), 9, 45, 89, 130
nuclear farming villages, 15

O'Brien, T.J., 103
Ostlund, Hjaldermar, 85

Painter, Sarah Jane, 33
Palmer, Asael E., 119
Palmer, Eldon, 48–9
Parliament of Canada, 29, 44
Parrish, John F., 139
Passey, Myrtle, 119
Paxman, Ezra, 78
Peterson, A.M., 112
Peterson, Hans, 148
Peterson, Lawrence, 112–13
Pierson, Ola, 156
Pierson, Olinda, 156
Pitcher, Frank H., 78
Pitcher, Nellie Hinman, 65, 78
Pitcher, Walter E., 108–9
plan of salvation, 17, 141
Plat of the City of Zion, 90–1
plural marriage: church's public confession of, 31; continuation of in Canada, 27–8, 43; and government surveillance of church, 45; and irrigation projects, 100–1; official requests for permission for, 37–40; opposition to in United States, 6–7; post-1892 Criminal Code, 44; and racialization of Latter-day Saints, 84; and woman suffrage in Utah, 56–7. *See also* First Manifesto; Fundamentalist Church of Jesus Christ of Latter-day Saints; monogamy; non-monogamy; polygamy; Second Manifesto; Smoot, Reed

polygamy: and Canadian criminal law, 38–44, 46, 48; among Indigenous peoples, 15, 27, 30, 33–4, 45; "monogamist polygamists," 32; post-Manifesto, 30, 122, 136; and slavery, 31; and women's rights activism, 64. *See also* 1892 Criminal Code; Edmunds Act (1882); Edmunds-Tucker Act (1887); Fundamentalist Church of Jesus Christ of Latter-day Saints; monogamy; Morrill Anti-Bigamy Act (1862); non-monogamy; plural marriage
postmillennialism, 111, 117
Prairie School, 129–30, 135–7, 140–6. *See also* Wright, Frank Lloyd
Pratt, Orson, 31
Pratt, Parley P., 5
premillennialism, 117–18
presiding bishopric, 138
prophecy, 55, 58, 60, 62, 72, 86–7, 144, 161; gendered relation to priesthood, 65; as source of authority, 64. *See also* spiritual gifts

ranching, 9, 23, 25, 90, 95, 102
Raymond Flour Mill and Elevator, 103
Raymond Meetinghouse, 129
Raymond Town Council, 109
Raymond Women's Institute, 82
Redford, John, 158
Redford, Sarah, 158
religious freedom, 31. See also *Reynolds v. United States*
Reynolds v. United States (1878), 31
Rigby, Lavinia Clark, 33

Rogers, Ruel, 84
Romanesque style, 131, 135, 141
Ross, Relva, 84
Russell, Adam, 71
Russell, Austin G., 148
Russell, Hannah, 71

sacred architecture, 129, 147, 156. *See also* Alberta Stake Tabernacle; Cardston Alberta Temple; Cardston Assembly Hall; Cardston Meetinghouse; Gothic Revival; Kirtland Ohio Temple; Laie Hawaii Temple; Logan Utah Temple; Manti Utah Temple; Mesa Arizona Temple; Nauvoo Illinois Temple; Prairie School; Raymond Meetinghouse; Romanesque style; Salt Lake City Utah Temple; Wright, Frank Lloyd
Salmon, Eva Dahl, 79
Salt Lake City Utah Temple, 131, 133, 144
Second Coming, 91, 117
Second Manifesto (1904), 46, 136, 161. *See also* First Manifesto; Smith, Joseph F.
Second World War, 14, 57, 76, 82, 86
Sex Sterilization Act, 84
Shaffer, Helen, 153
Short Creek Raid, 52. *See* Fundamentalist Church of Jesus Christ of Latter-day Saints
Shurtleff, Noah, 148
Smith, Don Carlos, 5
Smith, Hyrum, 6
Smith, Joseph F., 46, 65, 76–7, 97, 136–7
Smith, Joseph, Jr., 5–6, 10, 48, 50, 60, 67, 91, 135, 145, 152
Smith, Joseph, Sr., 5
Smith, Willard L., 50–1
Smoot, Reed, 20, 122–3

Snow, Chauncy E., 98
Snow, Eliza R., 152
Social Credit Party of Canada, 15, 47; in Alberta, 14, 19, 25, 107, 116–19, 121–4, 126–7, 162. *See also* Alberta Social Credit Party; House of Commons
social gospel, 22–4, 112, 123
socialism, 112, 116, 119
spiritual gifts: as mode of cultural negotiation, 55, 64; decline of, 57, 65, 73, 86–7; and health care, 71; as "othering" factor, 161; as reassurance, 58, 60–3; relation to private sphere, 80. *See also* assimilation; integration; domesticity; faith healing; prophecy; tongues, speaking in
Stevens, Stringham A., 118
St. George Utah Temple, 131, 144
Stirling Cemetery, 148, 156
Stringam, George L., 113
Stutz, Clara, 86
sugar beet farming, 23, 90, 102–4
Sullivan, Francis C., 137
Sullivan, Louis, 138, 143

Taber Riding, 113
Talmage, May Booth, 141
Tanner, Nathan Eldon, 122
Taylor, John, 5–6, 31, 48, 50
Taylor, John W., 37–8, 43, 99, 102, 128, 136
Taylor, Nellie, 43, 52
Taylor, Sarah Mercer, 102
Taylor Stake, 102, 109, 118, 139; Mutual Improvement Association of, 47; Relief Society of, 119; Sunday School Board of, 124
temple rituals, 77, 157
Temple Square, 144

Index

Territorial Grain Growers' Association (TGGA), 110
theocracy, 12
Thomas, Winnifred Newton, 77, 79
Timpson, Nettie, 53
tongues, speaking in, 58, 60–1, 63–5, 72, 161. *See also* spiritual gifts
Triennial National Council of Women, 63–4

United Farmers of Alberta, 82–5, 107–8, 110–16, 122–4, 126–7
United Farm Women of Alberta, 58, 64, 80, 82–7, 160
United Order, 20, 92–4, 102, 105, 118
Ursenbach, Octave W., 50

Village of Stirling, 91

Walker, James, 124
Walker, J. Harris, 77
Walker, Mary "Fannye," 77
western Canada, 7, 9, 13–14, 21, 29–30, 35, 131
Wheat Pool Committee, 113
Whitney, Orson F., 138
Wight, Charles Ora, 72
Wight, Cynthia, 72
Wight, Francis, 72
Wiles, Sarah Ann, 32
Williams, Florence, 49
Williams, Gwendolyn, 49
Williams, Sterling, 61, 75, 101
Woman's Exponent, The, 58, 67
Wood, Benjamin James, 105

Wood, Edward J., 101–2, 104–5, 118, 138
Wood, Forest, 50
Wood, Henry Wise, 111, 113–14
Wood, James Forest, 118
Woodruff, Wilford W., 42–3, 50, 77, 97
Woods, Easter, 49–50
Woodward, Martha, 148
Wooley, Lorin C., 48
Woolf, Absalom, 108
Woolf, Delia, 85
Woolf, Hannah, 53
Woolf, John A., 32, 43, 55, 101, 108
Woolf, John W., 101, 108
Woolf, Martin, 101, 108
Woolf, Mary, 62–3, 74–5
Woolf, Sarah, 53
Woolf, William L., 93
Woolford, Thomas H., 110
Woolford Provincial Park, 110
Woolford Ward, 124
Woolley, Emily, 47
Woolley, Phebe, 53
Woolley, Taylor, 135
Wright, Frank Lloyd, 129, 135, 137–8, 141–3

Young, Brigham, 6, 31, 43, 50, 53, 67, 71, 77, 132
Young Woman's Journal, The, 141, 153
Young, Zina D.H., 43, 52, 68, 133

Zaugg, Rosina Elisabeth, 32
Zimmerman, R. Scott, 52
Zion, 3, 18, 61–2, 98–9, 104, 117–18. *See also* Plat of the City of Zion